Collins Illustrated Guide to

EGYPT

Contributing Editor: Robert Morkot
Photography by Kazuyoshi Nomachi

COLLINS

8 Grafton Street, London W1
1988

(preceding pages) Tomb murals, Western Thebes
(following page) Queen Hatshepsut, Luxor

William Collins Sons & Co. Ltd
London • Glasgow • Sydney • Auckland
Toronto • Johannsburg

British Library Cataloguing in Publication Data

Collins Illustrated Guide to Egypt
1. Egypt — Visitors' guides
916.2'0455

ISBN 0-00-215227-4

Series Editors: May Holdsworth and Sallie Coolidge
Contributing Editors: Robert Morkot, John Owen and Robyn Flemming
Picture Editor: Carolyn Watts

Text by Robert Morkot and Lorenzo Martinengo
Additional text contributions by Dena Matar

Cover photograph by C.T.H. Smith, Images

Photography by Kazuyoshi Nomachi with additional contributions by
Lorenzo Martinengo (49 all three, 110 , 113, 235); CTH Smith, Images (130).

Design by Joan Law Design & Photography

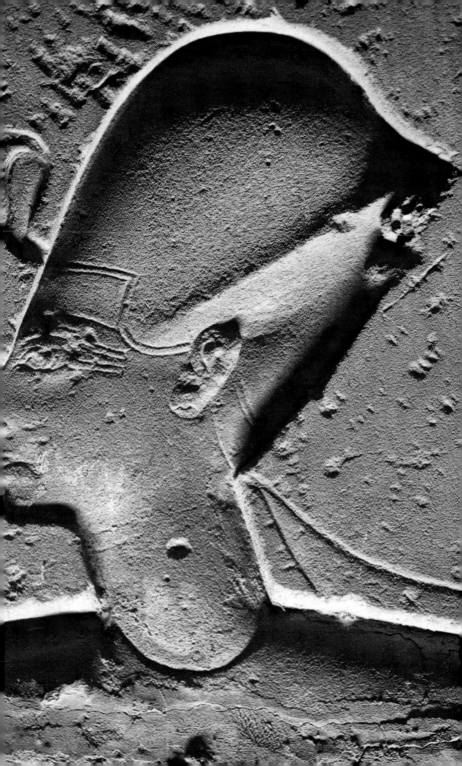

Contents

Maps

(top) An example of Coptic ecclesiastical art

(middle) Street vendor, Cairo

(bottom) Feluccas, Aswan

An Introduction

Ancient even to the ancients, Egypt was a great nation a thousand
years before the Minoan civilization was established at Knossos on
Crete. And it was viewed by the Greeks and Romans of 2,000 years
ago with the same awe with which we view ancient Greece and Rome
today. The name 'Egypt' (*Aigyptos*, from the Egyptian, meaning
'House of the Ka (spirit) of Ptah') was given to the region by the
Greeks, and it has stuck, prevailing over indigenous names and those
given it by other conquerors. To this day, districts are called *nomoi*, as
in Greece. After a tour of Egypt in the fifth century BC, the Greek
historian Herodotus said '. . . nowhere are there so many marvellous
things, nor in the whole world beside are there to be seen so many
things of unspeakable greatness.' His words were borne out by many
later writers who described the imposing pyramids, avenues of
sphinxes, soaring obelisks and colossal statues carved from stone. In
his book *An Egyptian Journal*, the British author William Golding
wrote '. . . perhaps for all of us, the supposed immortality of ancient
Egypt stood over the change which is the experience of daily life . . .
not quite a yearning for a lost paradise but certainly a yearning for
something or other.' A visit to Egypt today is like a journey back in
time. But Egypt offers the visitor much more than just its history.
Cairo is a bustling city, throbbing with people and traffic, and the
country offers many scenic attractions of awesome beauty.

A Geographical Overview

On a map Egypt resembles a rectangular trapezium. To the west, her
Libyan border corresponds to the 25th meridian and runs on a straight
line. To the south, the Sudanese border corresponds, with only slight
deviations, to the 22nd parallel through the Nubian Desert. To the
east, Egypt is bordered obliquely by the Red Sea, and to the north by
the Mediterranean Sea, almost parallel to the southern border. Only
Sinai, which borders Israel to the east and appears as an outcrop on
the north-eastern corner of the country, breaks the geometric pattern.
Because there is no point more than 250 kilometres (155 miles) from
either sea or river, communication in Egypt has been good.

The Egyptian territory, a little over 1,000,000 square kilometres
(386,000 square miles), is made up almost completely of desert: the
immense Arabian Desert (Eastern Desert) to the east, and the stark
Libyan Desert (Western Desert) to the west. Flowing from south to
north through this vast expanse of wasteland is the life-giving Nile to
which Egypt owes it essence, its culture and its life.

Climate

Egypt has a typical desert climate, except along the sparkling
Mediterranean coast. Rain is scarce and the skies tend to be clear all
year round. The winter months between November and March are
marked by a slight drop in temperature and an increase in humidity.
Rains at this time sometimes cause floods which block the roads and
destroy mud houses. Snow is unknown in Egypt and rain unheard of in
Upper Egypt. In a dry climate such as Egypt's, very hot temperatures
are more bearable than they would be in a humid climate.

Average temperatures at major tourist centres:

	Cairo min/max	Alexandria min/max	Luxor min/max	Aswan min/max
January	°C 8.6/19.1 °F 45/66	°C 9.3/18.3 °F 51/66	°C 5.4/23.0 °F 42/74	°C 8.0/23.8 °F 49/75
February	°C 9.3/21.0 °F 47/69	°C 9.7/19.2 °F 51/67	°C 6.8/25.4 °F 44/79	°C 9.4/26.1 °F 51/79
March	°C 11.2/23.7 °F 51/75	°C 11.2/21.0 °F 54/70	°C 10.7/29.0 °F 50/86	°C 12.6/30.4 °F 57/88
April	°C 13.9/28.2 °F 56/83	°C 13.5/23.6 °F 58/75	°C 15.7/35.0 °F 59/95	°C 17.5/30.4 °F 63/97
May	°C 17.4/32.4 °F 62/90	°C 16.7/26.5 °F 63/80	°C 20.7/39.3 °F 69/103	°C 21.1/38.5 °F 73/103
June	°C 17.9/34.5 °F 68/95	°C 26.2/28.2 °F 69/83	°C 22.6/41.0 °F 70/107	°C 24.2/42.1 °F 77/107
July	°C 21.5/35.4 °F 71/96	°C 22.7/29.6 °F 73/86	°C 23.6/40.8 °F 72/106	°C 24.5/41.2 °F 78/108
August	°C 21.6/34.8 °F 71/95	°C 22.9/30.4 °F 74/87	°C 23.5/41.0 °F 73/107	°C 24.7/41.3 °F 80/108
September	°C 19.9/32.3 °F 68/89	°C 21.3/29.4 °F 72/86	°C 21.5/38.5 °F 71/103	°C 22.2/39.6 °F 74/103
October	°C 17.8/29.8 °F 63/85	°C 17.8/27.7 °F 68/83	°C 17.8/35.1 °F 65/98	°C 19.3/36.6 °F 71/99
November	°C 19.9/24.1 °F 54/78	°C 14.8/24.4 °F 62/77	°C 12.3/29.6 °F 54/87	°C 14.5/20.2 °F 61/88
December	°C 10.4/20.7 °F 49/69	°C 11.2/20.4 °F 54/69	°C 7.7/24.8 °F 45/78	°C 9.9/20.5 °F 52/78

Flora and Fauna

The frescoes and bas reliefs found in and on Egypt's ancient buildings indicate that the country was a lush natural paradise during the time of the Pharaohs, almost 5,000 years ago. Aside from a plethora of plant life (the ubiquitous papyrus and lotus, for example), the most commonly represented figures are lions, leopards, monkeys, hippopotami, ibis and the sacred scarabeus. Today, most of these species are extinct along the banks of the Nile mainly due to man's development. The stretch of the river where seasonal floods once left tiny lakes and pools was an ideal habitat for a diversity of plant and animal life. Today, it is cultivated with imported plants. Nevertheless, the landscape has remained inviting. Palms and other trees grow in profusion along many of its sections, giving it a lush tropical appearance. On a boat ride down the Nile one can watch herons feeding, the languorous flight of the lapwing, and numerous other species of stilt-birds and waders. In the most sheltered bends and in the stagnant arms of the river, one can still find that very popular species of the waterlily, the lotus. But the Egyptian papyrus, which once flourished wild along the riverbank, now grows only in cultivated patches. The coastal lakes are important sanctuaries for ducks and geese, among which may be found the Egyptian goose, and in the cities as well as in the cultivated plains, there are numerous species of birds such as the turtle dove, the green bee-eater and the white kite, which is almost non-existent in Europe. In Cairo, it is interesting to observe how the hoopoe, which is rather bashful in the West, has become the uncontested queen of the city's grassfields, where it forms small groups to hunt worms and insects.

The Desert

Much of Egypt consists of the Libyan and Arabian deserts. The desert may appear to be a monotonous expanse of sand but, in fact, it is marked by a highly varied landscape, sometimes rocky, at other times sandy or pebbly, which is interspersed with oases. Reptiles are the true inhabitants of the Egyptian desert, having adapted themselves to the scorching daytime heat and the freezing nights and, above all, to the scarcity of water. Among the most common reptiles are the short-legged skinks and larger monitor lizards. Very few birds survive in harsh desert conditions, but a number of mammals have made it their home including camels and Dorca gazelles. Hyenas, gerbils, and small mice emerge only at night when the temperature drops.

The Sea

The Red Sea boasts a marvellous coral barrier reef teeming with diverse forms of life. Hurghada, a popular tourist centre situated at the confluence of the gulfs of Suez and Aqaba, makes an ideal point of departure for an interesting underwater exploration of the area. Along this reef live more than 800 colourful fish species, including the deadly stone-fish, the equally dangerous butterfly-fish, as well as surgeon fish and some species of sharks. Not far from the shore, which is overrun by small crabs in the evening, there are jellyfish such as cassiopeia, which attaches its head to the seabed, turning its tentacles into a perfect trap.

The Nile

'Egypt is the gift of the Nile', wrote Herodotus, for it was because of the Nile's annual floods which inundated the land that ancient Egypt became known as 'the granary of the world'. Formed by the meeting at Khartoum in Sudan of the White Nile, which flows out of Lake Victoria beneath the mountain ranges of equatorial Africa, and the Blue Nile, originating in the mountains of Ethiopia, the Nile paints a vivid strip of green through the barrenness of the desert before it branches off into Damietta and Rosetta some 20 kilometres (12.5 miles) north of Cairo. The Nile's banks slope upwards, allowing its waters to brim over the land, irrigating crops and leaving behind a rich mixture of fertilizing silt, algae and alluvial vegetation. The ancient Egyptians saw the annual flooding as a miracle which they attributed to the ram-headed god Khnum, the guardian of the underground caves in the Aswan Cataract, from which they thought the water flowed. Since ancient times, the Nile has held the Egyptians in its sway and many attempts have been made to control it. The irrigation system at el-Fayum, 80 kilometres (50 miles) south of Cairo, which was built during the Middle Kingdom (2040–1782 BC), is particularly ingenious, with canals set at different levels to utilize effectively the river's bounty as it rises and falls. In these areas, which have been cultivated for more than 5,000 years, the chromatic contrasts of the land are remarkable — greyish where there is fertile mud and reddish where there is sand. Today, the High Dam at Aswan, built in the early 1960s by President Gamal Abdel Nasser, has succeeded in controlling the river and protecting harvests from its annual floods. But whether the project has been a total success is debatable in view of the ecological changes it has brought about and its threat to many valuable monuments of ancient Egypt.

The People

Egypt has a population of more than 50 million people, a number that is increasing at the rate of 1 million every eight months. A third of the population lives in the fertile delta region, squeezed between the Nile's two branches just north of Cairo, while 15 million live in Cairo, making it one of the world's most densely populated cities. Attempts to curb the birth rate have so far been thwarted by pressure from traditional Islamic groups. The problem has not only created poverty and unemployment, but has also given rise to a new social situation and helped to breed a wave of Islamic fundamentalism in a country which has traditionally been tolerant of other cultures and religions. Many Egyptian women, who are amongst the most progressive in the Arab world, still wear Islamic dress, which allows only the head and hands to be uncovered, and an Islamic party won seats in the country's parliament in 1987.

The successive settlement of Egypt by various peoples has obscured many of the country's cultural roots. Its language now is Arabic and its religion Islam. The conquering Arabs called the inhabitants *'qubti'* which today is the term used to identify those who have retained their Christian faith, namely the Copts, whose language lives on only in their liturgy.

The only people to remain unchanged since ancient times are the Fellahin, descendants of the farmers of 3,000 years ago, who still work the soil using age-old methods and tools. Apart from the Fellahin, who inhabit the numerous small villages which dot the course of the Nile, the typical Egyptian in the major cities is characterized by a mixture of Libyan, Berber and Arab features. The most prevalent foreigners are Greeks, followed by Italians and a few English.

Because of the unwelcoming nature of the desert, the Egyptians tend to settle in one place. Apart from the Bedouins and the Nubian Bisharins, there are none of the large nomadic groups of the Afro-Asiatic deserts. With the exception of el-Fayum, the oases are scarcely populated, since they are far from each other and from the major cities, and to travel from one point to another is punishing even for camels. The only possible livelihood is the cultivation of the land along the Nile's banks; animal husbandry is impossible because of the absence of pasture lands.

Government

The Constitution, adopted through the national referendum of 1971, states that 'the Arab Republic of Egypt is a socialist democratic country that shall accordingly function till the full realization of the total unity of the Arab Nation of which it is an integral part, that Islam is the official religion of the state even if freedom of religion and thought are ensured and that the principles of Islamic law constitute the inspiring fount of legislation.'

Egypt is a presidential republic and its president is elected by popular vote. His mandate lasts for six years and is not renewable. It is the president of the republic who holds executive powers, who determines the country's policies, who nominates and revokes the vice-president, the prime minister and the five deputy prime ministers, as well as civil and military officials, members of the Consultative Assembly and the diplomatic corps. He is also the chief of the armed forces. Legislative powers are exercised by the Assembly, which is composed of 392 members, 382 of whom are elected every five years through universal suffrage; the remaining ten are nominated directly by the president. The Constitution states that 50 per cent of the body of the People's Assembly shall be selected from workers or farmers. There is also a consultative assembly, composed of 210 members, which has no decision-making powers. The numerous local councils collaborate directly with the president in determining the national policy. Egypt's administrative subdivision consists of 25 *mohafzats* (administrative districts), each of which is headed by a *mohafez* or governor. They are as follows: Cairo, Alexandria, Port Said, Suez, Ismailia, Behira, Damietta, Kafrel Sheikh, Caarbia, Dakhlia, Sharqua, Tahrir, Qalyubia, Fayum, Beni Suef, Giza, el-Minya, Asyut, Sohag, Qena, Aswan, the Red Sea, Matruh, Sinai and New Valley.

History

Geography very often has a great influence on history, and this is certainly true of Egypt. The Nile River, with its life-giving powers, winds it way through vast tracts of empty desert, and along this narrow valley of fertile soil grew an empire that has had few parallels.

The Beginning of Civilization

Near el-Kat (Upper Egypt) and along the borders of el-Fayum's depression, archaeologists have discovered tools dating back to the Neolithic communities who lived in the Valley of the Nile from the seventh to the sixth millenia BC. Their lives were devoted to hunting and the harvesting of the valley's produce. The first real transformation in prehistoric Egypt was brought about by the need for an organized system of food production and distribution from the fertile delta area and the region of el-Fayum to other parts of the country. The cultivation of cereals, wheat and barley was supplemented by the raising of animals. The agrarian way of life, which lasted for about 2,000 years, first spread through the oases in the Western Desert during the fifth century BC. Archaeological evidence shows how, from then onwards, the lifestyles of the peoples of Upper Egypt and the delta differed. The archaeology of Lower Egypt is less known since excavations are few and archaeological work has increased only recently. Based on evidence found in Upper Egypt, it is possible to reconstruct the main stages in the development of ancient Egyptians and their country. The earliest-known phase of the agricultural population was the so-called Badarian between 4500 and 4000 BC. It was characterized by a mixed economy and a livelihood based on animal breeding and cereal cultivation, although hunting and food gathering were still practised, as well as an embryonic form of artisan specialization concerning mainly the production of ivory artifacts. At the end of the fifth century BC social and economic transformations occurred, and archaeologists have unearthed evidence of Amratian culture, from a civilization identified for the first time at el-Amra near Nag Hammadi, which dates back to the beginning of the fourth century BC, indicating that the populations along the Valley of the Nile were agriculturally more advanced than the Badarians. The Amratians founded the first agricultural villages on the borders of the flood plain, although they maintained mainly a Badarian-type economy. They also specialized in artisan production, their work ranging from ceramics (such as the typical red vases with black tops) to flint weapons and hard stone objects. As barter and trade intensified along the river, social stratification began to emerge.

The annual flooding of the Nile, which assured the agricultural productivity essential to the country's economy, precipitated the demand for unification of Upper and Lower Egypt, which occurred at the beginning of the fourth millenium BC. At this time, the inhospitable deserts protected the valley, preventing invasion by other peoples. The first settlements along the Nile were on the heights above the flood level. It was not long before attempts were made to control the river, and soon irrigation projects were planned, with countless canals. The subsequent 'Gerzean' phase (3500–3300 BC) appears to have been a very structured society. Settlements grew up along the edges of the plain at the limits of the desert, and *necropoli* or burial vaults were dug in desert areas, such as at the predynastic site of Naqada and Hierakonpolis. The Gerzean economy was based mainly on agriculture and animal breeding, with some hunting and harvesting.

Artisan production increased further, as indicated by stone vases, decorated ceramics and other goods, and there is some evidence of copper manufacturing. The development of handicrafts and small industry was accompanied by an intensification of maritime trading activities, covering Nubia and the Near East.

The Advent of the Monarchy

The age of the Pharaohs has no written narrative such as Thucydides supplied for the Greeks, Livy for the Romans, and the Books of Kings for the Hebrews. Whatever information we have has been gathered from tomb inscriptions, paintings on temple walls, and prose, poetry and state records on preserved papyri. In about 3300–3200 BC, a proto-state was formed, with sovereigns resembling the Pharaohs of the First Dynasty. In addition to those from Hierakonpolis, artifacts such as the mace-head of King Scorpion and King Narmer's votive palette recall these proto-sovereigns.

Between 3200 and 3000 BC, the scattered tribes living along the Nile were united under one head, ruled by a formal government. The tribal leader of Upper Egypt (traditionally called Menes, though he has also been identified with Narmer) founded the first of Egypt's 30 dynasties and extended his control northwards, thus bringing about unification. Menes founded the city of Memphis near Cairo and established his capital there. Menes and his successors (18 kings of two successive dynasties spanning 400 years) who all ruled from Memphis, built tombs for their after-life and brought the two parts of the kingdom, Upper and Lower Egypt, together. It was from This (or Thinis), the capital of the unified kingdom near Abydos during the first two dynasties called the Archaic Period (3050–2686 BC), that the transformation of Egypt from a tribal society to a veritable state came about.

The Old Kingdom

The period between the Third and Fourth dynasties (2686–2181 BC), is conventionally called the Old Kingdom. During this time, the capital of Egypt and seat of the royal residence was still the city of Memphis, west of which, on the desert plateau, lay the vast necropoli of Saqqara, Giza, Abusir and Dahshur. The events of this age are known to us mainly through monumental archaeological remains. One of these is the complex of Zoser in Saqqara, which is evidence of the important cultural developments which occurred during the Third Dynasty. During this period, Egypt developed a number of complex institutions, on which the stability and wealth of the country depended. The king, crowned by divine right, held all the administrative, judicial, military and religious powers, and his authority was transmitted to peripheral bodies and to the officials in charge of different departments. This high degree of social organization enabled the country to make significant progress in other areas. The precise division of work provided abundant labour for public works, which consisted mainly of the building of Pharaonic and divine structures such as temples and pyramids. The three most famous funerary buildings, the pyramids of Cheops, Chephren and Mycerinus at Giza, are examples of Fourth Dynasty expansion. The economy also improved as a result of the intensive exploitation of copper and turquoise mines in southern Sinai and the frequent commercial expeditions to the Near East for precious wood, to Nubia (rich in gold mines), and to Punt (on the Sudan-Eritrea coast of the Red Sea). Religion was also defined by elaborate doctrines. During the Fourth Dynasty, the solar cult of Heliopolis spread, and gained ground during the Fifth Dynasty when solar temples were erected. During this period, the first Pyramid Texts were probably compiled, written for the first time in the Unas Pyramid (at the end of the Fifth Dynasty), then on royal sepulchres in the Sixth Dynasty. As well as religious literature, there was also a rich seam of scholarly and autobiographical works.

At the end of the Fourth Dynasty, a new social organization emerged, whose distribution of wealth and authority at first balanced then weakened the centralized power of the sovereignty. During the Fifth and Sixth dynasties, an entire sector of privileged high officials who were recipients of royal grants brought about the loosening of subordinate relations with the central authority, resulting in the establishment of 'feudal' autonomous areas in the country.

The First Intermediate Period

During the so-called First Intermediate Period (c.2181−2040 BC), central power disappeared and the whole country was divided among the local governors of the provinces who often fought each other. During the Ninth and Tenth dynasties (spanning 2160−2040 BC), the legitimate monarchy rose again in Heracleopolis in Middle Egypt, supported by the princes of Asyut. However, a Theban dynasty soon prevailed (the 11th Dynasty, with several kings named Antef and Mentuhotep), and declared its sovereignty. Thus, Egypt was once again unified under a central power during the Middle Kingdom (2040−1782 BC).

The Middle Kingdom

When Amenemhat I, Vizier of Mentuhotep III, founded the 12th Dynasty, the capital was moved north, to Lisht. The internal politics of the sovereigns, the Amenemhats and the Senusrets were highlighted by a series of important administrative and political reforms, among the most significant of which was the institution of the co-regency of the sovereign with his successor. The area of el-Fayum, with its rich agricultural resources favoured by the laws of these kings, became one of the economic centres of the country. Through military campaigns and the erection of imposing fortresses along the Nile south of Aswan, Nubia was conquered and has since been tied to Egyptian history. Intense commercial activity resumed in the east in the Syro-Palestinian area and in the south (Punt). There is also evidence of relations with the Aegean area. The arts and literature, in particular, flourished and the religious centre of Abydos, devoted to Osiris, became the major seat of an extremely popular cult.

The Second Intermediate Period

This period of prosperity was followed by the Second Intermediate Period (1782-1570 BC), which was marked by the invasion of the Hyksos from the Near East. They settled in the delta, where they founded their capital, Avaris, and spread their rule southwards. Egypt also partially lost its control over Nubia. During this time, the Theban princes Sekenenre and Kamose (17th Dynasty) prepared the way for the reunification of the country by initiating the fight for liberation from the Hyksos. Ahmose, the founder of the 18th Dynasty, finally completed the expulsion of the Hyksos from Egypt. The New Kingdom (from the 18th to the 20th dynasties) made Thebes its capital.

The New Kingdom

Under the sovereigns of the 18th Dynasty, Egypt created a vast empire whose influence and culture extended from the fourth cataract of the Nile in the very heart of Sudanese territory to the Euphrates and the confines of the powerful kingdom of Mitanni. Against this kingdom, Thutmose III (1504−1450 BC), carrying on the politics of his predecessors, Amenhotep I, Thutmose I and Thutmose II, completed 17 crowning military campaigns which are recorded in the Annals, incised, on his orders, on the walls of the Sanctuary of Amun in Karnak. Such large-scale expansion was also made possible by the profound innovations brought about by earlier contacts with other cultures. During the Hyksos occupation, for example, the horse, the war chariot and the new methods of metal-working were introduced into Egypt. At the same time, commerce with the cities in the Syro-Palestinian area and along the Aegean coast intensified. Under Makare Hatshepsut (1498−1483 BC), who ruled first as regent then as a queen in her own right, the Egyptian artistic renaissance began. Her architect, Senenmut, built a number of splendid monuments, including the mortuary temples at Thebes and the Temple of Deir el-Bahari, where reliefs document her expeditions to the land of Punt in search of exotic plants and products. After her death Thutmose III, in an act of revenge, destroyed or defaced many of the buildings erected for her by Senenmut. Thutmose III, the greatest conqueror Egypt was to produce, fought 17 campaigns to check the growing influence of the Hittites, a mixed people occupying most of Anatolia (modern Turkey), and the Mitanni, a Hurrian people, who inhabited the watershed of the Euphrates river. This period of conquest was followed by a series of alliances which were cemented by marriages between the daughters of the various royal families of the Hittites, the Mitanni and the Pharaohs, thus bringing a century of peace to Egypt. The empire reached its zenith under Amenhotep III (1386−1349 BC), who devoted his attention to building the temple at Luxor and a mortuary temple, of which nothing now remains save the Colossi of Memnon. Amenhotep's son, Amenhotep IV (1350−1334 BC) (who took the name Akhenaten), was little interested in the government of the empire. He established the cult of Aten, a form of god depicted as a solar disk, in a bid to diminish the authority of the powerful clergy of Amun, the leading god of Thebes. He also founded a new capital which he called Akhetaten or 'Horizon of Aten' in the area now known as Tell el-Amarna. These innovations, which affected every aspect of life, are best seen in the arts and literature of the time. After the king's death, there was an immediate restoration of earlier traditions. Amenhotep's successor, the boy-king Tutankhamun, became one of the most celebrated kings of this period when his tomb, filled with treasures of inestimable value, was discovered intact in the Valley of the Kings in 1922.

Military Campaigns

While Akhenaten and his beautiful wife Nefertiti stayed at Akhetaten to worship the new deity, the Egyptian empire declined and Egypt lost control of the eastern section of the kingdom. The last king of the dynasty, Horemheb, a general who was not of royal blood, did much to restore Egypt both at home and abroad. The rulers of the 19th Dynasty, however, found themselves confronted with uprisings and foreign interference. Ramesses II, who continued the plans and policies of his father, Sety I, brought off a series of military campaigns culminating in the Battle of Kadesh against the Hittites along the Orontes River in Syria. An alliance and peace treaty divided the Near East or Levant into two zones, one Egyptian and the other Hittite. The Battle of Kadesh is recorded in an ode and numerous reliefs in the Temples of Abydos, Luxor, Karnak, Abu Simbel and The Ramesseum. Egyptian political and economic activities were by this stage centred near the delta for reasons of defence and safety as well as to take advantage of the traffic of the Mediterranean. Ramesses II was succeeded by Merneptah, one of his sons, who faced a threat of invasion from the Libyans, but was able to expel them from the western delta. The rest of the 19th Dynasty was a period of confusion. Internal stability was not restored until the beginning of the 20th Dynasty and the reign of Ramesses III, who successfully defended the country against attacks from the Libyans and the so-called Sea Peoples, a mixture of Achaei, Sardinians and Philistines in a battle recorded in great descriptive detail in the Temple of Medinet Habu. The great Pharaoh was killed in a conspiracy in 1151 BC. (The Judicial Papyrus of Turin contains the proceedings of the trial of the conspirators.) By then, Egypt was becoming weak: it had suffered a number of invasions, and due to the significant decrease of tributes from the east, it was becoming impoverished and had numerous internal problems. Corruption spread amongst the ruling classes and royal tombs were looted. The office of the High Priest of Amun became a hereditary one, and it gradually acquired powers almost equal to those of the sovereignty, to the point where it virtually governed Upper Egypt during the 21st Dynasty. During this dynasty, the capital of which was Tanis in the delta, the rise of the foreign powers began. The first of these were descendants of the subjugated Libyans during the 22nd Dynasty, whose capital was Bubastis. They were followed by the Nubians during the 25th Dynasty, the Assyrians and then the Persians during the 27th Dynasty (525−404 BC), who brought about a century of prosperity.

A Brief Interval

An interval of independence and national rebirth occurred during the 26th or Saïte Dynasty (664−525 BC) ('Saïte' from the name of its capital Sais), when, with the Assyrian invasion, the Nubian kings of the 25th Dynasty were driven out of Egypt. Administrative reforms were put into effect and the country developed political unity and a national language, Demotic. The delta became the most important zone in the land, its maritime cities actively engaging in trade and commerce. By this time, Egyptian products such as cereal and papyrus were traded throughout the Mediterranean.

The Ptolemaic Period

Following the 30th and last Pharaonic Dynasty (380−342 BC), Egypt
was once again occupied briefly by the Persians, after which it was
conquered by Alexander the Great of Macedon in 332 BC and lost its
independence completely. As a result of Alexander's conquest and the
formation of the monarchy under his successors, the Ptolemies, Egypt
became part of the great Hellenistic Empire. The fusion of Egyptian
and Hellenic cultures bore rich rewards and resulted in a Ptolemaic
monarchy, the longest reigning of all the Hellenistic governments.

The Roman Conquest

In 30 BC, Egypt fell to the Romans after the Battle of Actium.
Because the new rulers respected Egypt's existing religious, economic
and political structure, stability was easily achieved, despite the fact
that Egypt's conservative internal environment was in sharp contrast to
the open ideology of Alexandria, an important centre of Hellenistic
humanism. The Ptolemies maintained good diplomatic relations with
Rome. In 168 BC they obtained Rome's protection against the
Seleucidae of Syria, thus establishing an early Roman presence in
Egyptian territory. Rome's continually increasing demand for a steady
and abundant food supply was a factor in Augustus' conquest and
annexation of Egypt as a Roman province, directly administered by the
emperor through his delegate, the Praefectus Aegypti. Egypt was then
known as the granary of Rome, and from that time on it became
important in the history of the Roman Empire. With the division of the
empire in the year 395, Egypt became part of the Eastern Empire and
lived through the Byzantine period until it was conquered by the Arabs
in 639.

Islamic Egypt

When Amr Ibn el-As, commander of Caliph Omar, entered Egypt
from Syria, he was welcomed by the Coptic population which was
sympathetic to the Arab conquerors because of the help they had given
in ridding the country of the Greek Melkites (Byzantines). The
conquerors established themselves in a fortified encampment, later
called Fustat, the first capital of Muslim Egypt. Fustat remained the
capital under the Ummayads who ruled from Damascus, and later
under the Abbasids who ruled from Baghdad. A slow Arabization
process began, and Islam was gradually embraced by many of the
Copts as the popularity of the Arabic language increased. As the
power of the caliphate waned, Ahmed Ibn Tulun, the Turkish
governor of Egypt, proclaimed himself an independent Sultan in about

870 and transferred his residence to the hill of Jechkar, north-east of Fustat. This stronghold later grew into the city of el-Qata'i, which witnessed years of growth and development under Ahmed Ibn Tulun. With his demise, however, Egypt underwent a period of political dissension and uncertainty which continued until the Abbasids were finally able to return in 905. They dominated the country from 939 to 969, and during this period Fustat regained its prestige while el-Qata'i was completely destroyed.

The Fatimids (969−1171)

The Fatimids, who claimed descent from Fatima, the daughter of Mohammed, came originally from Syria and settled in Kairowan in modern Tunisia. They had made several unsuccessful attempts to conquer Egypt, but in 969, Gawhar, commander of the forces of the Caliph el-Muizz, entered Fustat and met with little resistance. Upon its conquest, he deemed it a worthy enough place in which to establish a new city which would rival Baghdad, the capital of the Abbasids. Thus was conceived the city of Cairo, originally known as el-Qahira (the victorious). The early Fatimids also brought a period of economic stability to Egypt. Foreign trade expanded in Europe and India and the complex tax system was abolished. By 1079, the First Crusade entered Syria from the north-west, aiming to free Jerusalem from Muslim control. Jerusalem was captured in 1099 and the Crusaders then turned their attention to Egypt in 1168. The Crusaders' forays into Egypt were thwarted by the Kurdish general Salah el-Din, better known as Saladin, who set out to extend his power in Egypt in 1171, thus beginning a new period in Egypt's history which lasted until 1252.

After consolidating his power in Egypt, Saladin turned his attention to Syria, leading several campaigns against the Crusaders which finally led to the recapture of Jerusalem in 1187. Egypt, in the meantime, witnessed a period of prosperity and cultural growth and became a centre of theological studies. Saladin also fortified Cairo and built a citadel over a ramp of the Muqattam Hill, whose architectural features, though remotely of oriental derivation, are also strikingly typical of Crusade construction prevalent in Syria and Palestine.

The Mamelukes (1250−1517)

The Mamelukes, originally an army of Turkish slaves (mainly Kipchaks) brought from the region to the north of the Black Sea and installed by one of Saladin's brothers on the island of Roda in the Nile near Cairo, came to power through the marriage of the chief Mameluke, Aybak, to Shajar el-Dur, the wife of Sultan Ayyub who was herself proclaimed sultan after his death. The Mamelukes ruled for almost three centuries, centuries often marred by political turmoil.

The Reign of the Ottomans (1517–1805)

In 1517, a Turkish Dynasty (The Ottomans) occupied Cairo after having crushed the weak military opposition of the Mamelukes. The Ottoman governors (*pashas*) never enjoyed great popularity in Egypt; they were frequently recalled by the central government in Istanbul in order to prevent them gaining undue personal prestige. Throughout this period, Egypt declined as a cultural centre though it retained its importance as a religious fountainhead.

Napoleon's Expedition

Napoleon, who saw himself as the bearer of the ideals of the French Revolution, mounted his expedition to Egypt in 1798, landing at Alexandria. But while the French army was trying to gain control of Cairo in the Battle of the Pyramids, England's Admiral Horatio Nelson destroyed the French fleet at Abu Qir and the French were forced to retreat, leaving Egypt three years later. During this period, which was too short for Napoleon to put into effect his idea of *diwan*, a government assembly to reorganize the Egyptian government, a national awakening of sorts occurred in Egypt. By the time the French army had left, the country had emerged from the darkness and was revived by the discovery by French scholars and archaeologists of the great heritage of ancient Egypt. The discovery of the Rosetta Stone in 1799 allowed Champollion to decipher Egyptian hieroglyphic script in 1822.

Mohammed Ali and the Dawn of Modern Egypt

After the departure of the French, Egypt was again plunged into chaos and was only saved by an army revolt led by Mohammed Ali, a young Albanian officer in the Turkish army, in 1804. Though he acknowledged the Ottoman sultan as ruler, Mohammed Ali took control and remained in power as viceroy of Egypt for 40 years, during which the country witnessed modernization of its institutions and a wide-scale building programme, which included the construction of canals. By the time of Mohammed Ali's death, Egypt had attained international status and had begun attracting the attention of Western powers.

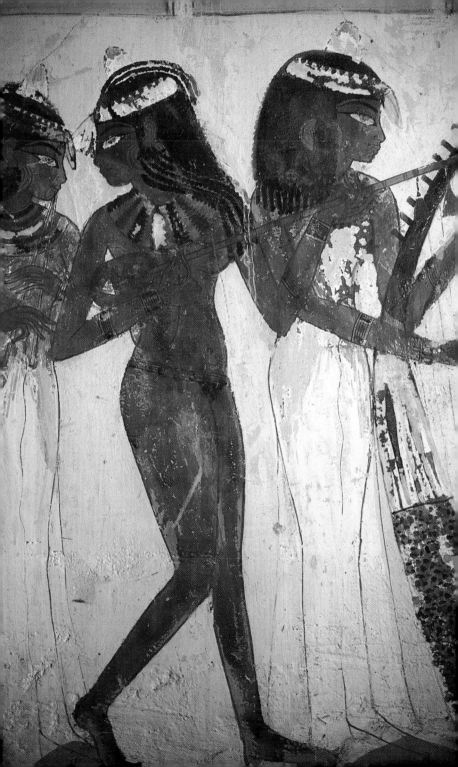

The Suez Canal and the British

Mohammed Ali's successors, who won for themselves the title of Khedive, continued his policies and, in 1875, took on total responsibility for the government of Egypt. During the rule of Khedive Ismail, the Suez Canal, linking the Red Sea and the Mediterranean, was opened in 1869 amid great celebrations. The project, designed by the French engineer Ferdinand de Lesseps, was so costly that an international fund was created to support it. Forty-four per cent of the shares went to Egypt. Six years later, Ismail was forced to sell his own interests in the canal company to British subscribers and, the following year, faced with bankruptcy, he was forced to agree to the setting up of a French-British condominium to manage his finances. In 1882, Britain sent an expeditionary force to Alexandria to quell disturbances caused by the economic situation, where it remained, thus beginning a period of increasing British influence in Egypt.

The Dawn of Nationalism

The British presence in Egypt did not stall the country's development, and with the founding of the Institute of Archaeology by Auguste Mariette in 1880, the Egyptians slowly became aware of their heritage. With the outbreak of World War I, Britain became conscious of the threat posed to the Suez Canal by the alliance between Germany and Turkey and so turned Egypt into a fully-fledged protectorate by law. In 1919, the King of Egypt attempted to win independence from Britain. This was granted in 1922 under a treaty which left the responsibility for the defence of the country and the Suez Canal with the British. Egypt was given a constitution and the Wafd Party, which had negotiated independence, was given the reins of government though the king retained his position. In 1936, Egypt and Britain signed a treaty which later allowed the British forces to carry out their North African campaign and to halt the advance of the Germans and Italians on Suez at el-Alamein in 1942. In March 1945, the Arab states of the Middle East met in Cairo and signed a pact creating the Arab League, which aimed at forming a unified front to pursue the aims of the Arab world.

Meanwhile, the internal situation in Egypt worsened and the monarchy was attacked because of the extravagance of King Farouk, who had assumed power in 1936. The creation of the State of Israel in 1948 and the emergence of a militant Islamic group (the Muslim Brotherhood) which advocated only Islamic rule, further discredited the monarchy. In 1949, the Israelis entered the Sinai Peninsula after defeating the Arab armies which tried to regain Palestine. This defeat angered the people and led to violent riots in Cairo. In July 1952, after three years of disturbances, Farouk was toppled by a revolt of army officers led by Gamal Abdel Nasser. He was forced to abdicate and seek exile in Italy. The Egyptian Republic was proclaimed in June 1953.

Nasser's main concern was to rid Egypt of Western influence and he successfully concluded an agreement with Britain which called for the evacuation of the British from the canal zone. Nasser also replaced the heads of foreign companies with Egyptians and, in 1956, he nationalized the Suez Canal, provoking armed intervention by Britain and France. This situation was resolved by a US ultimatum which won the Egyptian leader great prestige in the Arab world. In 1967, Nasser attempted an ill-fated attack on Israel which resulted in the seizure by the Jewish state of the West Bank and Gaza. He offered to resign, but crowds in Cairo forced him to stay. Nasser died in 1970 and his successor, Anwar Sadat, yet again changed the course of Egypt's history.

Sadat's major policy move was the scrapping of Nasser's treaty with the Soviet Union and the expulsion of Soviet experts. He turned to the West to help alleviate the country's economic problems and poverty, thus paving the way for an increased American involvement in Egypt, which began with the construction of the oil pipeline from Suez to Alexandria.

Conscious that the long-term success of his programme depended on the removal of the threat of Israel, Sadat launched a surprise assault across the Sinai in 1973. This was the turning point in Egypt's turbulent relations with Israel, paving the way for peace talks in 1978 and the signing of the Camp David accords and the peace treaty of 1979. Sadat was assassinated by Muslim zealots in 1981. He was succeeded by Hosni Mubarak, who has since sought to continue Sadat's policies while trying to reinstate Egypt in the Arab fold from which it was expelled in 1979 on account of its peace treaty with Israel.

The Religion of Ancient Egypt

The importance which the ancient Egyptians placed on religion has always intrigued visitors to the country. Upon visiting Egypt in the fifth century BC, the Greek historian Herodotus described the Egyptian population as the most 'highly religious' group he had encountered. Certain aspects of early religious history that we now term 'lay' may be identified in a cloudy mix of myth and 'pre-philosophic' thought expressed in a symbolic language.

When a more formal Egyptian religion was introduced at the dawn of the third century BC, it was characterized by more systematic mythical rituals which were derived from a number of groups in the ancient world. The Egyptians were always interested in finding more sophisticated ways to categorize and express their religious beliefs.

Cosmogony

In ancient Egyptian religious literature there is not one single account of cosmogony, or the creation of the world. It is only later, in the works of various schools of high priests, that such theories appear. From around 3000 BC, the most noted and influential cosmogonic beliefs were those developed in the cities of Heliopolis, Hermopolis and Memphis.

Popular beliefs

The foundations of many popular — as opposed to strictly religious — beliefs are found in the myths of Osiris, the king who, according to Plutarch, had imbued in his people the skills and techniques of agriculture, arts and sciences before being slain and cut into pieces by his brother Seth. His remains were then scattered to the far corners of Egypt. After the pieces had been recovered and recomposed, his wife Isis conceived from his mummy a son, Horus, who admirably avenged his father's death by defeating his uncle in a duel. Horus subsequently became king, later leaving his throne as a bequest to the Pharaohs.

The Egyptian gods were originally worshipped only in particular cities or provinces, but much later their cults became diffused over the entire country and some of them were put together in triads of families composed of father, mother and son (for example, Osiris, Isis and Horus, and Amun, Mut and Khonsu). The same type of reconciliation of beliefs allowed all the gods to share various attributes, so that from time to time it becomes difficult to distinguish one divinity from another.

The myth of Osiris inspired a divine ritual which was practised daily in the temples, and the belief in the cult of the dead included various ceremonies linked to embalming and other funerary practices designed to accompany the deceased on his voyage to the other world. The texts and images which appear on the walls of royal tombs belonging to the New Kingdom are neither descriptive nor commemorative nor merely artistic. They were designed to create a suitable ambience for the king's voyage to the other world and are taken from the abundant literature of that time known as 'Guides to the Other World'.

The Egyptian Gods

Amun Originally a secondary divinity venerated in Thebes, the god Amun and his cult were elevated to primary importance throughout Egypt with the expansion of the Theban dynasties which held power for several centuries. Known also in his syncretistic — or unifying — characterization as Amun-Ra, the God of the Sun, he was believed to possess all the properties of the solar demiurge (world creator) of Heliopolis, and was always represented with a crown of plumes.

Anubis Considered the protector of tombs, Anubis was represented by a jackal's head. (Jackals were often found wandering in the tombs.) He later became the patron of embalming. It was Anubis who recomposed the remains of Osiris and mummified him.

Apis The symbol of fertility, Apis was revered mainly in Memphis, in the form of a live bull which was also believed to be the incarnation of Ptah. When the sacred bull died, the priests carried out the embalming rituals which took 70 days, then buried the mummified bull in the Serapeum. The priests then looked for another sacred bull which had the precise physical characteristics of the original.

Aten Represented as a solar disk with rays becoming hands, Aten was believed to endow power and vitality on his followers. Amenhotep IV, under the name of Akhenaten, elevated the cult of Aten and considered this god as the creator of all things and the sole principle of any form of life. The cult of Aten declined after the death of Amenhotep IV.

Bastet The cat-goddess of Bubastis in the delta, Bastet was the peaceful form of the lioness Sakhmet. She had a great annual festival which was a time of much drunkenness.

Bes Bes was a protector of the household, particularly of women, whom he helped in childbirth. A bringer of good fortune, he was shown as a dwarf wearing a lion skin and often carrying a tambourine.

Geb Geb is the God of the Earth and married to Nut, Goddess of the Sky. Their children were Osiris, Isis, Seth and Nephthys.

Hapi Hapi is the divinity responsible for the Nile's beneficial floods which were considered extremely important for the earth's fertility.

Harpokrates ('Horus the Child') Harpokrates is one of the 'baby' forms of Horus, and is sucking his thumb. He became more popular in the last centuries of the Egyptian era. He was worshipped as the protecting god against dangerous animals, after his mother Isis had healed him from a scorpion's sting.

Harakhty ('Horus in the Horizon') Harakhty is represented by a falcon's head surmounted by the solar disk. He was particularly revered at Heliopolis.

Hathor The goddess with the cow's head who was the wife of Horus, Hathor was venerated, depending on the locality, as goddess of love and happiness, the protector of the dead, or the goddess of the sycamore. Her temple at Dendera was particularly important.

Horus Horus is the son of Isis and Osiris. Born after his father's body was skilfully mummified by Anubis, Horus was a divinity with various characteristics. Appointed by Anubis to avenge his father's death at the hands of the evil Seth, he was a symbol of the unification of the kingdoms and also the proud and powerful solar god with a falcon's head surmounted by the double crown. He was also shown as a winged sun-disk.

Ihy The son of Hathor, Ihy is depicted with the lock of hair denoting a child, and carrying a sistrum (a rattle used in the worship of Hathor).

Isis Osiris's sister and spouse, and mother of Horus, Isis was pictured as an attractive woman crowned with the hieroglyph for her name. As the goddess of pure love and the ideal mother and spouse, Isis became so popular in Egypt that her cult surpassed those of the other goddesses and found its way into the local faiths of other Mediterranean countries.

Khepri Pictured with a scarab for a head or a man with his head surmounted by a scarab, Khepri was another form of the sun god, signifying the morning sun.

Khnum According to Esna's theology, Khnum was the lord of creation. The artisan-god with the head of a ram, he reputedly modelled the human body with clay on his potter's wheel. He was particularly adored on Elephantine Island, where he was considered the controller of the Nile's water.

Khonsu A lunar god with a falcon's head, son of Amun and Mut, Khonsu was believed to be responsible for diseases and their diffusion through his genies. Much feared, Khonsu was believed to be merciless in his pursuit of the gods' enemies.

Maat The ithyphallic (licentious) god of fertility, Maat was honoured with propitiatory feasts of the harvests. Also considered the protector of travellers in the desert, he was represented as a mummy with a feathered crown and flail.

Nefertum Nefertum represented the primordial lotus from which the sun rose after the world's birth. Nefertum was Ptah's son with whom he formed, together with Sekhmet, a divine triad. He was believed to protect the eastern border of Egypt. He was represented by a lion's head surmounted by a lotus flower from which two feathers sprout.

Neith A very popular goddess in Northern Egypt in ancient times, Neith was considered the mother of the sun and the creator of the world. She regained her position of prestige during the seventh century BC with the advent of the Saïte Dynasty. Neith was always pictured with a bow and arrow and with the crown of Lower Egypt.

Nekhbet Vulture-goddess of Upper Egypt, Nekhbet was also considered the goddess of birth and the protector of buildings against intruders.

Nephthys Although married to Seth, the murderer of Osiris, Nephthys helped her sister Isis in the search for Osiris's body. She is shown mourning over the body with Isis, and is later a protector of the sarcophagus and canopic jars, along with Isis, Selket and Neith.

Nut Usually represented by a thin, arched body sprinkled with stars, Nut was the Goddess of the Sky and the wife of Geb, God of the Earth. Each day it was believed the sun and the stars followed the curve of her body. Her image was frequently carved inside sarcophagi to protect the deceased. She was the mother of Osiris, Isis, Nephtys and Seth.

Osiris Murdered by his brother Seth who was jealous of his wisdom and fame, Osiris was resurrected through the intervention of Isis and Anubis, but he was confined to the netherworld where he ruled. As supreme judge of the tribunal of the dead, Osiris was a very popular god and his cult flourished until the end of paganism in Egypt. He was pictured as a mummy with the white crown of Upper Egypt. He usually held a sceptre and a flail in his hands.

Ptah Considered in Memphis to be the creator of the world, Ptah's duty was also to protect goldsmiths and inventors. He was usually represented as a mummy with a tight white cap holding a sceptre in his hands.

Sakhmet A bellicose and dreadful lioness-goddess, Sekhmet was believed to be the cause of epidemics, which she spread with the help of her loyal genies. She massacred without mercy all those who threatened terrestrial or divine royalty, but her priests were taught the art of healing.

Seth Born as the God of the Oasis, Seth was respected because of his irascible nature until he rapidly lost esteem and popularity for his evil part in the legend of the murder of Osiris. After the Persian domination, Seth was usually identified with the hated invaders, but his popularity increased in the last period of paganism, returning him to his role as protector of the oases and their products. Seth is usually represented with a snout and long ears.

Sobek While he was considered the creator of the world in Kom Ombo, Sobek, the crocodile-god, remained a secondary divinity, the procreator and protector of fertility.

Thoth The God of the Moon, writing, time, weights and measure and mathematics, the wise Thoth was also a sorcerer. His major cult centre was Hermopolis. Thoth is usually pictured with the head of an ibis and a crescent moon on his head. He holds the scribe's tools in his hands.

Thoueris (Ta-weret) The peaceful hippopotamus-goddess, Thoueris became vicious when she was forced to punish troublemakers. She was considered the protector of mothers and children, aside from being the lady of pure waters. She was believed to reside along the narrow gorge of Silsila in the waters of the Nile.

Copts and Muslims

Inspired by profound religious fervour and impassioned by the desire to spread the message of Allah, the Arabs conquered Egypt in AD 639 and called its Christian inhabitants 'Copts'. Originally the expression 'Copt' was used to identify the entire population the conquering Arabs encountered in the newly-won land, but it later came to define only that part of the population which remained Christian. The Coptic Church does not differ from the Greek Orthodox Church except in the dogma concerning the nature of Christ. The Copts do not recognize the authority of the Pope nor the validity of ecumenical councils; instead, the Patriarch of Alexandria governs. Since the 11th century when, aware of the immense material advantages which assimilation into Islam assured them of, the Egyptians converted *en masse*, the patriarchate has had its seat in Cairo. Even so, the Egyptians retained the deep-rooted cultural qualities of their age-old nationalism. Thus, the country preserved a characteristic national identity as well as a certain political and cultural autonomy within the context of the Muslim religion. It was also an ideal starting point for the spreading of Islam across Africa.

Art and Architecture

For the ancient Egyptians, art had no aesthetic ends. It was functional, expressing the rationality according to which the world was ordered for them, and it was created for eternity and the divine. Likewise, the Egyptian artist was not an individual creator who transmitted his personality into his work; he was a specialized artisan who gave life to already-defined and selected forms.

The ideological basis of Egyptian art was the glorification of the deified Pharaoh, and magnificent tombs were built for that purpose. A preoccupation with the gods and their symbols was another dominant feature.

In Egyptian architecture, stone was used for those things which had to last for eternity, such as temples and tombs. Therefore houses, palaces and administrative buildings were made of unburnt brick, an easily available material, which could be easily renewed. Because this mud brick makes good fertilizer, many ancient town sites have been destroyed in the past, and consequently much less domestic architecture has survived.

Nature influenced architecture both in terms of spatial concepts and decorative elements. Temples and houses were built in the form of huts. They took advantage of natural light and used perishable materials such as tree trunks, papyrus bundles and reeds for structural members, and branches, mats and mud for the walls.

With the introduction of stone, previously utilized 'botanical' elements were imitated and worked into the new building material, which was considered eternal. Likewise, stone was quickly adapted for the construction of religious and funerary edifices. (Originally, tombs were simple graves dug out of the ground and covered with a mound of soil.) Space became neatly defined, following liturgical necessities.

Funerary architecture

The funerary architecture of ancient Egypt includes tombs, funerary statues, chapels or their annexed temples. The tomb is typically composed of three main parts: the body, constructed with brick or stone masonry or formed by a rocky declivity in the earth; the crypt, created within the body or beneath it, where the corpse and its funerary belongings were laid; and the sanctuary of the cult, which may be leaning against or included in the body or even isolated for offertory rites. In the sepulchres, there are always one or more statues of the deceased and stelae (carved stones) bearing his name, titles, religious funerary formulas and images. In Upper Egypt, the tomb is situated outside the inhabited areas along the confines of the desert so as to save arable land and to help preserve the corpse.

The most represented types of tombs are the *mastaba* (the ancient Egyptian tomb with sloping sides and flat roof), used from the First to the Sixth dynasties, the rupestral or semirupestral tomb (formed by a chapel carved out of the rocks, at the end of which there is a crypt), used from the Fourth Dynasty to the Middle Kingdom, and the royal tomb of the New Kingdom. A brief description of tomb architecture follows:

The *mastaba* The body of the *mastaba* is in the form of a parallelepiped with tapering sides and a crypt dug out from the ground, accessible through a ramp or a well which was filled up or blocked after the burial. Inside it were the altars, funeral offerings, multi-coloured reliefs or wall paintings with scenes from everyday life. It was the model for the royal tomb until the Third Dynasty. The *mastaba* was originally in mud brick, compact (such as the royal tombs of the First and Second dynasties in Abydos) or moulded (the *mastabas* of the sovereigns of the first two dynasties in Saqqara). During the Fourth Dynasty, *mastabas* were constructed in stone, at first compact (as at Giza), then composite with the characteristics of the moulded *mastaba* (for example Giza and Saqqara). Towards the end of the Fifth Dynasty, *mastabas* had numerous rooms, the walls of which were decorated with images of the deceased and scenes from daily life.

The rupestral tomb The rupestral (or rock-cut) tomb is the most common, especially in Middle and Upper Egypt, near rocky buttresses close to the Nile. It is formed by a chapel carved out of the rocks, at the end of which one descends to the crypt through a well or a ramp. The chapel may be at right angles, cruciform or longitudinal. The sanctuary of the cult is generally marked by a stele. Sometimes, these tombs have flights of steps outside and monumental façades which face the Nile. The interiors have notable decorations with colourful painted reliefs.

The pyramid The pyramid, the typical royal tomb of the Old Kingdom, was constructed in limestone with some elements in granite. First was the Step Pyramid of the Third Dynasty, followed by the geometric type during the Fourth Dynasty. In the Middle Kingdom (12th Dynasty), it comprised a brick and stone structure. The complex includes a 'valley temple', a landing pier for the fluvial or river procession, and a processional pathway leading to a 'high temple' which leans against the pyramid.

Funerary Literature

The ancient Egyptians' obsession with the after-life gave rise to a distinctive literature and writings associated with death. This 'funerary literature' was designed to facilitate and give guidance to the soul of the deceased person in its passage through the after-life.

The earliest-known examples of Egyptian funerary literature were texts inscribed on the walls of the Pyramid of Unas, built for the last king of the Fifth Dynasty, in Saqqara. The texts, referred to as the 'Pyramid Texts', are perhaps the most comprehensive and purest collection of the funerary literature of ancient Egypt. Originally, such texts were reserved for kings, but in the Middle Kingdom (2040–1782 BC) they were inscribed on coffins of noblemen and high officials, and by the New Kingdom (1570–1070 BC), inscriptions from what became known as *The Book of the Dead* were transferred to papyrus scrolls which were buried inside the swathings covering the corpse.

The Book of the Dead is today considered representative of all Egyptian funerary literature discovered in the tombs of the Pharaohs in the Valley of the Kings near Luxor. The book is a collection of more than 100 compositions on aspects of the after-life and ways to cope with it, some of which are among the most complicated literature of ancient Egypt. These were called by other names such as the *Book of What is in the Duat*, *The Book of the Gates*, the *Book of the Caverns*, the *Litany of Re* and the *Book of the Divine Cow*.

The Book of What is in the Duat is the earliest example of funerary literature of the New Kingdom. It is basically a manual of spiritual instruction which details in elaborate symbolic steps what must be done to ensure life in eternity, following the passage of the solar entity or king through the 12 hours of the night.

The Book of the Gates is apparently more recent and offers a variation on the theme of the solar entity going through the hours of the night, setting as Atum and rising as Khepri, the scarab. The word 'gates' stems from the belief that at the entrance of each hour of the night was a gate.

The Book of the Caverns is the most recent of New Kingdom funerary compositions. Here the theme of reward and punishment is obvious, particularly in reference to those who are enemies of Osiris.

The Book of the Divine Cow is the only one among the funerary texts which has not survived in a complete version. It tells a story that is interspersed with magic spells.

The ancient Egyptian funerary literature had no concept which corresponds to the word 'soul' for the Egyptians believed there was a variety of spiritual entities belonging to the same person. They believed there was the *ba* or *bai*, represented as a human bird, which could move in and out of the tomb at will; the *ka*, the person's double, represented by two raised arms; and the *akh*, an indestructible entity of the person which was usually depicted as a bald ibis in hieroglyphic script.

In predynastic times, Egyptians buried food and objects, such as weapons for a man and ornaments for a woman, with the dead. In the Old Kingdom, they buried models of servants who by some magical formula would carry out menial tasks in the after-life. In the Middle Kingdom, model boats and houses manned by servants were included in tomb equipment, but this was later phased out and replaced by *ushbati*, statuettes representing the dead person and inscribed with texts from *The Book of the Dead*, which they thought empowered them to carry out any work required of the dead person in the after-life.

Funerary wall paintings

The royal tomb The royal tombs of the New Kingdom were cut into the rock and sometimes extended for hundreds of metres into the limestone hillside of the western plain of Thebes.

Religious Architecture

Religious architecture as a general concept includes various types of temples. Aside from the royal funerary temples, the other types of temples dedicated to the gods are the solar, cell and peribolus temples. The solar temple was specially planned for offertory rites which were celebrated with the ceiling open for worshipping the solar divinity. The other two types were made for rites celebrated indoors. The various divinities worshipped indoors were represented by statues in cells.

Solar temples The earliest known temples dedicated to the solar cult of Ra date back to the Fifth Dynasty. The centre of this cult was Heliopolis, and very few vestiges of it remain. The best-preserved example is the Temple of Niuserra in Abu Gurob, in the area of Abusir north of Saqqara. This temple has three parts: the first is the main or real temple made up of a large court, at the centre of which is an altar fronted by a stone obelisk in two sections, the base and the actual obelisk; the second is a long corridor which descends from the court; and the third part is the valley temple with a landing pier in front of the Nile. Another type of solar temple is found at Amarna. It is formed by a succession of courts with a pillared entrance and rows of altars on the sides. At the centre of the last court is the principal altar, which is raised on a podium reached by a flight of steps.

Cell temples The cell temple creates a space which narrows to focus on the image of the god housed in the sanctuary. The simplest model, subject to variations and enlargements, is made up of a vestibule and a cell. This developed in the 18th Dynasty into its typical form which may be found in the great temple of Amun in Karnak, with the addition of a monumental pillared entrance, a court, and a hypostyle atrium. Only followers of the cult were allowed access to the court. The interior chambers were reserved for the king and high priests. A particular example of the cell temple is at Abu Simbel.

Peribolus temples Originally, the peribolus temple was a shrine or sacrarium annexed to the cell temple. It housed the sacred vessel of the temple god which was carried during processions of certain feasts. It is made up of a chamber encircled by a corridor, from which it derives the name peribolus. It has an entrance and an exit on opposite sides so as to create a continuous walkway. (An example of this is the White Chapel of Senusret I in Karnak.)

Other Structures

Other types of stone edifices such as *mammisi* (birth houses) and
kiosks were typical of the Late Ptolemaic and Roman architecture. The
work of the sovereigns of this period is manifested in the immense
complexes of sanctuaries with numerous annexes. Monumental
examples are best preserved in Upper Egypt, in Dendera, Esna, Edfu,
Kom Ombo, Philae and Kalabsha.

Alexandrian court life was based on the Hellenistic model and a
certain sector of the Egyptian upper class had Philhellenic (pro-Greek)
leanings. However, the temple remained free from foreign influences
and maintained its influence over the population. Consequently ancient
construction techniques were preserved in the cult sites. During the
height of the Roman domination and until the division of the empire
beween the east and the west, temples to the various Egyptian cults
were still being erected. Although they had no connection to Pharaonic
architectural models, they presented original aesthetic and spatial
qualities and a style which evoked the spirit of Hellenism.

Domestic Architecture

Domestic architecture is documented in the remains of layouts of city
palaces and private houses. Among the organized settlements, that of
el-Lahun in el-Fayum is noteworthy. It was founded during the 12th
Dynasty to accommodate the work force for the pyramids which were
under construction nearby, with separate quarters for the
administrators and the workers. Other interesting settlements are those
of el-Amarna and the village of Deir el-Medina. The capital of
Amenhotep IV (Akhenaten) in el-Amarna was founded in 1350 BC.
Sprawled along the Nile, without walls and protected by the river and
the mountain, the new city included a royal villa, a suburb with modest
houses, administrative quarters with government offices, a residential
section with villas, a royal palace and a temple. Houses for officials and
functionaries, barracks, storehouses and cult shrines were constructed
around the fortresses and within the city walls. These were built mainly
in the south for defence purposes following Egyptian territorial
expansion into Nubia. Materials utilized in the construction of civilian
edifices were mainly of unfired mud bricks and light supports such as
wood and reeds.

The Statue

Architecture was inseparable from the plastic and figurative arts, from
sculpture and painting. The statue was an important element in sacred

and funerary architecture. However, its purpose was not aesthetic, but religious. The statue had a substitutive function for the subject and was not commemorative or celebratory as its presence in the tomb or temple might suggest. The statue is a projection of the person who continues to live after death. In the mastabas, statues are hidden in the *serdab* or cellar and may be viewed through openings at eye level. In the valley temple of Chephren, the 23 statues of the sovereign lined along the walls were 'endowed with life' during the 'opening of the mouth' rituals. Aside from the magnificent examples of sculpture in stone and wood, the mastabas have yielded numerous painted limestone statuettes of servants which are also linked to the concept of the survival and, above all, comfort of the deceased in the other world. The wall paintings were created for the same purpose. As with the architecture, the statuary figures were created in semi-hard precious stones (granite, diorite and basalt) or soft stones (limestone, sandstone, alabaster) and multi-coloured wood and metal. The figurative, as opposed to literal, structure follows the same rules of painting and reliefs in accordance with a precise canon of proportions. Geometry appears as the expression of pure rationality. The full frontal pose is always respected. As well as the position or pose, external attributes such as dress, sceptres, insignia and crowns indicate the office the deceased held in life. Within the frame of such conventions, we find a developed figuratism which reached a secure equilibrium of forms at an early stage. Unfortunately, one cannot speak of 'portraiture' even though there is evidence of a keen observation of facial and bodily characteristics and some variety of individual expressions.

The Rediscovery of Egypt

Napoleon's expedition to Egypt in 1798 and the discovery of the Rosetta Stone in 1799 marked the beginning of systematic and methodical studies of the history of Egyptian civilization. A host of scholars had joined the expedition in order to make a systematic study and to publish any and all records of ancient and contemporary Egypt. But the most famous and important event was their accidental discovery of the Rosetta Stone (now in the British Museum in London), which contained the text of a decree made in 196 BC by a conclave of priests in Memphis in honour of Ptolemy V. It was written in hieroglyphic, Demotic and Greek. The attention of scholars, particularly of J.F. Champollion, the 'decipherer', was immediately focused on it, and it is considered to have given birth to the science of Egyptology as it is known today.

An Archaeological Awakening

At the start of the 19th century, Mohammed Ali, as part of modernization and economic recovery programmes for his country, opened Egypt to Europeans, many of whom established themselves around the court in Alexandria and in other major cities. Since it was not difficult to obtain an excavation permit, the newly appointed European consuls, diplomatic agents, engineers and businessmen also became archaeologists and antique dealers overnight. The treasures they accumulated became the nucleus of dazzling collections in European museums, and 'finds' made while digging major temples and pyramids out of the encroaching sands became the source of new excitement and impetus for the students of Egyptology.

The rich collection of Bernadino Drovetti, French consul-general to Egypt, was bought by Carlo Felice of Savoy and found a permanent home in Turin in 1824. A second collection of Drovetti's went to the Louvre in Paris. Giuseppe di Nizzoli of Trieste, Chancellor of the Legation of Austria, collected fine archaeological pieces from Lower Egypt which were later divided between the museums of Vienna and Florence. The English consul, Henry Salt, along with the Paduan Belzoni and the Genoese Caviglia, put together an impressive collection of Egyptian treasures which was later sold to the British Museum. Other antique collectors continued their excavation operations in Egypt during the early 1800s and their magnificent finds enriched the museums of Berlin, London and Paris.

The 'Gold Rush'

The operations of Bonaparte's French expedition continued with the arrival of more scholars. However, the true students of Egyptology were rare; the majority engaged in what became known as a period of unbridled pillage during which graves were plundered and tombs opened. When Champollion went to Egypt in 1828-9 with Rosellini, heading the Franco-Tuscan Expedition, he proposed that an office be set up to co-ordinate the study of the preservation of antiquities and to compile a list of all sites of archaeological interest in order of importance. As a result, one scientific expedition after another was mounted in the second half of the century. Interest in Egyptian archaeological research was also significantly increased by the concomitant growth of museums exhibiting rich Egyptian collections.

From 1842 to 1845, the Prussian Expedition of the Imperial Academy of Berlin, led by Karl Richard Lepsius, covered the entire Valley of the Nile and the deserts surrounding it, investigating chiefly characters carved in stone and drawn on papyrus. By the second half of the century, archaeological activities extended to the entire territory.

One of the most noteworthy archaeological discoveries of that time, that of the Serapeum of Memphis, is attributed to the French Egyptologist Auguste Mariette. Having seen the irreparable damage that antique dealers and art collectors were causing (approximately 700 tombs had been plundered between Abusir and Saqqara), Mariette strongly advocated the establishment of an institutional service for the control and supervision of antiquities. As a result, some rooms of the former River Company of Bulaq were set aside to serve as a museum and storage place for excavation finds. This represented a major step towards the eventual formation of the Egyptian Museum of Cairo. Mariette conducted excavation operations all over Egypt, particularly in the delta, and at Giza, Saqqara, Abydos, Dendera, Edfu, Karnak, Deir el-Bahari, Medinet Habu and Qurna. After Mariette's death in 1881, Maspero succeeded him as Director of the Office of Antiquities and of the Museum. The new director oversaw the opening of certain pyramids in Saqqara, most of which were badly ruined, but the mysterious interiors of which would reveal a number of important religious-funerary texts from which the name 'Pyramid Texts' is derived. In 1881 and 1891, a number of royal mummies and sarcophagi of the high priests of Amun were discovered in the vicinity of Deir el-Bahari.

Permanent Foreign Institutions

Until World War I, important and regular excavations continued all over the country. In 1881, the Antiquities Services Office granted excavation sites to foreign missions such as the English and the German, most of which founded permanent institutions in Egypt. Flinders Petrie introduced into Egypt a perfected methodology for the English excavations. The Germans on the other hand, under the direction of Borchardt, organized systematic and scientific excavations in Tell el-Amarna, the fruits of which may be found partly in the Berlin museums. A law passed in 1912 set up stricter and more rigorous standards for foreign excavations in Egypt.

Nevertheless, the practice of dividing finds into portions continued, despite the fact that foreign missions were no longer guaranteed half the finds. At the end of the 19th century and the beginning of the 20th century, and as a consequence of the discovery of lithic industrial products and Naqada ceramics, most attention was focused on Egyptian prehistory and protohistory. The construction of the first Aswan Dam between 1898 and 1912, which caused the seasonal flooding of Philae and other nearby temples, renewed archaeological interest in Nubia. After the slowing down of archaeological work during World War I, operations were resumed with the help of

Egyptian scholars. However, the direction of the Antiquities Services Office was still predominantly French. From then on, concessions were given only to scientific institutions such as museums and universities. The Museum of Cairo retained all finds considered unique, while the government decided on the division of the rest.

Tutankhamun's treasures, Egyptian Museum, Cairo

Post-war Euphoria

Post-war archaeological operations brought rich rewards, with, especially, the uncovering of the undisturbed tomb of Tutankhamun by Lord Carnarvon, a patron of the arts, and Howard Carter, an archaeologist, in 1922. The countless quantities of precious objects which made up the Pharaoh's funerary equipment remained in Cairo. In Saqqara, Firth and Lauer undertook the methodical excavation of Zoser's funerary complex and Lauer later continued the important work of reconstructing the monuments using the original blocks. From 1952, Egypt's archaeological efforts were focused on ways to save the ancient sites of Nubia, chiefly Abu Simbel and Philae, which would be flooded by the construction of the High Dam at Aswan. Excavations in Lower Egypt and the delta, made difficult because many historic sites had been buried by silt deposited by the Nile, also resumed with much more rigorous methodology, though to date few exciting finds have been unearthed.

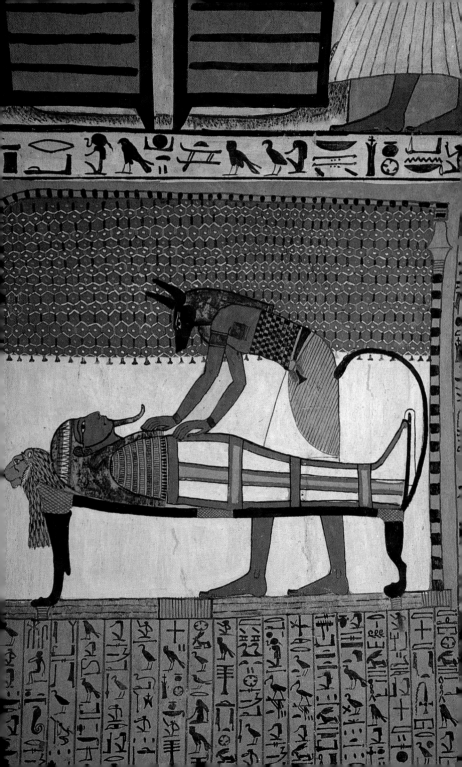

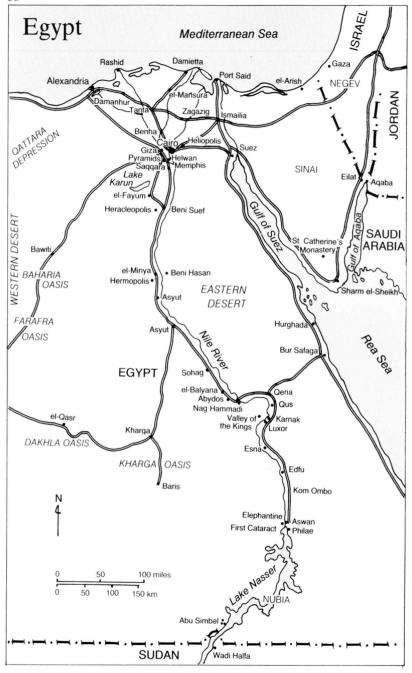

Egypt

Mediterranean Sea

ISRAEL

Rashid
Damietta
Gaza
Alexandria
Port Said
el-Arish
NEGEV
JORDAN
Damanhur
el-Mansura
Tanta
Zagazig
Ismailia
Benha
Cairo
Heliopolis
Suez
Giza
Helwan
Pyramids
Saqqara
Memphis
SINAI
Eilat
Aqaba

QATTARA DEPRESSION

Lake Karun
el-Fayum
Heracleopolis
Beni Suef
SAUDI ARABIA

WESTERN DESERT

Bawiti

BAHARIA OASIS

el-Minya
Beni Hasan
Hermopolis
EASTERN DESERT
St Catherine's Monastery

FARAFRA OASIS

Asyut
Gulf of Suez
Gulf of Aqaba
Sharm el-Sheikh

Asyut
Nile River
Hurghada
Rea Sea

EGYPT
Sohag
Bur Safaga

el-Qasr
el-Balyana
Abydos
Qena
Kharga
Nag Hammadi
Qus
Valley of the Kings
Karnak
Luxor

DAKHLA OASIS

Esna

KHARGA OASIS
Edfu

Baris
Kom Ombo

Elephantine
Aswan
First Cataract
Philae

N

0   50   100 miles
0   50   100   150 km

Lake Nasser
NUBIA

Abu Simbel

SUDAN
Wadi Halfa

General Information for Travellers

Getting to Egypt

When to go
The best time to visit Egypt is during the winter months, from
November to March, when the nights are cool and the days are not
oppressively sultry. However, prices tend to be higher at this time, and
the hotels are often fully booked.

April weather is unpredictable and often very windy; it is in fact
the season of *khamsin* or sandstorms. From May to September, the
weather becomes much warmer. Cairo can be very hot and Upper
Egypt particulary torrid. During these months, visitors are advised to
plan trips to archaeological sites during the cooler parts of the day,
either in the very early morning or late afternoon. However, most
hotels are air-conditioned and all first-class establishments have a
swimming pool. By October, the worst of the summer heat has
dissipated. During Ramadan, the holy month of fasting determined by
the lunar calendar, faithful Muslims abstain from both food and drink
from sunrise to sunset and the pace of life is generally slow.

How to get there
Egypt's strategic geographical position makes it a convenient and
important junction of the three continents of Europe, Asia and Africa.
Today, Cairo is the principal air terminal of the Middle East, and
Alexandria and the Suez Canal are the centres of maritime traffic. It is
rather difficult to reach Egypt by land. There are two roads to which
the Sudanese tract of the long stretch linking Cairo and Cape Town is
joined. The North African coastal road which starts from Tangiers
crosses Morocco, Algeria, Tunisia and Libya. The road in Libya is
known as the 'Road of Rommel'. A transit visa is required and is
obtainable only with a passport translated into Arabic beforehand. The
fact that Egypt and Libya do not have diplomatic relations can create
some problems for the traveller. The other coastal road leads east to
Jerusalem, Amman and Damascus, where it is joined by the road that
links Istanbul with Delhi. Use of these roads depends on the existing
state of relations beween the countries involved, so it is important to
keep well informed if you plan to travel to Egypt by road. Cars may be
ferried to Alexandria from Venice, Ancona, Naples, Marseilles and
Athens. The major companies which operate through these routes are
Adriatica, with offices in Venice and at 33 Sharia Salah Salem,
Alexandria, the Egyptian Maritime Company at 1 el-Hureya Avenue,
Alexandria, and DFDS, c/o Menatours, el-Nasr Building, el-Nil Street,
Giza, tel. 843160.

Cairo is linked by air to the United States via Rome or Athens, and many flights, both with and without stopovers, operate from the major European and Middle Eastern capitals. Cairo is the only Arab capital with regular flights to and from Tel Aviv, operated by El Al and Air Sinai. Other airlines which fly to Cairo are: Austrian Airlines, Gulf Air, TWA, Air Malta, Alitalia, Balkan Air, JAL, JAT, KLM, LOT, Olympic, Royal Air Maroc, Sabena, Swissair, Tarom, Thai, British Airways and Interflug.

Tourist information
Information on Egypt can be obtained through the various offices of the Ministry of Egyptian Tourism, the headquarters of which are at 5 Sharia Adly, Cairo, tel. 923000, or from the following overseas offices:

FRANCE: 56 Avenue D'Iena, Paris XVI, tel. 7205303
WEST GERMANY: Taunusstrasse 35, 6000 Frankfurt am main, tel. 252319/252153
UNITED KINGDOM: 62A Piccadilly, London W1, tel. 4935282
GREECE: 3 Vassilissis Sophias Avenue, Athens, tel. 606906
ITALY: Via Bissolati 19, Rome, tel. 4751985
LEBANON: Sahet Reyad el-Sulh, Hussein el-Ewainy Building, Beirut, tel. 254621
SPAIN: Alcala 21, Madrid 14, tel. 2213406
SWEDEN: 9 Strandvagen, 11456 Stockholm, tel. 634008
SWITZERLAND: 11 rue de Chantepoulet, Geneva, tel. 329132
UNITED STATES: 630 Fifth Avenue, NY 10020, New York, tel. 2466960; 3001 Pacific Avenue, San Francisco, CA 94115, California

Tourist Police Stations are located in all places of major interest, in ports, air terminals and stations. The Tourist Police, who can be identified by their armbands, will assist visitors in all sorts of situations such as giving information and directions, or intervening in disputes with taxi-drivers and merchants.

Organized tours
A popular tourist destination, Egypt is included in the programmes of most major international travel agencies. Organized tours are generally very helpful for those travellers who do not claim to be adventurous but who wish to visit the principal tourist sights and archaeological zones in comfort without having to undergo rigorous attempts at communication with the locals or painstaking research in the planning of an itinerary and means of transportation.

Organized tours can also prove to be time- and money-saving. Almost always, in fact, the total cost of an individual tour is considerably higher than that of a group. Major travel agencies offer a number of travel plans. The criteria you should keep in mind are: duration of stay, the season, the composition of the trip (how much time will be allotted for sightseeing and how much for free time), the means of transportation and the price. If you want to savour and discover Egypt, avoid hectic tours which visit dozens of sunny Mediterranean destinations and mystical Middle Eastern lands in just 15 days for they promise the tourist only fleeting contact with places which deserve to be visited at length. A brief listing of tour agencies appears at the back of this book.

Passports and visas

Visitors to Egypt are required to have a passport or equivalent documents valid for at least six months from the date of entry. A tourist visa may be obtained at Egyptian embassies or consulates abroad and is valid for 30 days, renewable for up to six months. The requirements for a visa application are a valid passport, a photograph and the payment of the entry tax which will be demanded upon arrival. The visa may also be obtained upon arrival at a port or frontier, but to avoid unnecessary queueing, it would be advisable to obtain one beforehand and to request a longer duration of stay to allow for some flexibility in your travel plans. Those who join organized tours will usually be included on a collective visa obtained by their travel agency. Visa extensions of up to six months can be applied for and are issued at the Passports Office, Mugamma, Palace of the Governor, Room 16, Midan el-Tahrir, Cairo.

Egyptian embassies abroad also issue special student visas valid for one year. Information on business visas or working permits may also be obtained from Egyptian embassies and consulates. Once in Egypt, visitors are required to register with the Mugamma or the nearest police station within seven days of arrival. Hotels register their guests; those who stay in pensions or private homes must register personally.

Vaccinations

An anti-smallpox vaccination is not now required. However, visitors from endemic zones must present a valid certificate of anti-cholera and anti-yellow fever vaccinations. The anti-cholera vaccination is valid for six months from the sixth day after inoculation. The yellow fever vaccination, on the other hand, is valid for ten years from the tenth day after inoculation. Health regulations are constantly changing to keep pace with worldwide epidemic trends and medical advances, and Egyptian authorities are very strict on public health. Visitors arriving from infected areas without proper certification must stay in quarantine for a certain period before they are allowed entry. Check beforehand with your local World Health Organization office for information.

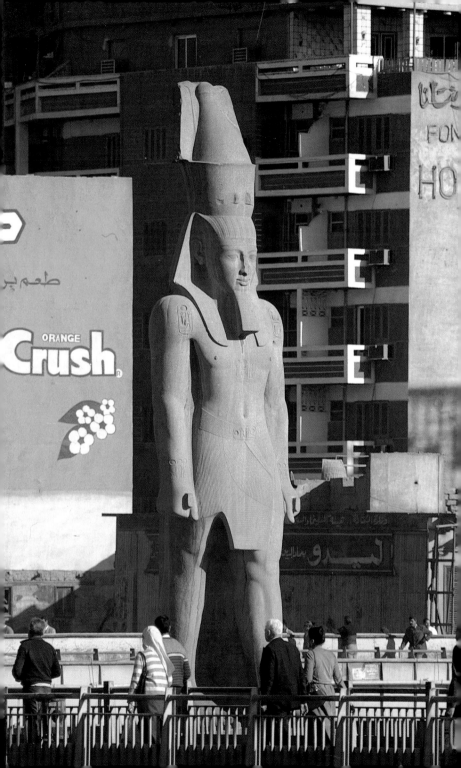

Dress

Although summer days are hot, the temperature drops in the evening and it is advisable to bring light sweaters or a shawl. Light, wide-brimmed hats offer protection against the heat, sunstroke and burns. Egyptian cotton is reputedly the world's best, and one will quickly discover the many benefits of a *galabeah*, the typical wide-sleeved, floor-length costume worn by the locals.

During the winter, the evenings become rather chilly and only major hotels offer heating facilities; however, jerseys and cardigans should offer sufficient warmth. A thin folding raincoat will be useful while an umbrella will seem superfluous. Regular spring wear will do for daytime. Laundry service is fast, efficient and inexpensive in Egypt, so it is unnecessary to bring a large wardrobe.

Whatever time of year one visits, it should be borne in mind that Egypt is a Muslim country and actually more conservative than it may seem at first. Women should dress modestly and avoid low necklines, miniskirts and skimpy shorts. Men should also avoid the latter. Improperly dressed visitors may be denied entry to temples, mosques and churches.

What to take

Do not forget to take sunglasses, suntan lotions and protective creams, as well as any necessary medications as they may be unavailable or sold under a different name. Cosmetics and toiletry products which are more or less internationally known are available, but at somewhat higher prices. It is a good idea to take along disposable wet towels, insect repellent and any special lotions you may require.

If extensive trips to archaeological sites are on your schedule, a canteen or a water-flask and an electric torch will be necessary. Take a photocopy of all important travel documents, including your passport, driver's licence and identification cards, and keep them separate from the originals throughout the trip.

Arriving by air

Cairo International Airport is a busy air terminal which can overflow with passengers during peak seasons. After submitting their arrival cards, visitors have to pass health and security checks. Visitors not travelling with a group or those without visas are required to change US$150 into local currency at the official exchange rate, after which a tourist visa will be issued. Keep all money-change receipts and the customs 'Form D' or other declaration forms (filled in on arrival) as you will be required to submit them on departure. Without exception, visitors are required to register with the Ministry of the Interior at the Mugamma within seven days of arrival and failure to do so will result in a heavy fine. When travelling outside Cairo, you must visit the local police station if you wish to stay for more than three days in any one place.

From the airport to the centre of Cairo is a distance of around 20 kilometres (12.5 miles). Taxis are available; there are also limousine services, run by Limousine Misr, which operate around the clock. They are a little more expensive than taxis but can be contacted by telephone on Cairo 831358 or 824539, and a car will be sent to the address required. If you decide to take a taxi, remember to bargain over the fare (which at the time of writing is about five Egyptian pounds to central Cairo) before leaving because taxi drivers will almost certainly not use the meter or may double the fare. Normally, it takes 20 to 30 minutes to get to Cairo by car from the airport. During rush hour, however, allow an hour and 20 minutes to travel to the city centre. Since entry formalities can be rather long and hotel transfers may require some time, it is best to arrive in the afternoon.

Arriving by sea
For visitors arriving by ship in Alexandria, procedures take place on board and only customs inspection follows upon landing. There are also telephones, a bank and post office in the arrival area. Tourist buses located outside the arrival area take on passengers with reservations to Cairo. Those who arrive without bus reservations may take a taxi to the train station. The three-hour train ride to Cairo is very pleasant as it passes through the fields of the Nile delta. It costs a few pounds for second class. The fare for first class, which is air-conditioned, is slightly higher. From the Cairo train station to the city centre is only 15 minutes by car.

Arriving by car
If you wish to bring a car to Egypt for a period of up to 90 days without paying import taxes, it is necessary to present the vehicle's international licence, the driver's international driver's licence, (valid at least 90 days from the date of entry), and the customs document ('Carnet de Passage en Douane') issued by any officially recognized automobile club. Customs authorities will then check whether or not the proprietor of the vehicle or driver is a resident of Egypt. A customs exemption certificate will be issued and should always be displayed on the windscreen. It is a good idea to ask your local automobile club for information regarding current requirements when you pick up the necessary documentation. If you intend to prolong your visit, contact the Automobile Club of Egypt at least a month before the 90-day expiry date and they will handle visa extensions. Beyond 90 days, an international driver's licence will not be sufficient. The driver will be

required to obtain an Egyptian driver's licence, issued upon presentation of three photographs, a medical certificate, the international driver's licence and payment of a modest fee. Those without a valid international driver's licence will also have to take a driving test.

Customs

Visitors may bring with them any form of personal articles they deem necessary for the duration of their stay, as well as 200 cigarettes or 50 cigars and one litre of alcohol. If you are in possession of more than one camera, it is advisable to register these using the 'Formulaire 54 KML' to avoid inconvenience when leaving the country. For the same reason, jewellery and other valuable items should be declared on a 'Form D'.

You may be required to pay an import tax on some items of high commercial value, but this will be refunded on departure if you show you are leaving with them. Any animal brought in should have a proper anti-rabies vaccination certificate and a medical certificate issued by a veterinarian stating that the animal is healthy and free of disease. On arrival, dog owners also have to pay a minimal entry tax for pets brought in and are issued with an identity medallion which should be attached to the dog's collar where it can be easily seen.

Firearms are forbidden. However, the Ministry of the Interior issues temporary licences for the importation of hunting equipment. To obtain this permit, a request addressed to the Ministry must be submitted with name, nationality, passport number, duration of stay in Egypt, plus a detailed description of the arms, two photographs and the official receipt of the covering fees. All arms thus declared must be re-exported upon departure. If, for whatever reason, a licence is not issued by the authorities, the arms will be consigned to the border or customs authorities and will be returned to the owner upon departure.

Travel Within Egypt

Currency The unit of currency is the Egyptian pound (LE), which is divided into 100 piastres. Notes come in 1, 5, 10, 20, 50 and 100 LE and coins in 5, 10, 25 and 50 piastres. Visitors will come across various currency forms of different weights and dimensions, but of the same monetary value. Some are marked only with figures in Arabic numerals. In Arab countries, Arabic numerals are different from what we call 'Arabic numbers'.

Visitors may bring in an unlimited amount of foreign currency, but not more than 20LE in Egyptian currency, which should also be declared on a 'Form D' upon arrival. This declaration form should be kept as it will be useful when changing foreign currency and also for re-exchange when leaving. In fact, all money-change receipts issued by banks should be retained throughout the duration of the stay. Upon departure, Egyptian pounds may be reconverted into foreign currency only upon presentation of valid receipts from banks or officially recognized money changers. The Egyptian government has successfully curbed the black market, and with a currently very favourable exchange rate Western visitors have no need to change money this way. However, many tourists take advantage of the black market, but laws exist against this, and, if applied, they are rather severe. Travellers' cheques may be changed easily at banks or official money changers. Although credit cards are gaining in popularity in Egypt, their use is limited at the moment to large hotels, luxury restaurants, and shops with a regular tourist clientele.

Time zone Egyptian Standard Time is two hours ahead of Greenwich Mean Time, seven hours ahead of the east coast of the United States (Eastern Standard Time) and ten hours ahead of the west coast (Pacific Time). Egyptian Summer Time from May till September is three hours ahead (GMT+three).

Accommodation During the last few years, a number of hotels have been built, reconstructed or renovated, many of which are affiliated with international hotel chains. However, there is still insufficient accommodation especially during the peak winter season, so it is important to book well in advance. Egyptian hotels are divided into five categories, from one-star to five-star. Luxury-rated and top-grade hotels compare favourably with their counterparts in other parts of the world. Some of the pensions are very reasonably priced, though many are rather spartan and not very clean by foreign tourist standards. They are usually only used by backpackers and very low-budget travellers who do not mind some discomfort, noise and overcrowding. Unfortunately, hotels in Egypt are concentrated only in certain places. Beyond Cairo, Alexandria, Luxor, Aswan, Hurghada and Port Said, there are only very small hotels. A selected list of hotels appears at the back of this book.

Working hours As in most Islamic countries, Friday is a public holiday.

Holidays The following dates are official public holidays:
1 January — *New Year's Day*; 22 February — *Union Day*; 1 May — *Labour Day*; 18 June — *Anniversary of British Evacuation*; 23 July — *Anniversary of the Egyptian Revolution*; 6 October — *Egyptian Military Forces Day*; 24 October — *Anniversary of Suez*; 23 December — *Victory Day*.

Islamic festivals and holidays follow the Muslim lunar calendar and are observed 10−12 days earlier each year. The following Muslim holidays are observed: Mouled el-Nabi (the 'Birth of the Prophet'), Eid el-Adha (the Bairam celebrating the end of the annual pilgrimage to Mecca); Eid el-Fitr at the beginning of the Hegira (Islamic calendar).

During Ramadan, practising Muslims fast from sunrise until sunset. Hence, activities slow down or come almost to a standstill. It is a period when visitors can expect to find all sorts of inconveniences. Thus, it would be most advisable to avoid visits to Egypt (and to other Muslim countries) during this period.

Festivals Aside from the Cairo International Fair, which takes place in the first half of March, an even more interesting spring event which dates back to the time of the Pharaohs is the Sham el-Nessim, literally the 'Scent of Spring', a traditional festival which takes place on Easter Monday following the Coptic Easter. Ancient Egyptian men observed this feast by presenting a lotus flower to their ladies. Families would take leisurely cruises down the Nile on flower-decked feluccas. Today, the entire population celebrates this festival with family picnics in the parks and gardens along the Nile. The feasts celebrated in the Muslim calendar are also observed.

Language While Arabic is the official language in Egypt, many educated people are fluent in English and French. In major hotels and restaurants patronized by tourists, staff almost always speak English and French and, very often, German and Italian as well.

Postal and telephone services In Cairo, the Central Post Office located in Midan el-Ataba is open 24 hours a day. All other post offices are open from 8.30 am until 3.00 pm every day except Friday. Stamps are also available in hotels. If you wish to send a package abroad, an export certificate must first be obtained at the Central Post Office. Often, however, the store from which the item was bought will handle these formalities for an additional service fee. Letters sent to tourists whose exact addresses are not verifiable may be forwarded to the city's Poste Restante. Telegrams in foreign languages are accepted by the PTT offices on Sharia Adly, Sharia el-Alfy, Sharia Ramses, Midan el-Tahrir and by the branch offices of Maadi, Dokki and Zamalek. Note that the forwarding address and the signature of the sender are also counted in the cost and that after 21 words the cost per word increases.

In spite of recent improvements, the Egyptian telephone service is far from perfect. In order to avoid line interferences and wrong numbers, dial numbers slowly. Public phone booths may be found around stations, in main squares and hotel lobbies. Insert ten aluminium piastres, not brass. Stores and other establishments may also permit limited phone calls to be made. Long-distance or overseas calls can be made through telephone offices or much more easily in major hotels. In both cases, it is advisable to book the call in advance and to expect delays. In public telephone offices, numbers are assigned and called out when the connection is confirmed. It is not possible to make reverse-charge calls from Egypt.

Health Although Egypt has a healthy climate, some basic precautions may prevent a number of problems. Pay strict attention to food hygiene and be extra careful when eating food sold in the market, on the streets and in open squares. Fruits and fresh vegetables must be washed or peeled. Avoid eating salads and open sandwiches. Although the major hotels and cities claim that their tap water is potable, it is better to be cautious and to drink only bottled water. Make sure that it is a properly sealed bottle and that it is opened in your presence. Resist the temptation to drink freshly-squeezed fruit juices from street vendors.

After a few days in Egypt, many tourists suffer from 'gypy tummy' or the 'Pharaoh's curse', a type of diarrhoea which, though uncomfortable, is not serious. Prescription medication such as Lomotil will alleviate the symptoms. (It is wise to take it with you.) It is also a good idea to take an effective anti-bacterial drug obtained from your doctor for more serious cases.

It is always wise to take vaccines against typhus. There is no danger of catching malaria. Do not bathe in the Nile or the canals, where there is a risk of catching bilharzia, a disease caused by a parasite found in stagnant water which attacks the liver. For those with delicate complexions, stay in the shade; the Egyptian sun can be quite punishing. In cases of severe sunburn, yoghurt applied to the affected parts gives instant, temporary relief. You can buy wide-brimmed hats locally, but set off with sunglasses, beachwear and more important, anti-mosquito lotion or spray. Salt tablets are unavailable in Egypt and are worth bringing, particularly during the hotter periods of the year.

Low-budget and student travel For those who know how to adapt to new and varying conditions, Egypt is an economical destination, particularly with regard to food and transportation. Living the Egyptian way and avoiding hectic itineraries ensures an interesting experience and an unforgettable holiday.

Direct contact cannot be made in the same way by seeing the country's sights from aboard a tourist bus or by staying in a luxury

five-star hotel. Egypt has 14 youth hostels located in Cairo, Alexandria, Aswan, Luxor, Mersa Matruh, Port Said, Sohag and the Suez. They are well maintained and very reasonably priced. However, the main problem is finding a free space. Some hotels in Cairo offer discounts to students with a valid International Student Identification Card. (This ID entitles the holder to discounts on transportation and a 50 per cent reduction in entrance fees to museums, monuments and archaeological sites.) The Youth Hostel Association, with offices at 7 Sharia Doctor Abdel Hamid Said, Marouf, Cairo, assists youth travellers and facilitates their accommodation in the various hostels.

The Youth Travel bureau, on the other hand, organizes discount tours and excursions to destinations both popular or different and offbeat. Some of these tours are offered only by travel agencies. Campsites are not yet well developed in Egypt. The few that exist are simple and generally annexed to resorts and bungalows. It is not advisable for reasons of hygiene and security to set up camp indiscriminately.

Women travelling alone Much progress has been made by Egyptian women in the last two decades. Compared with others in the Arab world, they enjoy more freedom and mobility. Young women now work in offices, hotels and banks as well as in the fields of teaching and nursing. Women have also won seats in the Egyptian parliament and joined the cabinet.

Women in Egypt are free to wear what they wish provided they retain some decorum in line with the country's Islamic tradition. In the past few years, however, more young women have begun wearing the Islamic dress which leaves only the face and hands bare.

Women wishing to travel alone in Egypt will have no particular problems as the crime rate, despite widespread poverty and unemployment, is low. However, if you have the choice, it is advisable to travel with a group. The greatest hazard for women travelling alone, especially Europeans and Americans, is being stared at or talked to by men, though physical harassment is uncommon.

Travelling with children Egypt is a fascinating country for children. They are much loved by the population, allowed anywhere and will not find it hard to make friends. Some restaurants have a special section reserved for children, complete with games and other amusements. There are some children's amusement parks in Cairo where adult participation makes for a most enjoyable experience.

When in very warm and popular places, be very careful about the food. Children are generally attracted to food sold on the streets or in open squares and because of the generally insanitary conditions, it is advisable to inspect the food closely before making a purchase. Other precautions described under 'Health' should be followed even more strictly for children.

A family pediatrician should be consulted regarding any necessary vaccinations before embarking on the trip. If travelling with very young children or babies, it would be advisable to avoid the summer months and the hot southern areas of Upper Egypt.

Babysitters, known locally as 'nannies', are not widely used and there are no agencies. However, some of the major hotels offer these services to their guests.

Photography Egypt offers endless photographic subjects. Its magical cities, the awe-inspiring pyramids, the drama of life in the bazaars, the faces of children and older people who resemble ancient Egyptian portrait-heads come to life, the powerful Nile and the luxuriant oases are only a few of the many beautiful facets of the land. Remember to bring along plastic bags or a camera case to protect you camera from the dust and sand which penetrates everything. The sun is very strong and can be searingly bright. Over-exposure errors are common. Under-expose a little during the middle of the day and use a polarizing filter. Taking pictures with a flash is permitted in almost all tombs and archaeological sites. A small fee is charged for taking photographs and video films inside the pyramids, tombs and museums. Fees for commercial filming are much higher. Photography with a flash is not permitted in the Cairo Museum. Although a ticket can be purchased for ordinary photography in the museum, the lighting is so poor it is hardly worth taking photographs. It takes a few days to develop black and white film and at least ten days for Ektachrome and Agfacolor. It would be advisable to develop film on your return home, as the results are not always consistent in Egypt. Do not take pictures of military zones, industrial areas, bridges and other such installations, or military and official personnel. Strategic areas such as the Aswan High Dam may be photographed only from a certain angle. Ask permission before attempting to photograph people, especially women or older people. On arrival remember to fill in a 'Formulaire 54 KML' form for the eventual re-export of cameras and accompanying equipment.

Electricity supply In the major cities such as Cairo and Alexandria, electric current is 220 volts, whereas in other zones it is 110 volts. Electrical plugs are of the European type. Cycles are 50, hence American appliances running on 60 cycles require the use of adaptors.

Domestic flights The national carrier, Egypt Air, links Cairo to all the major Egyptian cities and places of interest to tourists. It would be advisable to book flights well ahead for they are usually full and may even be overbooked. Be at the airport early, as a first-come-first-served policy is followed. There are daily flights from Cairo to Aswan, Luxor and Abu Simbel, and several flights a week to Asyut, Hurghada and the New Valley (oasis of Kharga). Air Sinai flies to St Catherine, Sharm el-Sheikh and el-Arish, handling the Sinai network. It also operates flights to Hurghada and Tel Aviv. Air Sinai offices are located at the Nile Hilton Hotel, tel. 760948.

Trains The Egyptian railway system covers over 7,000 kilometres (4,350 miles). The principle routes connect Cairo with Alexandria, Port Said, the Suez and Aswan. There are three categories, and it is not recommended to take the third class which is spartan and rather uncomfortable. Second class is advisable only for short-distance trips. First class provides air-conditioning, dining-car facilities and sleeping cars for major routes. There are also refreshment services offering sandwiches, sweets, pastries, coffee and other beverages. Though Egyptian trains may be slow, they are always on time. Reservations may be made directly at the station of Midan Ramses in Cairo or the Central Station of Alexandria or through any travel agency. They should, however, be made in advance, not only for sleeping berths but also for seats on regular trips.

Visitors travelling to Luxor and Aswan by train are rewarded with a view of the beautifully varied landscapes of the scenic Nile valley. Return trips may be made by air or better still, by cruising down the river. First-class fares are generally a little less than double those of second class. Sleeping compartments for two are available only on first class; sleeping berths may be reserved also for second-class passengers. For information, reservations and a timetable for the principal train routes, contact Ramses Station in Cairo, tel. 753555.

Nile cruises A Nile cruise is probably the highlight of most visits to Egypt. A variety of ships run from Cairo to Aswan and vice versa. Major hotels also have their own boats offering various services and facilities. Smaller than regular cruise vessels, Nile boats can accommodate from 20 to 150 passengers in relatively spacious cabins. Other than the regular service facilities, bigger boats offer swimming pools, solariums, capacious recreation areas, evening entertainment, laundry and beauty parlour services. Cruises depart from Cairo, Luxor and Aswan and last from three to 16 days depending on the route and itinerary. Almost all of the bigger boats are equipped with air-conditioning, making these trips very pleasant even at the height of summer. However, it is still advisable to travel in Upper Egypt during the cooler months since sightseeing ashore can be very hot unless you visit in the very early morning or at the end of the day. Fares during the summer are considerably lower, sometimes only a little more than half the fares in winter, because of the intense heat. The largest number of cruise boats operate between Luxor and Aswan, with stops at Esna, Edfu and Kom Ombo to see the Ptolemaic temples. This cruise usually takes four days. Some cruises add a short northward cruise, to include Dendera and Abydos, but only a small number go the whole distance between Cairo and Aswan. Those that do, make stops at the interesting sites of Tell el-Amarna and Beni Hasan, and see the rich agricultural region of Middle Egypt.

The following are the major companies which operate cruises on the Nile:

Eastmar Travel: 13 Qasr el-Nil, Cairo, tel. 753147

Cairo Hotel & Nile Cruise: 23 bis, Ismail Mohames Street, Zamalek, tel. 651511

Nile Hilton: Corniche Street, Cairo, tel. 740880

President/Concorde Hotels: 13 Maraashly Street, Zamalek, tel. 800517

Pyramid Tours: 1 Midan Talaat Harb, Cairo, tel. 758655

Sheraton Hotels: 48 Giza Street, Horman Building, Cairo, tel. 987200

Trans Egypt Travel: 21 Aziz Abbas Street, Zamalek, tel. 744313

Other major hotels such as the **Cairo Marriott Hotel** and the **Oberoi** offer the same services.

Buses It is best to avoid public buses as they can prove to be uncomfortable and time-consuming. There are, however, tourist (excursion) buses offering excellent services operated by agencies which run package tours from Cairo to Aswan with stops at places of archaeological interest. These efficient buses are air-conditioned and have a maximum capacity of 40 seats. Other companies ply the Sinai and the principal destinations of the delta. Trips are reasonably priced and are comparable with the prices of first class train tickets.

Listed below are some addresses:

Intra-City Bus Service: ticket office and departure from Midan el-Tahrir for Luxor and Aswan; **Shark el-Delta Line:** departure from Kolai Terminal for Sinai, St Catherine's Monastery.

The points of departure for major destinations are:
Suez, Ismailia, Port Said: el-Olali, in front of Ramses Station
Hurghada and other Red Sea cities: Ahmed Helmi, behind Ramses Station. Oases of Baharia, Kharga and Dakhla: Sharia el-Azhar.
(Note: buses are without air-conditioning and permits to visit the area are needed.)

Travelling by car Visitors who intend to travel in Egypt by car should be prepared for the usually chaotic state of local traffic. The highway

code is not strictly observed and drivers are given to blaring their horns, not to mention committing other more serious traffic offences. Road signs are usually in Arabic only. In the major cities, quick reflexes and strong nerves are indispensable. It is advisable on arriving in a major city like Cairo or Alexandria to park the car in a safe place and to use public transport around the city; this will save time and ensure a calm disposition and a more enjoyable visit. If confusion and risk are created mostly by other motorists in the major cities, beyond the urban areas the greatest hazards on the road are trucks, hand-carts, barrows, children playing and donkeys. In any case, prudence and caution are your only defences. Drive at moderate speeds. Be very alert and do not hesitate to use the horn. Do not always trust in your right of way, since generally it is not observed. Do not attempt to drive at night. For assistance and information, contact:
Automobile Club Egypt: 10 Sharia Qasr el-Nil, Cairo, tel. 743355
Touring Club of Egypt: 8 Sharia Qasr el-Nil, Cairo.

Road network The Egyptian road network is approximately 45,000 kilometres (27,963 miles) long, the principal branches of which are Cairo — Alexandria, Cairo — Port Said — Ismailia, Cairo — Suez, Cairo — el-Fayum, Cairo — Aswan, and Suez — Hurghada. All of these routes are asphalted and in quite good condition. The other main roads are also asphalted but are in need of repair. The rest are dirt roads. In addition to these roads, desert tracks lead to the secondary oases, but they are recommended only for highly skilled drivers with knowledge and experience in desert driving. Drivers should be properly outfitted for the journey and equipped with spare parts, compasses and other orientation instruments as well as sufficient food and water supplies. It is useless to try to enumerate all the risks and dangers to which a driver is exposed. However, it is always advisable to travel with other vehicles. The next few years will see a marked improvement in existing roads and the construction of new ones, especially in areas of major tourist interest. The Cairo-Aswan route is part of the major artery which will link the Mediterranean to Cape Town. From Aswan, vehicles may be ferried to Wadi Halfa by boat.

Petrol Called 'benzene' locally, Egyptian petrol is cheap but of low-grade octane. Super, which is the only recommended type, has only 85 octanes, like Normal elsewhere. It is therefore advisable to regulate the carburation of your vehicle on arriving in Egypt. Distributors and filling stations are abundant in the principal cities but rather scarce in the rest of the country. Plan carefully before setting out on long journeys and always have some reserve petrol.

Travel permits There are no problems for motorists using the major routes in Egypt. These include Cairo — Alexandria, the main roads of the delta, Cairo — el-Fayum, Cairo — Aswan, and the routes from Cairo to the principal cities of the Suez Canal, to Port Said via Damietta, and the coastal road. Certain roads of lesser interest to tourists may be used only if you are in possession of permits, which may be obtained from the Travel Permits Department, located at the corner of Sharia Sheikh Rihan and Sharia Nubar in Cairo. These routes include the secondary roads of the delta, the coastal road to Libya, the track along the Suez Canal between Ismailia and Suez, the Sinai, and St Catherine's Monastery. Some roads leading to the oases, especially those to Siwa and Baharia, are also restricted.

Traffic and road signs In Egypt, right-hand driving is observed. Road signs are almost always in Arabic, except in some tourist areas. Owing to difficulties in transcribing Arabic into English spellings, certain names may be seen written in two or three different ways.

Insurance Because the Green Card or International Motor Insurance Form is not recognized in Egypt, you are required by law to take out an insurance policy locally.

Repair Egyptian mechanics are generally skilful, clever and highly inventive, having been trained in the techniques of adaptation and reutilization of auto parts because complicated import laws and regulations make it very difficult to obtain original spare parts. However, it is advisable to bring along the necessary spare parts such as spark plugs, various filters, headlights, rear lights, fuses and other electrical components. Major repair shops and authorized auto concessionaires have their own specialized offices.

Car hire It is very economical to hire cars in Egypt. This is also a convenient way of avoiding the red tape involved in bringing one's own vehicle. Major international car hire companies have offices and outlets in the principal hotels and airports. Hiring a car with a driver is a wise alternative which will prove to be time-saving as well as economical. Because of Cairo's chaotic traffic, it is the most convenient and relaxing way to travel, and for excursions out of the city, it is enjoyable to have the freedom to stop off whenever and wherever you like.

Taxis While taxis are largely an urban form of transportation, their low cost and the inconvenience of other means make them a recommended mode for excursions of both long and short distances. Travelling by taxi is undoubtedly the best way to visit the pyramids around Cairo and destinations further afield such as el-Fayum, Beni Suef or el-Minya. For these journeys, it is advisable to bargain and settle on a figure before starting, agreeing on the condition that the driver waits while you tour and that the fare is paid only at the end of the trip. If all goes satisfactorily, leave a generous tip.

The gharry In some places such as el-Minya, Luxor, Esna, Edfu and Aswan, the gharry (horse-drawn carriage) actually functions as a sort of taxi. Decked in the romantic trappings of another age, it is a very pleasant contraption which can accommodate as many as five passengers.

Bicycles Bicycles are very much in fashion in Luxor where they can easily be hired. They may be hired for a whole day from establishments which allow reasonable freedom of movement even for those travelling with an organized tour. Remember, though, that the heat can become truly oppressive. Besides taking breaks, it is advisable not to be too ambitious and not to overwork oneself. Take along a canteen or a flask so as to avoid unsafe drinks with ice.

Horses For those who already have a certain familiarity with horses, this should be a fascinating and unforgettable way to visit the pyramids of Giza and Saqqara. The local horses are smaller in stature than Western ones and may be difficult to control.

Camels In the vicinity of the pyramids, camels equipped with saddles are rented out to tourists for rides, although they serve more usually as props for souvenir photographs.

Donkeys In Luxor, donkeys for hire are a very popular and are an ideal means of tranportation to the Theban reliefs. The standard excursion, a half-day affair, includes visits to the Valley of the Kings and other funerary temples in the vicinity, taking the same route which ancient artists and craftsmen followed 1,000 years ago when they worked on the royal tombs. In the course of the excursion, there are a number of places which offer breathtaking views of the valley and sweeping vistas of the entire ruins. These are some of the many things which make the trip most rewarding.

It is also possible in other parts of the country to travel by donkey accompanied by a guide.

Feluccas These flat-bottomed boats powered by white sails are an essential part of the river scene. Besides being a major tourist attraction, these boats are an irreplaceable means of transportation, especially in the areas of Aswan and its numerous islands.

Hydrofoil services Hydrofoil services link Aswan to Abu Simbel in approximately five hours. Runs are rather infrequent; the first return trip to Aswan is always the following day. For information and reservations, contact Misr Travel Agency which has offices in Aswan in the vicinity of the tourist bazaar. Misr Travel also has offices in the major world capitals: in London these are at 40 Great Marlborough Street; in New York at 530 Fifth Avenue, Suite 555.

Etiquette and Customs

In spite of the rapid growth of industrialization and the rise of big cities, every Egyptian maintains and upholds convictions and attitudes which attest strongly to his deep-rooted rural heritage. A tenacious sense of conservatism tending to exalt the values of the past, a natural predilection for making decisions on instinct rather than reason, and a certain lack of concern about punctuality are general characteristics. These are counterbalanced by a deeply comforting warmth and humanity, courtesy, love and attachment to the family, kindness to children, and a profound sense of friendship and hospitality. Added to these characteristics is a deeply embedded loyalty to Egypt's Islamic heritage. This holds true for all other Arab nations where religious faith is deep-seated, and it has also influenced non-Muslims like the Christian Copts. National pride is another strong Egyptian characteristic. Burdened by millenia of foreign domination, the country, now finally independent, is intent on building a great nation which can offer a better standard of living to its citizens.

The simplest and most important rules of conduct for all visitors are not to offend local people with displays of wealth or strong negative reactions to the inconveniences inherent in a developing society; and to avoid entering mosques during hours of prayer. Eating and drinking in public during the fasting hours of the Ramadan are also considered to be very inconsiderate.

Cuisine

Egyptian cuisine, though heavily influenced by Arab, Turkish and European (French and Italian in particular) culinary traditions, is very distinctive. The country's geographical position favours the growth of all types of fruit throughout the year. The catches from the Mediterranean and the Red Sea are excellent, though Nile fish should be avoided. Koranic precepts regarding food are not strictly observed here, and even though Muslim Egyptians do not eat pork, some drink alcohol which is also produced locally. Local wines are quite good and so is the beer. Among the ingredients of Egyptian cuisine, the *ful* (broad beans) are the most popular, followed by lentils, various cereals and Mediterranean vegetables such as tomatoes, squashes, aubergines, peppers, onion, okra and other local vegetables unknown in Europe. Many ingredients such as sesame, spices, grapes and olives characterize local dishes. Among meats, veal is the most popular, followed by chicken and pigeon. Fish and shrimps are less popular.

The traditional Middle Eastern meal consists of a number of dishes which can be meals in themselves. The most typical appetizer, *felafel* (also known as *taameya*), is mashed white bean balls fried with spices and olive oil. *Baba ghannoug* is mashed aubergines with sesame paste, flavoured with spices, olive oil, lemon and garlic and served with bread. *Tahini* (sesame seed paste) and the wonderful local yoghurt, *leban zabadi*, thicker and creamier than the common kind, are often used as a base for cold sauces used with bread and various types of vegetables. The national dish is *ful medames*, which is made from beans cooked in a thick sauce with tomatoes and spices. This dish varies with the locality and with the origin of the chef. *Melukhiyia* is also popular, a glutinous soup made with a mint-looking and spinach-tasting local vegetable and chicken, served with rice. It does not always suit Western tastes. *Ooshari* is made of rice and small macaroni in a lentil, onion and ginger sauce. Meat is more often served as *shish kebabs* (grilled veal cubes). The same method of cooking is also used for *kofta* (balls of minced lamb), marinated in onions, lemon, parsley and marjoram. Another favourite meat is that of the pigeon, which is widely bred in the country. Other rice dishes make the base of normal meals, which are completed by desserts, several from the rich Middle Eastern cuisine. In addition to the various Turkish-Lebanese cakes (usually very sweet and covered with honey), grapes and dried fruits, there is a wide variety of ice-cream, including *dondurma* and many others which are easier to appreciate than to describe.

Among the best of the local wines are 'Gianaclis Village' (dry white), 'Omar Khayyam', 'Chateau Gianaclis' and 'Pharaons' (red), and 'Rubis d'Egypte' (rosé). The quality corresponds to the price, so be careful with the cheaper brands. The beers are also good: 'Stella' (and 'Stella Export,' which is more expensive and rather too sweet for Western tastes), and 'Marzen' which is only available in the spring months. Another very popular alcoholic drink is *zibeeb*, a sort of aniseed drink which, like Pernod, is a good aperitif on the rocks or diluted with water. Imported spirits are very expensive in hotels and restaurants, so it is advisable to buy one or more bottles at airport duty-free shops before arrival. Fruit juices and sugar-cane juice are prepared on the spot at special stands all over the country. *Karkade*, a red infusion made from hibiscus flowers from Aswan, is pleasant and thirst-quenching when drunk either hot or cold (a good alternative for those who cannot take coffee, which is offered many times a day). Egyptian coffee is made Turkish-style, with finely ground coffee boiled in water and poured (with the sediment) into the cup. There are three types of coffee: *sadeh* (bitter), *maazbut* (medium), and *ziyadah* (extremely sweet). Tea is served in small glasses.

Music and Dance

As in other Arab countries, music is popular throughout Egypt. The big-name Egyptian singers, who are idolized by the public, almost always sing sad and mournful songs of suffering and resignation. The country's most famous singer was Umm Khulthum. She was so loved by the Egyptians that when she died in 1976, more than three million weeping admirers and fans followed her funeral cortege.

Recently, traditional Egyptian music has been adapted into a more Western style by Muhammad Adb-el-Wahab, who is currently one of the most noted musicians in the Arab world. Drums, tambourines and the Oud (oriental guitar) are the main musical instruments used for effect in the repetitive tunes which are peculiar to Arabic music.

Belly dancing is another form of entertainment which has attained a worldwide audience. Shows are held nightly in night clubs and cafes along the road leading from Cairo to the pyramids at Giza. Interesting folk dance and musical performances are staged during peak seasons at the Umm Khulthum Theatre in Cairo.

Sports

Cairo offers first-rate sports facilities, most of which are annexed to big hotels or are part of sprawling country clubs. Most five-star hotels allow non-guests to make use of their facilities for a daily fee. Country clubs and sports organizations accept membership applications for limited time periods. Public centres are few and often crowded.

Golf There are two golf courses in Cairo. Gezira Sporting Club in Zamalek offers an 18-hole course, and Mena House Oberoi Hotel has a nine-hole course set against the dramatic backdrop of the pyramids. Gezira Sporting Club hires out equipment and also offers the assistance of instructors to both members and guests. The Alexandria Sporting Club in Alexandria also offers an 18-hole golf course.

Tennis Tennis is played on the clay courts of major hotels and private clubs. The rules and regulations are rather formal, requiring players to wear the traditional white tennis outfit. Among Cairo's best clubs are Gezira Sporting Club, Maadi and Tewfikia Tennis Club, where the annual Open Tennis Championships of Cairo are held.

Riding A horseback ride around the pyramids is an exciting and unforgettable experience, especially in the moonlight. However, this sport is recommended only to those who have some riding experience, as Arab horses are somewhat difficult to control, particularly in the tricky, sandy desert terrain. Two or three stables in the vicinity of the pyramids offer more tame and manageable horses for beginners and also organize cross-desert excursions on horseback from Giza to Saqqara (approximately five hours) for fit, well-trained and hardy riders. The Ferrusea Riding Club near the Gezira Club has horses and instructors for both experts and beginners. Telephone 800692 for information.

Rowing Rowing is a prestigious sport in Egypt. The floating headquarters is at the Egyptian Rowing Club, situated in front of the Sheraton Hotel, Cairo, tel. 982639.

Sailing Egypt offers an excellent variety of sailing facilities. Whether in the open Mediterranean, on the Nile, or in the Red Sea, aboard a felucca complete with Nubian riggings or an ordinary sail-boat for two, one is assured of a fascinating experience of unforgettable seascapes and shorelines of the most varied types. The principal clubs are in Alexandria, Hurghada and Cairo. All hire out boats and most offer organized sailing lessons. In Cairo, the most well-known are the Maadi Yacht Club at 8, Sharia Demeshk, Midan el-Maadi, tel: 35091 or 34925 (which also has baby-sitting services for children from four to eight years old), and the Cairo Yacht Club at Sharia en-Nil, Giza, tel: 984415, where regattas and competitions are held.

Aquatic sports The sailing clubs in Cairo and in the other resorts offer water-skiing facilities. Avoid wading or bathing in the Nile (it is highly polluted) or where there is a risk of catching bilharzia. Major hotels, sports centres and private clubs, as well as some of the bigger Nile cruise boats, have swimming pools. The sandy beaches of the Mediterranean are crowded with local and tourist bathers, especially around Alexandria and Mersa Matruh. The Red Sea provides an underwater paradise. Considered one of the richest seas, it teems with myriad varieties of fish in different shapes and colours. Its crystalline water is highly recommended for serious divers or plain snorkellers who wish to observe the marvellous underwater fauna at first hand. Diving equipment can be hired in Hurghada and Safaga.

Football (soccer) Followed avidly by a large percentage of the population, football is the real Egyptian national sport. When the principal teams of Cairo meet for the derby, the city is deserted, only to explode after the games in the rowdy victory parades of the winning team. The city streets are filled with banners and the sound of terracotta drums. Information regarding hours and dates of matches may be obtained from your local porters.

Horse racing There is a strong tradition of horse breeding and training in Egypt. Horse races are held every Saturday and Sunday from October until May at the Gezira Sporting Club and the Nadi Etehad el-Gomhuriyat (better known as el-Shams Club) in Cairo. Races are announced in the foreign-language dailies. It is possible to bet, but it would also be rewarding simply to watch and enjoy the splendid spectacle of flying Arab horses at their best.

Other Useful Points

Baksheesh (tipping) The problem of tipping is somewhat magnified in Egypt. The tourist zones swarm with characters importuning foreigners for *baksheesh* (meaning 'alms' in Arabic, it is also the word for 'tip'). It becomes more difficult when one leaves the hotel and has to distinguish who among the many chambermaids, waiters, head-waiters, assistants, and assistant assistants have actually been of service. There remains no alternative but to give something to everyone, though this should not total more than ten per cent of the bill. As a rule, give five piastres for small services, such as watch-your-car services, 10−20 piastres to porters for each piece of baggage and to barbers or beauty parlour assistants, and 25−50 piastres for those who render a satisfactory or excellent service. Be courteous but firm with all others. No service, no *baksheesh*, but always smile!

On arriving in Egypt, it is advisable to ask about the current scale of charges for porters, shoeshine boys, keepers in sacred monuments, and tourist guides.

Cigarettes The local brands of cigarettes, which generally cost less than half the price of imported ones, include Cleopatra, Giza and Nefertiti, all of which are filtered and comparable to American cigarettes. Belmont, Boston, Capital and Florida are like Pall Malls. Port Said are mentholized, while Boustany are more like a Turkish blend.

Toilets Cleanliness and hygiene in toilets exist only in five-star hotels. Always have on hand your own supply of tissue or toilet paper because it is usually not available in the bathrooms of bars, restaurants, stations, airports and other public establishments.

Taking a break

Newspapers and magazines Three foreign-language dailies are published in Egypt: *The Egyptian Gazette* in English, *Le Progres Egyptien* and *Le Journal d'Egypte* in French. An English monthly, *Cairo Today*, is also available at newspaper kiosks in the city centre, together with other magazines and newspapers from abroad.

Dragomen Tourists have been visiting Egypt for centuries. It was the first country to have tourist guides (dragomen), who once dressed in loose tunics and turbans (today these are worn only by the older guides). They are a common sight in the vicinity of archaeological sites, guiding tourists and narrating the history of the monuments. They have a tendency to exaggerate, to tell tall tales and to freely embellish colourful events. The modern dragomen are generally more competent but less picturesque than their predecessors.

Shopping and Handicrafts

Egypt offers wonderful shopping. Choices vary between sophisticated boutiques and shops and characteristically colourful bazaars. In Egypt, every big city and each little village has something unique to offer the visitor. Shopping or mere browsing through the countless curio items on sale can become an engaging activity which may easily occupy days. Though not practised in the modern elegant shops, haggling over prices is certainly the order in Egyptian markets, stores and the bazaars. Remember that if you buy merchandise at the first price indicated by the vendor, this is taken as a sign of inferiority. Negotiate over prices. Aside from being an experience, it is also very rewarding as the last price is often 60−70 per cent lower than the initial one. If you decide not to purchase anything after a prolonged transaction, the vendor will not feel affronted; it is part of the game.

Brand new 'antiques' Egyptian handicrafts are varied, beautiful and interesting, though much of what one finds today is specially made for tourists. Some are miniature reproductions of the famous Pharaohs in heavy colours and are in rather poor taste. There are much better items, however, such as the faithful copies of ancient objects done with great artistic skill and workmanship which can only be identified as reproductions by an expert. Do not purchase items sold as ancient objects or antiques at very high prices because authentic ones are simply not available. Handicrafts stores deal only in reproductions. If by luck, however, you chance upon an authentic piece you will encounter enormous problems regarding its export. Egyptian customs authorities are very strict about the export of antiquities and sometimes search the baggage of departing tourists thoroughly.

Cotton Do not forget the world-famous Egyptian cotton fabrics. Considered the world's best, they are available in various designs and colours at very reasonable prices. Among the many cotton goods is the *galebeah*, a full-length garment traditionally worn by men, but which is popular with women as casual dress. Cotton is available in pastel colours, with or without stripes and, being very sturdy, it may be used for mattresses, as tea-cloths or for other domestic uses. Names may be embroidered on them in hieroglyphic characters within a cartouche (scroll or tablet). Every type of garment may be made to order in a few days at very reasonable prices. The only challenge will be explaining the cut or pattern to a tailor who may not speak English.

Good luck charms and other accessories The scarab beetle is probably the most famous charm, together with the sacred eye of Horus, better known as Udjat, which is supposed to drive away misfortune and enjoy the protection of Ra. Amulets are very popular and are usually found mounted on bracelets, rings, earrings, or as pendants. Exquisite gold jewellery is also available for those in search of more valuable souvenirs. Marked by excellent workmanship and intricate designs, the bracelets and earrings are patterned after traditional models which still constitute part of the dowry of Egyptian brides. They may be showy and gaudy at times but, even so, tend to be rather thin and do not cost too much. Names may be engraved within a cartouche on cufflinks or other such objects. Silver is also an excellent buy and is worked into trays, platters, candle-holders, cigarette cases, boxes and jewellery cases. Similar objects in brass and copper, often with inlay work, are also available. It is advisable to compare merchandise from one store to another before making your purchase.

Wood, leather, carpets and rugs Wood is beautifully inlaid with mother-of-pearl, ebony and ivory and transformed into wonderful boxes both large and small, chess boards and other objects. Look for the very rare *mushrabiyah*, panels carved out of wood, generally salvaged from old houses or palaces which have been demolished.

Other items are rugs and carpets in beautiful colours, seat cushions of hide, beaten leather, ladies' bags and purses (beware of imitation crocodile bags), attache cases, wallets, camel saddles, oriental babouches and shoes, all of which abound in the bazaars and markets.

Spices, perfumes and gems Inexpensive but certainly worth taking home are the following exotic spices: saffron, sesame, cumin, nutmeg, hot and aromatic black pepper and other spices less-known in Europe, as well as the excellent *karkade*, perfect hot or cold. *Henna* gives hair an exotic copper-red shade. This substance is extracted from a common North African herb which is also used by Arab women to paint their palms. Look, too, for a special type of vegetable sponge called *lifah* for a soothing and toning massage under the shower. Oil-based oriental perfumes also make superb buys. Among the precious and semi-precious stones available are topaz, turquoise, aquamarine and pearls. These should be bought only from the more reputable stores.

Colourful wool tapestries, prepared and designed by children, are a cheap and interesting buy. These are sold throughout Egypt but are made primarily in villages near Cairo, particularly Harraniya along the canal road on the way to Saqqara, and Kardassa, off the Pyramid Road to Giza.

Cairo and Surroundings

Cairo, once dubbed 'the mother of the world', is the starting point of all tours in Egypt. It is the largest city in Africa and the Arab world and has a daytime population of 15 million people, when workers from the nearby delta flock to the city for employment. Cairo has always attracted people from the delta and surrounding villages, but it owes its recent growth to the damage inflicted on the city of Suez during the 1967 Arab-Israeli war and the later conflict in 1973.

During rush hour, Cairo appears to be gasping for breath. Buses threaten to collapse under the weight of people scrambling through doors and windows or clinging on outside. Stations are crowded and the streets are an endless cacophony of blaring horns and shouting people interspersed with the call for prayer of the muezzin.

Even as early as AD 330, the celebrated Arab traveller Ibn Batuta described an overcrowded Cairo: 'There are but so many inhabitants, so much that the multitude seems to move itself in waves, making the city appear almost in such desperate straits and anguish to contain all this, like a sea in perpetual agitation.'

Present-day Cairo has its roots in el-Qahira (the victorious), built by the Fatimids in 969. You can still trace the city's history from the east bank of the Nile opposite Roda Island, where the Romans built a fortified camp for the Mamelukes, Turkish slaves brought to serve in the Egyptian army who eventually came to power in the 13th century.

Opposite the walls that now enclose the old Coptic quarter of the city was the city of Fustat. The first Islamic capital of Egypt, built in AD 639, it was destroyed in a 54-day fire in 1168, which was deliberately started to prevent its occupation by the Crusaders.

The route from the airport, the usual entry point for most tourists, passes through the residential area of Heliopolis with its modern luxury villas and apartments and the squalid buildings of the working class. Cairo is now undergoing considerable change in a bid to improve transport and its complex road system. A multi-million dollar project for an underground railway (metro) is one of the biggest projects in the city. Even the scenic Nile corniche has not escaped modernization; huge multi-storey buildings now dot the river's banks. But you can still see graceful feluccas sailing along the river in the early mornings or afternoons, bringing a sense of tranquility and images of the past.

The Egyptian Museum

In 1858, the eminent French Egyptologist Auguste Mariette, originally assistant at the Louvre's Department of Egyptian Art in Paris, was

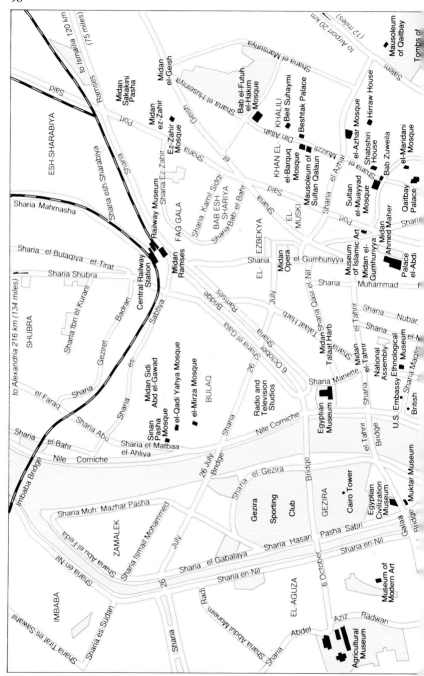

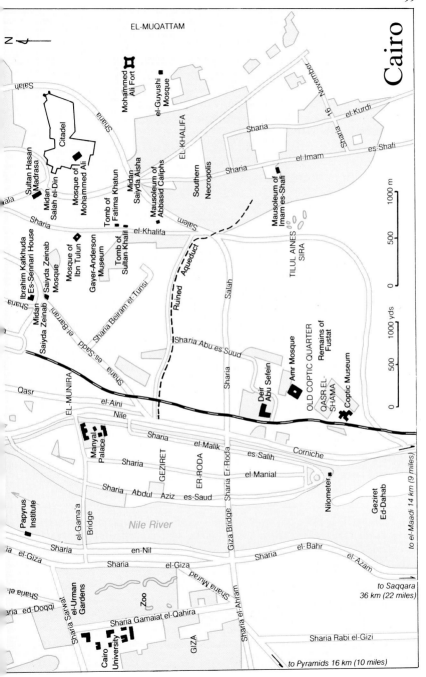

Cairo

EL-MUQATTAM

N

Mohammed
Ali Fort

el-Guyushi
Mosque

Citadel

EL-KHALIFA

Salah el-Din

Sharia

Sultan Hasan
Madrasa

Midan
Salah el-Din

Mosque of
Mohammed Ali

Midan
Saiyda Aisha

Mausoleum of
Abbasid Caliphs

Southern
Necropolis

Sharia

el-Imam

Sharia

es-Shafi

el-Kurdi

Nomran

Tomb of
Fatima Khatun

el-Khalifa

Salem

Mausoleum of
Imam es-Shafi

Sharia

Ibrahim Katkhuda
Es-Sennari House

Mosque of
Ibn Tulun

Tomb of
Sultan Khalil

Ruined   Aqueduct

TILUL AINES
SIRA

1000 m

500

0

Saiyda Zeinab
Mosque

Gayer-Anderson
Museum

Midan
Saiyda Zeinab

Sharia

el-Barrani

Sharia

es-Sadd

Salah

1000 yds

500

0

Sharia Beiram el-Tunsi

Sharia Abu es-Suud

Qasr

EL-MUNIRA

el-Aini

Nile

Sharia Abu es-Suud

Sharia

Amr Mosque

Deir
Abu Sefein

OLD COPTIC QUARTER

Remains of
Fustat

QASR EL-
SHAMA

Coptic Museum

1000

500

0

Manyal
Palace

Sharia

GEZIRET
ER-RODA

el-Malik

es-Salih

el-Manial

Corniche

Sharia

Sharia Er-Roda

Nilometer

Geziret
Ed-Dahab

to el-Maadi 14 km (9 miles)

Papyrus
Institute

el-Gama'a

Bridge

Sharia

Abdul   Aziz   es-Saud

Giza Bridge

Nile River

Sharia el-Giza

en-Nil

Sharia   el-Giza

Sharia   el-Bahr

el-Azam

to Saqqara
36 km (22 miles)

Sharia Sarwat

el-Urman
Gardens

Zoo

Sharia Murad

GIZA

Sharia el-Ahram

Sharia Rabi el-Gizi

Sharia ed-Doqqi

Cairo
University

Sharia Gamaiat el-Qahira

to Pyramids 16 km (10 miles)

made Director of Works for Antiquities in Egypt. As head of this pivotal office, he dedicated himself to the documentation of monuments and archaeological sites and the collection and categorization of excavated objects in the halls of the former headquarters of the River Company in the area of Bulaq. He transformed four rooms into exhibition halls which he himself embellished with mural paintings. This repository of ancient Egyptian treasures steadily expanded and was later housed in a new edifice constructed in neo-Egyptian style with a garden for statues. This building, also in Bulaq, was destroyed by a devastating flood in 1878. The collection was transferred temporarily to the Palace of Giza and then, in 1902, to its present site on Midan el-Tahrir. The museum has been expanded and modified to accommodate the increasing wealth of treasures brought in by prolific excavation work. This impressive museum contains the world's largest and richest collection of Egyptian antiquities, from prehistory to the Roman occupation.

It is impossible to cover the museum in one visit as it is badly organized and poorly lit. The display of almost 100,000 items is divided into two main sections. On the ground floor, sculptures are arranged in chronological order. On the upper floor, there are relics and artifacts collected from various tombs, especially those from the tomb of Tutankhamun. The selected listings which follow are presented in chronological order and do not correspond to the conventional route followed in the museum.

Prehistory (3150−3050 BC) The last phase of Egyptian Prehistory is well represented by a wide selection of vases. Typical of the Amratian Period (Naqada I) are red vases accentuated by black lids, an art which later disappeared. Also characteristic of the Amratian Period are red vases with decorative motifs of white geometric or figurative designs generally of aquatic animals such as crocodiles, fish and hippopotami, all of which tend to be highly stylized. Immediately following is the Gerzean period (Naqada II) , which rose exactly at the twilight of the fourth millenium BC. Representative of this period are unglazed and unfired ceramics embellished with red designs of animal or human forms and themes recalling the Nile, such as oared vessels. Some, however, are simply decorated with geometric designs.

Protodynastic Era (3050−2686 BC) The Predynastic or Protodynastic Era is represented by valuable examples of votive palettes which were used for pulverizing minerals for use in the preparation of cosmetic creams. Their figurative themes depict thanksgiving feasts and divinities. The most celebrated of these is the Palette of Narmer, which commemorates the union of Upper and Lower Egypt. This palette was found in Hierakonpolis. Narmer later came to be identified with Menes, the first ruler of unified Egypt, a personage glorified to mythical heights by history.

The early dynasties (3050−2649 BC) One of the most remarkable discoveries from the early dynasties was the First Dynasty funerary treasure from the Tomb of Hemaqa, Vizier of Udimu, in Saqqara. Numerous disks of stone, alabaster, limestone, copper and soapstone encrusted with alabaster and schist were found in round wooden cases. The real purpose of these items has never been defined; they may have been used simply for amusement. Flint knives and other weapons were also found.

Uncovered from the funerary apartments of the pyramid of Zoser in Saqqara was a panel with matted coverings and composed of blue glazed tiles, now restored. In a *serdab* (cellar) annexed to the pyramid was uncovered a portrait-statue of Zoser in white limestone; an exact copy of the piece today stands on its original site.

Fourth Dynasty (2613−2498 BC) The Old Kingdom's royal and private statuary collection is well documented in an array of masterpieces. The statues of Rahotep, who is believed to be the son of Snefru, and his wife Nofret, date back to the Fourth Dynasty, and were found in their tomb in Medum. These statues, in perfect condition, are of painted limestone with inlaid eyes. In fact, the workers who discovered these pieces in 1871 were awed by the brilliance and life-like qualities of the eyes.

The celebrated Pharaohs of the Fourth Dynasty, builders of the pyramids, are all represented in the museum. Cheops lives on in the image of a small ivory statuette. His successor, Chephren, is represented in a splendidly sculpted statue of black diorite with white veins, which was uncovered from the pit of the temple at the foot of the pyramid. His royalty is manifested through symbols such as the falcon's protective wings spread out behind the king's head and the motif of the union of the two territories of Egypt on both sides of his throne. The museum houses three of the four surviving triads representing Mycerinus with the goddess Hathor and the personification of an Egyptian province. The fourth is housed in the Museum of Fine Arts in Boston. There were originally 42 of these triads, one for every province to signify the Pharaoh's sovereignty over the whole land. Carved out of dark schist, the pieces were all recovered from the temple below the king's pyramid in Giza. The practice of placing a so-called reserve-head in the chamber of the sarcophagus was established during the Fourth Dynasty, particularly under the reign of Cheops. This substituted the funerary statue to guarantee the survival of the deceased in the after-life. The museum exhibits some good examples of these with characteristic skull-caps crowning the limestone heads.

Fifth—Sixth dynasties (2498—2181 BC) Among the first examples of colossal statuary is a pink granite head of King Userkaf, dating back to the Fifth Dynasty, uncovered from the temple of his pyramid in Saqqara. The private statuary of the Fifth Dynasty is presented here in an impressively wide variety of grand-scale examples, depicting scenes from the lives of aristocratic familes. The image of the high official 'Kaaper' in sycamore with inlaid eyes was discovered in 1860. The legs and staff are restored. It was nicknamed 'Sheikh el-Balad' (village chief) by its excavators, due to its resemblance to their own village chief. From the same tomb was also uncovered the wooden statue of the 'Wife of Sheikh el-Balad' and the image of Ra-nofer, prophet of Ptah. The museum has two painted limestone statues of the same personage, one with a wig and the other without. The latter's clothing and modelling of figure vary slightly. It was common practice at that time to place many statues of the same person in one tomb.

Also from Saqqara is the portrait statue of Ti, in painted limestone. In the same material, but with inlaid eyes, is the image of the Scribe. The use of the Scribe as a representation of the owner of the tomb dates back to the Fourth Dynasty and originated in court circles, as it deals with more 'noble' activities. Characteristic of this period are the figures of servants which are added to, and sometimes even substitute for, wall paintings of tombs. Through the repeated scenes of activities on the tomb's walls, the deceased is reassured in his desire to attain eternal life. Among the most common themes are the milling of wheat, the preparation of bread and the brewing of beer. From the Sixth Dynasty were found the exceptionally important statues of Pepy I and his son. Made of thin plates of hammered copper rivetted to a base of wood, these constitute the only examples of metal statues of such dimensions known in Egypt. They were found in the temple of Hierakonpolis.

Another group is that of the midget Seneb and his family, in painted limestone, dating back to the Sixth Dynasty and also uncovered in Saqqara. Seneb was an important functionary, being the head of the royal weaving factories.

Reliefs and paintings of the Old Kingdom are documented in a range of excellent examples, such as the wooden panels embellished with reliefs from the tomb of Hesira in Saqqara, belonging to the Third Dynasty. Other fine examples are the famous Fourth Dynasty tempera masterpiece (the Geese of Medum), and the panels with painted reliefs in the tombs of Saqqara from the Fifth to the Sixth dynasties.

Among the funerary treasures which exemplify the applied arts of that period is one of extraordinary workmanship, uncovered intact and considered unique among the Old Kingdom's funerary treasures: the tomb equipment of Queen Hetepheres, mother of Cheops, replete with a canopied bed, seats, sedan-chair in wood with gold trimmings, a jewel-case, jewels and toiletries. It is housed in a room on the upper floor.

Representing the goldsmith's art is the sacred falcon's head, the god Horus, in hammered gold-plate with obsidian eyes, found at the temple of Hierakonpolis.

Eleventh Dynasty (2060—1991 BC) Between the First Intermediate Period and the Middle Kingdom, statues and models with new subject matters were introduced, notably those depicting the daily activities of the Egyptians. One fine example is the painted statue in stuccoed wood of a woman 1.23 metres (four feet) in height, with an offering of a basket of bread on her head, which was uncovered from a tomb of the end of the 11th Dynasty in Deir el-Bahari. The best examples of such works are those from the tomb of Meket-re in Deir el-Bahari, in the vicinity of the monumental tomb of Mentuhotep, to whom Meket-re was a high functionary. Here you can see a model of a garden, a house, a weaving workshop and a carpenter's booth. A section of the uncovered works are housed in the Metropolitan Museum of Arts in New York.

In the temple of Nebhepetre-Mentuhotep of the 11th Dynasty in Deir el-Bahari was found a statue of the king in painted grey sandstone. This statue was uncovered from a funerary hollow in the temple where it was kept wrapped in bandages like a mummy. The king is represented by a black body wrapped in a short white mantle and a red crown. A series of eight statues had been placed in the garden before the temple.

Military themes are also typical of the First Intermediate Period. Models in painted wood from Asyut, around two metres (six feet six inches) in height from the base, represent 40 marching soldiers armed with spears and shields. Another group from the same tomb shows 40 archers.

Twelfth Dynasty (1991—1782 BC) This dynasty is documented by an important royal sculptural collection. One of the most beautiful is a statuette of Senusret I in painted cedar wood with a white crown, uncovered from the tomb of a vizier near the pyramid of Senusret I in Lisht. A similar copy of the statuette is in the Metropolitan Museum in New York. Also on exhibition is a series of ten statues of the enthroned king in white limestone discovered in a hastily constructed underground chamber in the north-west area of his funerary temple in Lisht. Each statue stands 1.90 metres (six feet two inches) high, and is an almost exact replica of the others, differing only in facial expression and in the design on the sides of the thrones. These depict the unification of Upper and Lower Egypt which are personified in two figures stepping on the shovel-shaped hieroglyph for 'unity' as they knot together the lotus and the papyrus. On five of the thrones, the two figures are personifications of the Nile in the shape of fertility deities depicted as male but with large breasts. On the other five, the two figures are the gods Horus and Seth in human form, but with a hawk and aardvark head, respectively.

From Tanis is a pair of statues of Queen Nofret, the wife of Senusret II, in black granite. Also in black granite is a head of Senusret III from the temple of Medamud near Thebes. It is interesting that sphinxes of Tanis represent the face of Amenemhat III with a name instead of a royal headdress. Discovered in 1860, they caused much controversy regarding their origins; they were initially attributed to the Hyksos Period because of their strange typology, but on their bodies are scroll ornaments of the kings of the 19th and 21st dynasties. Markedly different from established sculptural styles are porters bearing offerings of fish, perhaps from the two Niles of Upper and Lower Egypt, attributed to the era of Amenemhat III. There is a large series of statues of this sovereign uncovered in Hawara in the Fayum. From the pit tombs in the vicinity of his pyramids in Dahshur is a gilded wooden statue of King Hor. This king is not historically documented, although it is suggested that he was a co-ruler with Amenemhat III. The representation of the Ka (the person's double), with a pair of two arms raised towards heaven, is superimposed on the statue's head.

The jewellery made during the Middle Kingdom shows the height of its refinement. Crowns, armlets and breastplates in gold and rough stones found in Illahun and Dahshur are superb examples. Noteworthy also is the 'Treasure of Asia', which consists of metal cases bearing the name of Amenemhat II.

Eighteenth Dynasty (1570–1293 BC) From the beginning of the 18th Dynasty comes a most impressive treasure, that of Queen Aahotep, mother of Ahmose (liberator of Egypt from occupation by the Hyksos). Her tomb contained a bonanza of precious objects, the most interesting of which are a golden votive axe plated with copper and inlaid with stones and glass paste, bearing her son's name and the 'Golden Fly' military decoration.

From the chapel of the goddess Hathor, patroness of the Theban necropolis, comes the statue of the heifer identified with the goddess,

and here it is shown coming out of a papyrus pond at the foot of the
Western Desert. She is the protector of the king, nursing him to ensure
survival in the after-life. The principal kings and rulers of the 18th
Dynasty are represented in the museum by statues, including those of
Thutmose III, Amenhotep II in offertory, Thutmose IV with his
mother, the colossal group of Amenhotep II and Tiye, among others.

Amarna Period (1350—1334 BC) An entire hall is dedicated to the
Amarnan Period. It boasts objects gathered from Tell el-Amarna and
finds dated to this period from other sites. The colossal statues of
Akhenaten, originally four metres (thirteen feet) high, in sandstone
with traces of polychromy, was uncovered in Karnak, where around 30
such statues were erected at the beginning of his reign. Showcased are
a series of royal portraits, markedly finer in style: a plaster-cast mask
of the king, the king with an offertory table, a head of a princess, finely
crafted profiles, a group representing the king holding a daughter on
his knee, an unfinished but splendid head of Queen Nefertiti in
quartzite, a relief from the royal tomb depicting the king followed by
Nefertiti, and two princesses in adoration of the god Aten.

Numerous other interesting objects were uncovered in the
exploration of the city, including necklaces, rings, cases, decorative
items, toys (a pair of monkeys riding a cart pulled by dogs) and
fragments of pavements with floral designs. Important historical
documents are the terracotta tablets with texts written in cuneiform,
which constituted the diplomatic archives of Amenhotep III and
Amenhotep IV in their relations with Asian kingdoms. Another
remarkable item is the coffin of Smenkhkare (found in tomb 55 in the
Valley of the Kings), with a death mask in gold and inlaid with
lapis-lazuli, turquoise, enamel and carnelian. A model recreates a
typical Amarnan house with secondary buildings.

King Tutankhamun's Treasures The most spectacular section of the
museum glitters with the treasures discovered intact in the tomb of
Tutankhamun in 1922. This find left the world wondering about the
wealth and riches of the greater and longer-ruling Pharaohs of his age
for Tutankhamun was only a minor king who ruled from 1334 to 1325
BC, just as he was coming to manhood. The treasures have remained
entirely in Cairo since the contracts beween the Egytian government
and the discoverer, Lord Carnarvon, assured Egyptian ownership of
the finds, while guaranteeing Carnarvon and Carter, another
Egyptologist, rights to publication. The casket (in quartzite) and the
largest of the sarcophagi have remained in the tomb.

A splendid array of the treasures is exhibited on the first floor of
the museum, where there are four grand, gilded catafalques in wood

with ornaments in the shape of amulets in blue enamel, one inside another, mounted directly on the tomb around and above the quartzite casket. The first of these measures about six metres (nearly 20 feet) in length. Originally positioned between the first and second catafalques was a canopy with supports of gilded wood with gold rose designs and adorned with a veil. The second sarcophagus is in gilded wood with inlays of glass paste shaped into wings. Weighing 200 kilograms (440 pounds) is a third sarcophagus of gold, again with inlaid semi-precious stone. Finally, over the face of the mummy is a solid gold alabaster hood or coffer, with four images of the protecting divinity on the edges contained within an aedicule in gilded wood.

The *ushabti* (small, wooden figures of servants which were made in order to serve the dead in the after life) of which there were originally over 400, are represented here. The ceremonial beds in gilded wood are shaped in the form of heifers, lions and hippopotami. Then there are the military carts, bowls, shields, and a dagger in gold and iron, which is one of the first examples of the use of iron in Egypt. Its sheath is adorned with decorative depictions of palms and animals in swift motion. Interesting objects are the feather fans, tunics, sandals, cloth, gloves, leather, alabaster vases, head-rests (one of which is in lapis-lazuli and gold), toys, as well as the jewels such as rings, necklaces, armlets, breastplates, crowns and diadems found on the mummy and in the tomb. Battle scenes of Asians and Nubians are depicted on a beautifully painted coffer in wood and another inlaid with ivory, and constituting one of the most refined products of the cabinet-maker is a grouping of elegant seats, one with the king sitting casually as the queen pours ointments over him. There are also small royal statues, some of which are on model boats. Finally, two statues in gilded wood stand in the hall.

Nineteenth—Twentieth dynasties (The Age of the Ramesses) (1293—1070 BC) The 19th and 20th dynasties (the Age of the Ramesses) have left a host of artifacts. Ramesses II employed the land's skilled and talented artisans and artists throughout the duration of his reign. Aside from the grand statuaries he commissioned, of primary importance are historical documents such as the Stele of Israel of Merneptah. The products of the applied arts include earthenware with motifs of foreign inspiration, and numerous examples of jewellery. Noteworthy are the designs of papyrus, the *ostraca*, some of which contain rough sketches for paintings, as well as funerary papyri containing the texts of the *Book of the Dead.*

The Later Years The period from the end of the New Kingdom until the Ptolemaic Period witnessed flourishing reigns and a wealth of artifacts. From the royal tombs of Tanis, belonging to the 21st and 22nd dynasties, gold and silverware were uncovered as well as some remarkable examples of sarcophagi such as the large granite one of Psusennes and two others in silver. The Ethiopian domination of the 25th Dynasty is documented here with the Stele of Piankhi, which relates the conquest of Egypt with details of the siege of Memphis. The extremely expressive statue and bust of the governor of Thebes, Montuemhat, are of the same epoch. The remains of his funerary temple can be found in Thebes. Art of the Saïte Period (664−525 BC) expresses the period of renaissance during which ancient Egypt enjoyed its last moments of independence.

Graeco — Roman Period The art of this period shows a fruitful cultural encounter which produced a particular style called Graeco-Egyptian or Roman-Egyptian. Among the most characteristic artworks of the period are the funerary masks and portraits of mummies with encaustic paintings on tablets of wood placed between bandages on the face. These constitute one of the rare examples of Hellenistic painting which have been well preserved. A collection of royal mummies is assembled together in one hall of the museum.

Islamic Cairo

Islam in Egypt began at Fustat, the first Arab city in Egypt, and later mushroomed into a great civilization with its most beautiful monuments in Cairo. Egypt was one of the first countries to be conquered by the Arabs after the death of Mohammed. Facing minimal resistance, the army of Amr Ibn el-As conquered the weak fortress city of Pelusium by siege. Its location was crucial: posted at the extreme east of the Nile delta, this gateway city opened the rest of the land to subjugation. Large numbers of the local population, dissatisfied with Byzantine rule, were converted to Islam so that Christianity was slowly reduced to a minority faith, thereby losing importance and secular influence in politics, economics and culture. The skilled Christian craftsmen and artists, however, did not hesitate to offer their services to the new rulers; they contributed to the embellishment of old structures, sometimes changing the style to conform with the distinctive Islamic use of arches and clear open geometric courtyards.

On the site of Amr Ibn el-As' encampment, which later became Fustat, rose the mosque of Ibn el-As, which has lost some of its original features because of continuous remodelling and embellishment over the years. Nonetheless, its present structure is considered Cairo's oldest mosque. This section is known as 'old Cairo' and is populated by artisans and dealers of all varieties.

The Mosques of Cairo

The mosque is the place where the Muslim community gathers for the ritual prayers on Fridays; they are the only prayers that are recited in public or in communion. From the beginning, the mosque has always had a political as well as a religious importance. In fact, before reciting prayers, the faithful engage in political discourses. This encourages social integration since each locality has only one main mosque. The function of the mosque may be compared to that of the Christian cathedral in history. The main difference, however, is that the mosque is not considered by Muslims as a house of God, as the Christians believe the church to be, but rather as a house of believers, a haven where people gather in observance of the rites of prayer.

The mosque as an original architectural form is derived from the house of Mohammed in Medina. In its most traditional form, it is composed of an open interior court off which are located various rooms and chambers, at times also adorned with elegant porticoes. Under the rule of the Umayyads and Abbasids (between AD 650−860), Fustat occupied itself with the enrichment and embellishment of its structures, erecting new monuments and buildings, all of which are unfortunately lost today. Outside its fortifying walls grew the suburbs of el-Askar, meaning 'the army'.

In about 870, Ahmed Ibn Tulun, the Turkish governor of Egypt, proclaimed himself an independent sultan and transferred his residence to the hill of Jechkar north-east of Fustat where, after having destroyed both the Christian and Hebrew cemeteries, he constructed a citadel, the primitive stronghold which then grew into the city of el-Qata'i. This city witnessed glorious years of growth and development under Ahmed Ibn Tulun. In its ancient splendour, it is said to have had 100,000 houses under its protective wing. It counted among its most resplendent and impressive buildings the palace of el-Maidan and the hospital or *maristan* of el-Askar. Today, not a trace of these splendid buildings remains. Aside from battered vestiges of private homes and palaces, only ruins of the aqueduct of el-Basatin and the grandiose mosque of el-Qataiya still stand.

Designed and built by a Christian architect, the beautiful **Mosque of Ibn Tulun** follows the lines and style of the Abbasid type, which is generally characterized by pilasters on which slightly pointed arches are applied. Soaring gracefully in front of the mosque is a minaret which originally had the same spiral characteristic as those of Samarra found in Mesopotamia. It was transformed into its present form in 1297 by the sultan, Lagin. The stucco-work which adorns the mosque is a revival of the style and technique found in Samarra. It is interesting to note, however, that certain designs and motifs are taken from Coptic art.

The first Fatimid monument in Egypt was the **Mosque of el-Azhar**, along the southern edge of Cairo, constructed by General Gawhar in 970. It has undergone so many restorations and reconstructions, especially after the devastating earthquake of 1303, that today it is impossible to make out its original structure. The mosque was entirely built on columns which were part of older monuments, and its style was strongly inspired by the cult edifices already existing in Tunisia and Spain.

The mosque of el-Azhar, a highly regarded and respected centre of theological studies, immediately gained prestige in the Arab world. Its university is in fact still the most prestigious centre of learning for a devout Muslim; its students are highly esteemed and, having been educated in the most traditional Koranic disciplines, are then sent out to spread the revelations of Mohammed.

The second-most important mosque of the Fatimid epoch in Cairo, the **Mosque of el-Hakim**, was founded by el-Aziz in 990. The project was continued by his son el-Hakim between 1003 and 1012, following not only the planimetry but also the artistic forms of Mesopotamian styles which also characterize the mosque of Ibn Tulun. The name of el-Hakim (996−1021) is associated with some rather grotesque scandals, such as the prohibition of numerous drinks and dishes, some particularly dear to the Egyptian palate; the imposition of a strict ban which forbade women to loiter in the streets; and the slaughter of dogs because their howling disturbed his solitary promenades around the city. In a fit of rage, he ordered an entire quarter of Fustat burned and pillaged.

The Kurdish general **Salah el-Din**, better known as **Saladin**, supplanted the last of the Fatimids. This brilliant sovereign was a generous and honoured patron of the arts and culture; he brought about the elevation of Cairo to the most respected intellectual capital of the Islamic world. Testifying to this was the foundation of a *madrasa*, a theological school which followed strictly the disciplines of the Sunnis, the main sect of Islam.

Saladin also proved himself to be an invaluable innovator in the city's architectural and urban planning. The city walls which enclose both the old and the new sections of Cairo provided a sense of security for its inhabitants. His most important work, however, was the **Citadel**, constructed in 1179 over a ramp of the Muqattam hill. Many of the architectural features of this edifice are of remotely oriental derivation, but they are also strikingly typical of the Crusade construction prevalent in Syria and Palestine. The primitive fortress has undergone

various expansions and transformations in the course of the centuries. A Turkish-style mosque was built within its walls by Mohammed Ali, who demolished the ancient palaces which once stood on the site.

A new impetus for architectural and artistic development in Cairo came from the Mameluke sultans who held the country for almost three centuries. Under their patronage, Cairo was enriched and beautified with a number of monuments, including the vast architectural complex consisting of a mausoleum, mosque and maristan of Sultan Qalaun, and the splendid **Mosque of Sultan Hasan**, erected beween 1356 and 1362 — one of the masterpieces of Islamic art.

Cairo found new stimuli for growth and development in the vitality and force of Mohammed Ali. Through his initiatives a new city sprang up, with residential sections and zones delineated for administrative buildings patterned on European cities. Among many other architectural works constructed was the **Mosque of Mohammed Ali**. Also referred to as the **Alabaster Mosque** (its walls are covered entirely by a splended alabaster finish from Beni Suef) its style is greatly influenced by the mosques of Istanbul. There is a panoramic view of the city from the terraces behind.

The large number of splendid art objects collected from various mosques and other ancient buildings in Cairo led, in 1880, to the foundation of the modest Museum of Arabic Art in the court of the mosque of el-Hakim. With generous art donations from the private sector, it was necessary to build a new museum, and Bab el-Khalq was inaugurated in 1902. In 1952, its name was modified to the more appropriate **Museum of Islamic Art**, since numerous pieces from non-Arab nations such as Turkey and Persia were also exhibited.

The 23 halls are organized according to type of object and in chronological order. It is most rewarding to follow the defined routes and not to miss any part of the exhibition. Recent archaeological excavations (some in the vicinity of Cairo) have provided, amongst other treasures, precious examples of figurative art from the Fatimid and Tulunite eras. Other excavations around Cairo have also yielded many ceramic fragments and even some exceptional vases and plates in an excellent state of preservation, which reveal the high level of refinement attained by artisans of the ninth and tenth centuries. Among the most beautiful examples of Islamic ceramics here are those finished with the characteristic technique of 'metallic lustre', which is probably of Egyptian origin. There are also some rare examples of Hispano-Moorish ceramics.

Near the bazaar of Khan el-Khalili in south Cairo rises the imposing Mosque of el-Azhar, an important centre for worship and study for the whole Muslim world. Other monuments located along

Sharia el-Muizzli Din Allah to the north are the **Madrasa** (mosque), **tomb and Maristan** (hospital) **of Qalaun**, a sultan who lived in the second half of the 13th century. Of particular beauty are the mausoleum and the tomb, the latter rich with a colourful play of light on the magnificent structure and splendid wall decorations; its mosaics are among the most celebrated in Cairo.

Not far away are the **Madrasa of Mohammed el-Nasser** (son of Qalaun), with its beautiful façade, and the **Madrasa of Sultan Barquq**, an elegant building dating back to 1386. Towards the Mosque of el-Hakim is **Beit Suhaymi**, the ancient manor of a 17th-century sheikh, situated on a minor side street to the right. The mosaics, *mushrabiya* (wooden lattice-work screens) and the fountain are very interesting. Past the square containing the **Mosque of el-Hakim** (see also Islamic Cairo) and the **Museum of Islamic Art** is **Bab el-Futuh**, or 'Conquest Gate', a portion of which is buried four metres (13 feet) underground. The vault decorations are clearly of Byzantine influence. Rising on the other side of the mosque is **Bab el-Nasr**, or 'Victory Gate', which is built in the Graeco-Roman style.

A short distance to the west of el-Azhar is the complex of **el-Ghuri**, consisting of a *madrasa*, a mausoleum and a caravanserai which today houses a school of traditional arts and crafts. A visit to this pleasant and interesting school is recommended.

The house of **Gamal Eddin Ed Dahabi** is a remarkable example of civilian architecture of the 1600s. Going on along Sharia el-Muizzli Din Allah, one reaches the gate of **Bab Zuwayla**, also called **Bab el-Mitwalli** which once marked the southern boundary of el-Qahira. Legend has it that a very famous healer who performed miracles used to live here.

The **Mosque of el-Muayyad** (15th century), the two minarets of which are incorporated within the towers of Bab Zuwayla, is one of the most beautiful in Cairo. Its portal in black and white marble and doors of thick wood are richly embellished with bronze plaques. The interior is also splendidly adorned, though some of the friezes have been replaced with modern copies.

From the Bab Zuwayla, the main road, Sharia Darb el-Ahmar, runs south-east (becoming Sharia el-Tabbana and then Sharia Bab el-Wazir). It passes many notable buildings, including the mosque and tomb of the emir Qagmas el-Ishaqi (also known as the **Mosque of Abu Huraybah**), the **Mosque of Altunbugha el-Maridani** and the **Mosque of Aqsunqur**. This last, built in 1346−7, was partly destroyed by an earthquake and restored in 1651, when it was decorated with tiles, hence its most common name, the **Blue Mosque**.

Another area rich in interesting buildings is that enclosing the mosques of Sultan Hassan and Ibn Tulun, and the Citadel, extending towards Old Cairo. The mosques are east of **Midan Saiyda Zeinab** at the bottom of **Sharia Bur Said** or west of **Midan Salah el-Din** below the Citadel. The **Mosque of Ibn Tulun** (876−9) is not only endowed with rich and splendid decorations, but also holds the distinction of being the most ancient of the mosques still in a good state of preservation. Adjacent to it is the beautiful **Gayer-Anderson Museum**, an annex of the Museum of Islamic Art. It consists of two former houses restored and refurbished by an Englishman before World War II. The museum has irregular levels, winding corridors and galleries with *mushrabiya*.

To the north-east is the magnificent **Mosque of Sultan Hasan** (built 1356−62), representing the most vigorous period of the Muslim Middle Age. Its decorations are austerely applied on bare surfaces, creating a noble and mighty complex overlooked by imposing minarets. The gate is majestic and leads to a cross-shaped vestibule. In the central court is a fountain crowned by a great cupola which was once painted blue. Notwithstanding the passage of time and human negligence which have stripped it of part of its original beauty, the mosque stands unique in the panorama of Islamic art. Nearby stand mosques of minor importance (all of which face Midan Salah el-Din), and **Bab el-Azab**, the entrance gate into the Citadel, which encloses various mosques and a military museum within its mighty walls.

On the same level as the southern tip of Roda Island, a few blocks from the right bank of the Nile, is the ancient district of **Qasr el-Shama** or **Old Cairo**, where the main Christian religious buildings and the Coptic Museum are clustered. Also included within the Roman walls are numerous Christian cemeteries belonging to the various orthodox sects of the Orient (predominantly Greek), Roman towers, and the ancient **Mosque of Amr** built in 642 by Amr Ibn el-As (see Islamic Cairo) which has many legends revolving around it. The column enclosed by a grill is said to have been miraculously transported from Mecca by the order of Mohammed himself. In addition to the most famous Coptic churches, one can admire the walls surrounding the Christian cemeteries. There are also some less famous convents and churches which have both charm and spiritual intensity. Among these are the convent and church of Abu Sefein and the church of Amba Shenuda.

East of the Citadel are two large Muslim **necropoli**, also called 'the city of the dead'. Following to a tradition which was certainly influenced by the creeds of ancient Egypt and very uncommon in the Islamic world, tombs and burial places were built and furnished as if they were proper homes. On feast days it is customary for entire families to visit the tombs of their loved ones, enjoying picnics or even spending a few days in and around the tomb. The richest tombs also provide the housing of servants and keepers, stables etc, and at a glance the cemetery looks like a normal residential area. It is distinctly gloomy and colourless on closer inspection. After the Arab-Israeli wars of 1948 and 1967, many people from the war zones found refuge in the cities of the dead and only a small portion of the necropoli are visited by tourists.

The northern cemetery, or **Tombs of the Caliphs**, is located east of Sharia Saleh Salem, between el-Azhar and the Citadel, and comprises many mosques and sultans' tombs. Among the most interesting is the **Mosque of Ibn Barquq** (1400–11), which was restored a few years ago. It has twin minarets in the Mameluke style and two beautiful cupolas with a zig-zag decoration (probably the first in Egypt to be built in stone). At the entrance, a stone with mutilated hieroglyphics is used as a doorstep, allowing the symbolic act of trampling on paganism before entering the house of worship. A real masterpiece is the **minbar** (or pulpit) in sculpted stone and also particularly beautiful are the decorations of the two domes. The second-floor porch offers an impressive view of the vast necropoli.

The **Mausoleum of Barsbay** on the left-hand side of Sharia Gawhar el-Qa'id (el-Muslim) as you go north-west, is more modest, but has a very beautiful minaret made of ivory-inlaid wood forming arabesques, and a beautiful dome.

The **Mausoleum of Qaitbay** is a 15th-century masterpiece of Arabic art, delicate and harmonious in proportion and decoration. The southern cemetery or **Tombs of the Mamelukes** is a large expanse stretching from the Citadel to Maadi. Its most interesting monuments are the **Mosques of Imam el-Layth** and **Imam el-Shafii** and many tombs of the Abbasid caliphs. Most of the other mosques are inaccessible to non-Muslims, and are badly preserved.

Coptic Cairo

You can reach Coptic Cairo from Midan el-Tahrir by taxi or by train from Bab el-Luk station. The number of Copts living in primitive, nuclear villages founded by the Arabs (constituting the foundations of present-day Cairo) has been documented accurately only from the Roman period, when the Romans constructed the fortress of **Babylon** on the island of **Roda.** Within these ancient walls are the sprawling quarters of the Copts (later renamed Qasr el-Shama by the Arabs), where they enjoyed relative protection. Here the heirs of what was once a unique oasis of Christianity in the heart of a Muslim city still live. Throughout the centuries, the Copts have generally been allowed to co-exist peacefully alongside the Muslim majority. The Coptic churches were occasionally subjected to the religious intemperances of fanatic adversaries however, but the Copts were never actually persecuted by the Muslims in Egypt. In the quarters of Qasr el-Shama, better known as Old Cairo, Muslim houses may be found interspersed with Coptic homes and buildings. There is an old synagogue here, too.

The most ancient and interesting of the remaining Coptic churches are situated in the heart of Old Cairo. The primitive Coptic churches of Egypt were usually constructed according to a Roman basilica plan which must have originated in Alexandria. Today all traces of the original churches have disappeared. The traditional Coptic church normally consists of the narthex, the choir, the sanctuary, and a baptistry, almost always situated at the far end of the north wing. The nave is divided into three parts by double colonnades, the north wing being reserved especially for women. At the end of the nave is the choir, separated by a chancel screen. The sanctuary, on the other hand almost always consists of three chapels, each of which has its own altar. Placed exactly behind the principal altar is the tribune, marked by a throne for the bishop and seats for the officiating clergy. The typical primitive Coptic church, devoid of columns and paintings (elements introduced much later), was extremely simple and rather plain. The entrance façade often, if not always, had only one narrow doorway, in order to conceal the presence of a religious building in a sea of houses.

Constructed over the ruins of two towers of the Roman fortress of Babylon, the **Church of St Mary**, dating back to the fourth century, was called **el-Moallaqah**, meaning 'overhanging or suspended', owing to the peculiarity of its construction. Laid out on a basilica plan with a single nave, it has a splendid baptistry. Destroyed in the ninth century, el-Moallaqah was later restored and, after numerous renovations, it was chosen as the seat of the Coptic patriarch in 1039.

The original **Church of St Sergius (Abu Sarga)** dedicated to St Sergius and St Bacchus, two soldiers who suffered the agonizing trials of martyrdom under the reign of Maximiah, probably dates back to the fifth century. It was destroyed in the fire of Fustat in the reign of the last Umayyad caliph, Marwan II, in around 750. It is based on a basilica plan, but is made more beautiful by an elegant narthex that takes devotees into a vast central hall divided by two lines of pilasters into three naves. The Church of St Sergius brings to mind religious structures in Rome and Constantinople. The crypt, definable as another church, is situated right under the centre of the choir and dates back to the fifth century. This is certainly among the most interesting parts of the entire complex of buildings which belong, for the most part, to the Fatimid era of the tenth and eleventh centuries.

Although the **Church of St Barbara** in Old Cairo was dedicated to St Cyrus and St John, the church is now known as the Church of St Barbara after the chapel which contains her remains. St Barbara was the young martyr of Nicomedia who died at the hands of her own father whom she tried to convert to Christianity. Of basilican type, the church probably dates back to the fifth century, and, like the church of St Sergius, it was reconstructed in about the eleventh century. Particularly interesting and pleasing is the wooden architrave running over the capitals which is one of the more characteristic features of Coptic architecture. In the 15th century, the Arab historian Maqrizi celebrated this particular church in his writing, describing it as the largest and most beautiful Coptic church of his time.

Of the other Coptic churches in Old Cairo, three are worth a special mention. **The Church of the Virgin (Haret Zuweila)**, constructed in 350 and destroyed in 1321, was later restored and became the seat of the Patriarchate until 1860. **The Church of the Virgin (Haret el-Rum)** built in the sixth century, has undergone countless alterations. The **Church of Sts Peter and Paul** is one of the most exceptional of these Coptic churches. Constructed in 1910 following the wishes of the family of Boutros Ghali Pasha, it has the typical features of primitive Egyptian churches.

The building which currently houses the **Coptic Museum** is situated to the south of the southernmost walls of Old Cairo, rising over one of those places identified by tradition as the setting of legendary battles between Horus and Seth. It is a site which is particularly fascinating and evocative even for modern Egyptians as it contains the world's richest collection of Coptic art and treasures. Founded in 1908 with treasures and materials from mostly private collections, the Coptic Museum has witnessed a notable rise in importance. It has been designated a state institution, and was granted the dazzling collection of Coptic documents once held in the Egyptian Museum. The Coptic Museum is well lit and well ordered. There are also excellent funerary stelae from ancient churches and monasteries here. The textile industry of the Copts has real artistic value both for its technique and for its mastery of design. It drew admiration from Muslims who later used Coptic models in their work. The superb murals and the vast series of icons on wooden tablets deserve special attention.

The Centre of Cairo

Midan el-Tahrir or **Liberation Square**, just north of Old Cairo, is the focal point of the modern tourist town, surrounded by the Egyptian Museum, a large number of the main city hotels, airline offices, ministries and government offices. Close to the Nile, the square is linked to **Gezira Island**, where numerous museums and sports clubs are located. The northern part of the island is occupied by the modern residential area of **Zamalek** where wide well-lined avenues offer a change from the crowded centre of the city.

Not far from Midan el-Tahrir, northwards along Sharia Soliman Pasha (its official name, though little used, is Sharia Talaat Harb), is **Midan Talaat Harb**, another square dense with traffic, shops and offices. It is crossed by **Sharia Qasr el-Nil**, an avenue full of luxury shops, and branch offices of international companies and banks. Sharia 26 July, a main road link, crosses the river at two points and passes through Gezira Island before following the left bank.

At the opposite end, the avenue leads eastwards to the **Ezbekiya Gardens**, which are often packed with people. The gardens retain their charm, nonetheless, and of particular interest are the numerous little stands selling secondhand books. Adjacent to the gardens is **Midan Opera**, in the square where the Opera Theatre stood until 1971, when it was destroyed by fire. To get to **Khan el-Khalili**, the bazaar area, cross the old and interesting quarter of **Muski**, which is full of markets and colourful commercial establishments.

With a character all its own, the bazaar of Khan el-Khalili is exactly what an oriental bazaar should be and more. It is laden with various kinds of goods, crowded with tourists, craftsmen and local people and filled with exotic odours. Its alleys, so narrow that the roofs block most of the sunshine, form a labyrinth in which it is easy to get lost. If you lose your bearings, there is no need to become alarmed; the local people are invariably ready to help in providing directions. If the atmosphere approximates that of the past, the goods on sale cater for the tourist with a taste for cheap souvenirs and imitations of ancient models. However, the shops still resound with the hammering of coppersmiths and old-style sewing machines with which competent tailors can fashion every conceivable kind of garment within a few hours.

Bargaining is a must and is widely practised by foreigners and residents alike. Plan at least a half-day visit to the bazaar, and before buying anything compare prices among the different shops. A relaxing respite from shopping can be found at **Fishawi**, an authentic and characteristic cafe close to the Mosque of el-Hasan.

The Outskirts of Cairo

Heliopolis Heliopolis (or Masr el-Gadida, which means 'New Town' in Arabic) is 20 kilometres (12.5 miles) from Cairo, on the road to Suez. Today, it is a modern residential quarter, but in ancient times it was one of the most famous cities of Egypt. Though without great political significance, it was of great religious importance. The **Heliopolis Temple** detailed an entire doctrine based on the cult of the sun (Ra, Harmakhis, Atum), its principal gods, and the dogma of primeval Ennead (the nine creator gods). Its prestige lasted even through the New Kingdom period, when the Theban god Amun became important, and up to the fifth century when Greek philosophers went there to study. Later, the temple lost its importance and columns and obelisks were removed to Alexandria and Rome.

Heliopolis is often mentioned in the Bible as it sheltered the Holy Family during their escape into Egypt. Here you can see an age-old sycamore called '**The Virgin's Tree**' which, according to legend, gave shelter to Mary (in reality, the tree was planted in the 17th century to replace an older one). There is nothing left of the old monuments today.

Helwan Helwan is about 25 kilometres (15.5 miles) south of Cairo on the eastern bank road of the Nile. North of the town are the residential quarter of Maadi and the Tura Hills, the source of the stones used to build the pyramids of Memphis. Some votive works are still visible today. The technique used to cut the large blocks of stone is still used today in the rural areas. Once the block's shape was defined, narrow slits were made into which were inserted dry wood slivers. These slivers expanded when wet, causing blocks to split apart. (We still do not know how the ancient Egyptians transported such large blocks to the site.)

Helwan is famous for its thermal sulphurous waters, which gush out at 30°C (86°F) and are believed to have curative powers for rheumatism, kidney problems and skin infections. Among the local attractions is the **Wax Museum**, which illustrates scenes from Egyptian life from the time of the Pharaohs until the last century. It also holds a collection of traditional dolls from all over the world. A **Japanese garden**, the only one of its kind in the Arab countries, strikes an odd but welcome note for the visitor, with its Buddhas, artificial lakes and small pagodas. **The residence of King Farouk** (1936–1952) is now a museum open to the public. Nearby is the **Astronomic Observatory**, founded in 1903, which is used for housing meteorological records. Helwan is also well known for its industrial installations.

Giza Sprawled across a calcareous tableland which is surrounded by the long chain of Libyan mountain ranges and rimmed to the north and south by two wadis is Giza, 11 kilometres (6.8 miles) south-west of Cairo. Although it is associated with the grandeur and tradition of the Fourth Dynasty, recent archaeological excavations south of the pyramids here have uncovered remains of a settlement with tombs and

The Pyramids of Giza

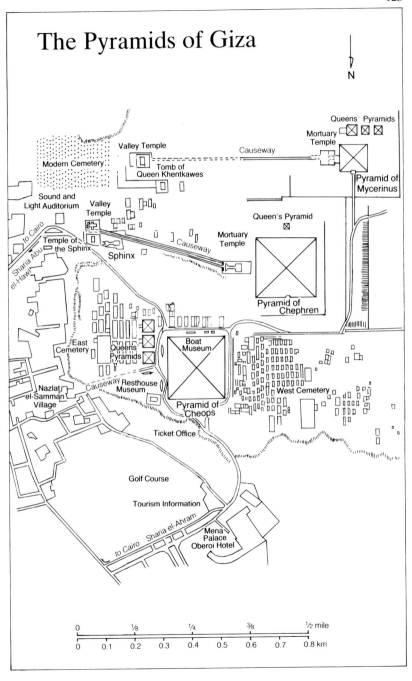

N

Queens' Pyramids
Mortuary Temple
Pyramid of Mycerinus

Causeway

Valley Temple
Tomb of Queen Khentkawes

Modern Cemetery

Queen's Pyramid

Sound and Light Auditorium

Valley Temple

Temple of the Sphinx

Sphinx

Mortuary Temple

Causeway

to Cairo

Sharia Abu el-Hawl

Pyramid of Chephren

East Cemetery

Queens' Pyramids

Boat Museum

West Cemetery

Nazlat el-Samman Village

Causeway

Resthouse Museum

Pyramid of Cheops

Ticket Office

Golf Course

Tourism Information

Sharia el-Ahram

to Cairo

Mena Palace Oberoi Hotel

0	⅛	¼	⅜	½ mile
0	0.1	0.2	0.3	0.4	0.5	0.6	0.7	0.8 km

dwellings dating as far back as the First and Second dynasties in the Thinite Era. Punctuating its seemingly infinite expanse are the three celebrated pyramids of Cheops, Chephren and Mycerinus, the funerary temples of which are linked to the Sphinx and the mastaba camps constructed in parallel lines according to a regular plan. This rigid skyline was later softened by the addition of new constructions. First among these were the tombs of civil and religious functionaries of the Fifth and Sixth dynasties, followed by those of important personages of the Saïte Era (26th Dynasty) and of the Persian Period (27th Dynasty), who desired, for reasons both social and religious, to be buried with pomp and dignity alongside the majestic pyramids.

Giza is part of the White Wall *nome* or province, which had Memphis as its main town. Though linked to the largest necropolis of Memphis, Giza has always retained a certain characteristic homogeneity. Rich historical records of this vast area are preserved in the travel writings of Greek, Roman, Arab and Western travellers. It was first scientifically and methodically explored in the early 1900s when the first important archaeological excavations began. The area soon became overrun by American, German, Austrian, Italian and Egyptian excavation teams. Excavation and research work continues today. The three pyramids of Giza represent classic models of the type of construction practised during the Fourth Dynasty which served as the pattern for other structures until the end of the Old Kingdom.

The Pyramid of Cheops This magnificent funerary complex, designed and executed by the architect Hemiunu, has inspired countless pseudo-scientific theories as to the reasons for its dimensions. However, the dimensions are probably the best solutions to construction problems. The angle of inclination of the sides (51°52′), permits an equal distribution of weight. Now rising 137 metres (450 feet) high, the structure originally stood 140 metres (460 feet). Its sides measured 230 metres (755 feet). The pyramid appears to be intact, although its surface layer of fine Tura limestone was stripped by invaders for use as construction material. Like the exterior, the interior is structured in grand style. The project was modified three times in the course of its construction before the builders arrived at a definitive form. The first plan included a 'Queen's Chamber', which was excavated from the centre on the apex line, but left unfinished. Then followed various alterations for unknown reasons, such as the excavation of a room for the sarcophagus, much higher and slightly askew to the apex axis. It is reached by crossing a grand gallery with walls notched at the top, so that roofing blocks rested individually against the wall. (This prevented the weight from resting on one spot.) The granite funerary chamber contains an unadorned, lidless sarcophagus also in pure granite slabs, and is protected from the weight of masonry by five relieving spaces. The actual entrance of the pyramid, 15 metres (49 feet) above the original entry, winds across a narrow tunnel excavated by thieves and looters of the tombs.

Of the temple annexed at the eastern side of the pyramid, only the basalt flooring remains, though its actual layout and plan have been reconstructed. The processional ramp with its once richly-decorated walls has also been largely destroyed. Three small pyramids along the eastern side probably belonged to queens and princesses.

Another important archaeological find east of the pyramid of Cheops, uncovered in 1925, was the tomb of Queen Hetepheres, wife of Snefru and mother of Cheops. The richly glittering furniture recovered from the site is now on exhibition at the Museum of Cairo.

A most exceptional discovery in 1954, was that of two boats in Egyptian sycamore and cedar from Lebanon. The funerary vessels had been disassembled and carefully deposited in separate air-tight pits along the pyramid's southern side. One of the vessels has been fully reconstructed and is housed in a museum near where it was found. As in other pyramids, air-tight pits for sacred funeral vessels may be found in the eastern face of the pyramid or on the side of the ramp. The significance of these vessels is unknown. They were believed at first to be the solar barque of Cheops, thus equating the deceased Pharaoh with the sun god Ra. Recent studies, however, show that the boats were used by the priests in the funerary rites of Cheops to make pilgrimages from one site to another.

The Pyramid of Chephren This pyramid is situated in a quarry from which came part of the material used for its construction. Protected on the north and west by a natural rocky barrier with rock tombs, Chephren's pyramid, originally reaching a height of 145 metres (476 feet), now stands at 136 metres (446 feet), about two metres (six feet six inches) shorter than that of Cheops. It appears taller, having been built on higher ground which has preserved its limestone top covering, and blocks of red granite at the base. The interior, which was also a result of two successive projects, was extensively explored by the Italian explorer Belzoni in 1818, who uncovered a granite sarcophagus and transcribed an inscription testifying to a violation committed by Arabs in 1200. On the west side of the pyramid is a series of lodgings for the workers employed in the construction of the funerary complex. The funerary temple leaning against the foot of the pyramid on the east side is not easily identifiable in all its particulars but it is recognizable in its essential functional structures which are divided into two distinct parts: an entry hall and an open court accessible to

Mummification

Mention of the ancient Egyptians usually brings to mind the practice of mummification — preservation of the body of a dead person or animal. The Egyptians were masters of this craft in ancient times, and their mummies have been the subject of fascination both because of the science of the craft and the macabre images they evoke.

There is no concrete evidence as to when this practice started. Finds dating back to the predynastic period (3050−2686 BC) show that corpses were put in shallow tombs in the fetal position. By the Third Dynasty (2686−2613 BC), there are signs that the body was dismembered and the limbs wrapped to represent the dead person. The first known example of mummification, however, dates back to the Fourth Dynasty (2613−2498 BC); yet it was only during the New Kingdom (1570−1070 BC) that the art of embalming was perfected, as the well-preserved mummies of Sety I and Ramesses II show.

The word 'mummy' comes from the Arabic word *mummiya* (bitumen), the substance in which the body was soaked. Various methods were used at different times, but those of the 18th and 19th dynasties were the most effective. The process of mummification itself is complex. Seventy steps carried out over a period of 70 days were required, although there was one case of an Old Kingdom queen whose mummification reportedly took 285 days. The following are the main stages of mummification:

1. Extraction of the brain through the nostrils.
2. Removal of the viscera through an incision in the flank.

Tutankhamun's tomb, Valley of the Kings

3. Sterilization of the body and viscera.
4. Cleaning, treating, dehydrating and anointing the viscera with resin.
5. Packing the body with natron, a natural dehydrating and preserving agent (the body was then left for up to 40 days).
6. Removal of the natron packing.
7. Packing of the limbs with sand, clay or other earthy material.
8. Packing of the body with resin-soaked linen, myrrh and cinnamon.
9. Treatment of the body with unguents, then packing it with fine linen gauze.

This process was followed by the actual burial, in which the mummy would be placed in a coffin, often made in the shape of the corpse. Shaped coffins were sometimes nested one within another, and the coffin or coffins then placed inside a stone sarcophagus. The viscera were treated separately and placed inside canopic jars, usually made of alabaster, which were later placed in the tomb chamber near the mummy. Originally, mummification was reserved for kings and members of the royal family; the poorer people were simply wrapped in linen shrouds and buried in sand or stone tombs.

Mystery surrounds the purpose of mummification, but it appears to have grown with the belief in Osiris (God of the Underworld), resurrection and reincarnation. Ancient Egyptians sought to impede the decaying process; they believed that by preserving the body or physical vehicle, the soul was able to continue its existence in the *duat* (underworld). Osiris appears repeatedly as a motif in sarcophagi.

Most of what is known today about ancient Egypt comes from the study of mummies, coffins and sarcophagi. Coffins, usually made of wood, were placed inside the stone sarcophagi which were usually limestone, basalt or granite. A third type of material, especially common during the Third Intermediate and Graeco-Roman periods, was cartonnage, which was made by placing successive applications of linen and glue around a model mummy and painting it with bright watercolours. The Cairo Museum has several fine examples of wooden coffins painted to resemble the dead.

Decoration of the tombs which were basically rectangular or anthropoid (mummiform) in shape varied according to the period. Anthropoid coffins with feathered wings were characteristic of the 17th Dynasty, while white coffins with bands were common in the 18th Dynasty. During the last part of the New Kingdom, the use of decorations, scenes depicting various deities and texts became more prevalent. Anthropoid sarcophagi, made of dark hard stone, were perfected during this same period.

From the end of the Middle Kingdom onwards, more funerary statuettes, known as *ushabti*, were added to the funerary equipment. By the end of the 18th Dynasty, these statuettes began to resemble the mummy itself and usually carried inscriptions from the text of *The Book of the Dead*.

devotees; and the actual sanctuary which was strictly dedicated to the cult. Chephren's valley temple, linked by a processional ramp, is the best-preserved temple of this type and was used for purification and embalming rites. It also includes the landing pier for the river procession which bore the remains of the deceased. The principal hall, reached through a vestibule with a double entrance, is a pillared room laid out in an inverted T-plan. The roof is made of granite slabs which permit strips of light through its narrow apertures to wash the interior with mysterious shades of yellow and ochre. These slabs are supported by 16 monolithic pillars in red granite, and the perimeter is covered with slabs of alabastrine limestone. Twenty-three statues of the sovereign lined the hall's black granite walls. A diorite statue of Chephren (Khafre) with a falcon with outspread wings, uncovered from a pit excavated in this hall, is currently housed at the Cairo Museum. The external walls of the temple are slightly tapered. In its totality, and most particularly in its façade, the temple was made to resemble a monumental mastaba. The pyramid of Chephren is not aligned to its valley temple; hence, to avoid the irregularity of the landscape, a rocky bridge which crosses obliquely over the sunken parts of the terrain all the way up to the tableland was used as a base for the processional ramp which rises to the pyramid.

The Sphinx, famous because of the mystery surrounding it, is partly natural and partly man-made. For the grand-scale construction of the Sphinx, blocks and boulders from the limestone quarries north of the valley temple were excavated. They were shaped into a leonine body with a human head which bore the features of Chephren. The Sphinx measures 20 metres (65.6 feet) in height and 57 metres (187 feet) in length. This was to emphasize the divine nature of the king, as the solar divinity was believed to manifest himself in the lion and in the king. In front of the Sphinx was erected a temple of enormous limestone blocks, probably originally covered with granite, with an ample central court marked by decorative pillars. It was not designed for funerary purposes but was dedicated to the divine cult and perhaps also used during coronation anad investiture ceremonies. Between the Sphinx's paws, Thutmose IV erected the 'Dream Stele' which commemorates the clearing of sand and restoration of the monument ordered by the Pharaoh who dreamt, under the Sphinx's shadow, of the sun divinity's lamentations at being abandoned.

The Pyramid of Mycerinus This pyramid is of smaller dimensions and rises to around 66 metres (216.6 feet). It is covered by red granite blocks from Aswan to a height of 16 layers, although the upper part is unfinished. On the northern side is a noticeable breach cut by the

Mamelukes in their attempt to discover the entrance to the sacred halls. The funerary apartment is reached by crossing a descending gallery, the entrance of which was only discovered in 1817, opening into the sacrifical room in granite finish crowned with false vaults. The magnificent basalt sarcophagus was lost in a storm at sea while being transported to Britain. An anthropoid coffin in wood uncovered on the site and belonging to a later period is probably a Saïte or Persian work of restoration common in this area. Along the southern side of the pyramid are three smaller satellite pyramids, all of which are tombs of queens and princesses. Of smaller dimensions, these pyramids follow the typical structural features of larger pyramids with interior funerary apartments and cult rooms reduced to essential elements. Granite sarcophagi were placed inside these funerary rooms.

The funerary temple of Mycerinus, situated east of the pyramid, was constructed partly during his reign and was completed, like the rest of the complex, by his successor Shepseskaf with mud brick and limestone facing, instead of the intended black granite. From the valley temple schist statuary groups representing the king accompanied by a divinity and by the personification of a province or with the queen were uncovered. The smaller dimensions and the inferior workmanship of this complex reflect the waning of royal power, which ended with the passing of the Old Kingdom.

The area around the pyramid of Mycerinus is devoid of the usual tombs of dignitaries which dot the surroundings of other pyramids. At the end of the Old Kingdom, the area was left in a state of abandonment, though maintenance and restoration operations continued, led by high priests who took charge of the funerary cult and to whom the earnings of royal endowments to the temple were given. In the First Intermediate Period, the entire area was sacked by thieves and looters. Kings and leaders of the 12th Dynasty continually took blocks and other fragments of the pyramids as material for their own pyramids. The pessimism and cynicism of the literature of that era decry the vanity of such constructions which, though impressive and pleasing to the eye, could not endure the trials of time and weather. It was only during the New Kingdom that this necropolis regained importance, influenced by the growing centres of Memphis and Heliopolis which, to counterbalance political and religious influences of the Theban clergy of Amun, led a renewed development of its solar cult. The restoration of monuments, and of the Sphinx in particular, became central to believers in Harakhty (Horus in the Horizon), and during the Saïte rebirth (26th Dynasty), the ancient royal cult was re-established.

Not far from the pyramid's ramp, a very important complex of Saïte and Persian tombs (unfortunately badly preserved) may be found. During the Graeco-Roman period, the place took on a tourist character as can be seen by the descriptive notes left by travellers as well as other evidence showing the care which visiting rulers took to preserve its legacy.

Memphis

The unification of Upper and Lower Egypt and the foundation of the city of Memphis by Menes mark the beginning of Egyptian dynastic history. In fact, Menes was probably a half-mythical king, a composite of a number of rulers who brought about the unification of the country. Nevertheless, the Egyptians regarded Menes as the founder of the state, and Memphis was to remain Egypt's major administrative city throughout its history. Situated close to the junction of the delta and the valley, it was in a prime position to govern the two lands.

The original name of Memphis was 'the White Walls', from its fortress enclosure. In later times it was referred to using the name of the pyramid of Pepy I, meaning 'established and beautiful' (in Egyptian, 'Men-nofer', which became 'Memphis' in Greek).

During the Old Kingdom, Memphis was the chief administrative city, while Heliopolis, not far away on the eastern bank of the river, was the major centre for the worship of the sun. Ancient Egyptian cities were not like modern ones; each king built himself a new palace and the government buildings gathered around this. In the Fourth Dynasty, the city of Memphis was probably near Giza, moving further south to the valley below Saqqara in the Fifth and Sixth dynasties. Of course, the major temples of Ptah and the other local gods, as well as shipyards and harbours, remained in the same place. The mounds of the ruins of ancient Memphis today cover a huge area, but much of what can be seen dates from the New Kingdom and the Late Period.

The rulers of the Middle Kingdom chose the southern districts of Memphis, standing between the river valley and the entrance to the Fayum, as their residence and burial place. These kings did much to expand the agricultural potential of the Fayum region, cutting canals and extending irrigation, so that from this time on it was one of the most important parts of Egypt.

Memphis lost some of its importance during the periods of disunity (the First and Second Intermediate Periods), but with the advent of the New Kingdom it again became a major city. From here the kings of the 18th Dynasty set out on their campaigns to Asia, and to the city's ports came the products of the conquered lands. The temple of Ptah was probably as big as that of Amun at Karnak, but much of the stone in the city's ruins was carried off in the Middle Ages in order to build Cairo. The Alabaster Sphinx, and the colossi of Ramesses II hint at the now-lost glories of Egypt's first city.

In the Late Period, Memphis had large foreign communities, each with their own districts; Jews, Phoenicians, Syrians, and later, Greeks, all resided here, with their own temples and cults. The great importance of Memphis as a religious centre in the Late and Ptolemaic periods is shown by the many dedications in the Serapeum, the burial place of the Apis bulls, and the other animal cemeteries at Saqqara. Memphis was a centre of pilgrimage, a place for oracles, and for healing. The Ptolemies promoted the worship of Serapis, and his association with the Apis bull, as a means of uniting Egyptian and Greek elements in society, and the kings were crowned in the temple of Ptah.

The chief deity of Memphis was Ptah, a creator god who spoke and all things came into being. He was associated early with another local deity, Sokar, a god of death and fertility. The main temple of Ptah was connected by canal with the temple of Hathor in the south of the city, along which the god would sail on an annual visit to his neighbour.

The Saïte Dynasty Under the prosperous Saïte Dynasty, Memphis underwent an overall revival, becoming cosmopolitan with the presence of Phoenician, Hebrew and Syrian colonies. In 525, the Persian emperor Cambyses conquered the city. In the following years under Greek-Roman occupation, the city kept its primary role, resting on its famed religious and political prestige. Notwithstanding Memphis' unimpeded rise as a truly cosmopolitan city, ancient Egyptian cults thrived as well; in fact, the high priests of Ptah exercised a strong influence over the ruling Greeks. But today there are very few vestiges of the splendours of the ancient capital. It was devastated by the great floods during the Mameluke Period. The gracious palm tree, thriving since the time of Pliny, slowly choked the land between the ruins. The first excavations dating back to 1820, focused on selected portions because the greater part of Memphis lies under silt from the Nile. Memphis suffered extinction when the Arab conquerors pillaged its stone to build Cairo 15 kilometres (9.3 miles) to the north. The modern village of Mit-Rahineh is the site of the Temple of Ptah, whose cult was founded in Memphis as far back as the First Dynasty.

The Temple of Ptah The original layout of the temple which now lies half covered with water in the village of Mit-Rahineh, is difficult to reconstruct visually because of its battered state. It was a marvellous construction during the Old Kingdom and underwent glorious

expansion in the time of Ramesses and embellishments in the Saïte era. Near the southern entry were discovered a number of colossi of Ramesses II, one of which, sculpted from a single boulder of limestone (the first discovered in 1820 by Caviglia and Sloane), has been preserved in the prostrate position in which it was found, measuring 10.3 metres (33.8 feet) in height and without feet. Its name is incised on the right shoulder, on the pectorals and on the belt buckle. A double crown and the characteristic names adorn its head. Another colossus in pink granite was transported to Cairo and stands in the station's square. Another important discovery made by Petrie in 1912 was an alabaster sphinx without inscriptions, probably posted at the entrance of the temple and believed to date back to the beginning of the New Kingdom. Still to be found within the confines of the same site is a grand commemorative stele with a decree promulgated by Apries in the 26th Dynasty regarding royal endowments in favour of the Temple of Ptah. Nearby, within the same archaeological delimitation, a small chapel of Sety I, dedicated to Ptah, was uncovered in 1948. The interior is beautified by an impressive group of statues representing the god Ptah with two goddesses and the king positioned at its knees.

Besides these relics, there are other remaining religious and civil buildings, such as the temple of Neith, lying at the extreme north of the archaeological site, and the palace of Apries, with a military camp adjacent to it.

Saqqara

The archaeological area of Saqqara, 32 kilometres (19.9 miles) from Cairo or six kilometres (3.7 miles) north-west of Memphis, spreads out over a vast, barren tableland seven kilometres (4.4 miles) in length and includes various necropoli and sepulchral monuments which have left valuable testimonies of all the principal periods of Egyptian history. The northern sector is the oldest part of Saqqara. This ancient zone accommodates tombs of kings of the archaic epochs (the Thinite era from the First to the Second dynasties), grand mud brick *mastabas* with mouldings, among which is that of King Hor Aha, identified through the marks of his official seal on clay caps of terracotta jars found in large quantities, and that of Hemaka, Vizier of King Udimu, which yielded an array of games, arms, unique instruments and utensils currently preserved in Cairo Museum.

The grandeur of Saqqara The area of Saqqara owes its importance as a royal necropolis to the **funerary complex of Zoser** (Third Dynasty) with its imposing structures which, to this day, never fail to command

North Saqqara

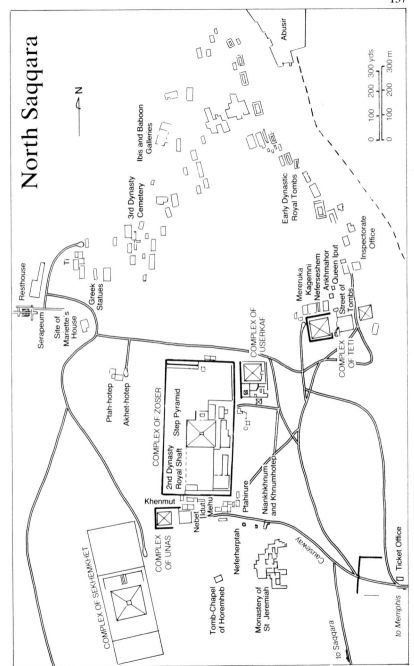

N

COMPLEX OF SEKHEMKHET

Tomb-Chapel of Horemheb

Neferherptah

Monastery of St Jeremiah

Causeway

to Saqqara

Ticket Office

to Memphis

COMPLEX OF UNAS

Khenmut

Nebet
Idut
Mehu

Niankhkhnum and Khnumhotep

Prahirure

Ptah-hotep

Akhet-hotep

COMPLEX OF ZOSER

2nd Dynasty Royal Shaft

Step Pyramid

COMPLEX OF USERKAF

Mereruka
Kagemni
Neferseshem
Ankhmahor
Queen Iput

Street of Tombs

COMPLEX OF TETI

Inspectorate Office

Serapeum

Site of Mariette's House

Resthouse

Ti

Greek Statues

3rd Dynasty Cemetery

Ibis and Baboon Galleries

Early Dynastic Royal Tombs

Abusir

0   100   200   300 yds

0   100   200   300 m

awe and admiration. Successive periods, starting from the Fourth Dynasty, saw Saqqara's prestige and importance diminish with the rise of Giza as a new site of royal burial grounds. It was only at the close of the Fifth Dynasty that systematic construction of royal pyramids, private tombs and *mastabas* recommenced in Saqqara, giving the necropolis its magnificence and richness.

After this period, no particular monuments or edifices were constructed until the New Kingdom, although the cult of the ancient kings which continued through this period permitted, through constant maintenance operations, the preservation of numerous precious tombs and monuments.

Eighteenth — Nineteenth dynasties With the dawn of the 18th and 19th dynasties, Saqqara enriched itself anew with the erection, south of Zoser's enclosure, of tombs of high officials of the state. A fine example is the tomb of the general Horemheb, the future sovereign (his other tomb is in the Valley of the Kings), marked with splendid bas reliefs, parts of which are housed in the Archaeological Museum of Bologna in Italy and in the Museum of Leiden in the Netherlands. During the 19th Dynasty, consistent restoration and reconstruction operations were put in motion. The plan to care for and preserve ancient monuments was led by Khaemwaset, son of Ramesses II and the High Priest of Ptah in Memphis, and by his brother Merneptah, the successor of Ramesses II.

Years of desecration During the following years, with the fall of Egypt to repeated foreign invasions, the desire to preserve the royal necropolis at Saqqara waned. In fact, some temples came to be used as quarries for construction materials. In later years, the cemetery of the sacred bull of Apis was extended. Its origins date back to the 18th Dynasty and it was known by the Greek name Serapeum. During the 30th Dynasty and under the Ptolemaic rulers, it was transformed into a monumental architectural complex, with religious and funerary edifices flanked by administrative buildings, as well as schools, inns, a market and a sanitorium. To the vestiges of the Graeco-Roman period were added inscriptions of the Coptic epoch. The monastery of St Jeremiah flourished here from 430 until the second half of the tenth century.

The Necropolis of Zoser The Necropolis of Zoser, which dominates the site of north Saqqara, is the largest of such complexes of the Old Kingdom. The necropolis surrounds the royal tombs with a mock palace so the king's *ka* (spirit) could pursue his life in the other world. It was designed by the famous architect Imhotep, surgeon and administrator of Zoser, who was later deified for the excellence of his knowledge in all the arts, venerated as a patron of the sciences and medicine, and subsequently identified with the Greek Asklepios (see Philae). The architecture is unprecedented: it is the world's earliest known structure made entirely of stone, but it retains general characteristics and methods of primitive constructions in mud brick, wood, and bundled reeds.

The complex, reconstructed by Lauer following archaeologists' conceptions, is dominated by the **Step Pyramid** and enclosed within a belt of walls with ramparts, creating the effect of fortified walls which bear a resemblance to the 'White Wall' of Memphis. Measuring approximately a kilometre and a half (about a mile) in length, and originally 10 metres (11 yards) high, it occupies a rectangular area of about 15 hectares (37 acres). It has a single entrance along the south-east corner, and at intervals in the indentations are carved out 14 gateways, of which only one gives access. On the upper parts of the wall, small rectangular hollows simulate the ends of reinforcement beams high above rough walls.

The court The passageway leading to the grand court of the pyramid is marked by a colonnade formed by two lines of 20 columns (with traces of pink paint), simulating reed bundles. The colonnade opens into a wide open space delineated on the north by the pyramid and along the south by the surrounding walls. Adorning its three sides is a beautiful wall with mouldings, of which very little stands today. At the centre of the court are two elements in the form of the letter 'B', around which the king followed a ritual course during the jubilee ceremony. Near the pyramid stands an altar. A smaller side court, oblong-shaped and flanked by chapels of the deities of Upper and Lower Egypt, was reserved for jubilee rites.

The 'Houses' of the North and South The houses are marked by four slim, fluted columns incorporated in the façade with characteristic capitals of two hanging lanceolate leaves. The cornice which lines the upper section follows the arch. Inside is a small cruciform chapel. Along the corridor of the 'houses' from the south entrance, two Hieratic inscriptions by visitors from the New Kingdom contain the first mention of Zoser.

The Step Pyramid, a novel form of architecture involving an original construction technique, shows how the royal tomb in the form of the mud brick *mastaba* evolved to the geometrically defined pyramid of the Fourth Dynasty. The Step Pyramid was the result of six successive studies and projects, the first three of which were influenced by the design of *mastaba*. From the third project, the original *mastaba* was enlarged to incorporate the galleries and funerary pits of the royal family dug out in continuation along the east side, thus beginning the most radical innovations: the *mastaba* became the base of a pyramid, first with four and then six levels or 'steps', rising approximately 60 metres (197 feet) over a base of around 140 × 118 metres (460 × 387 feet). While the original plans and construction technique were followed, the placement of blocks in horizontal beds laid one on top of the other created an inclined structural covering.

The interior of the Step Pyramid is not open to the public. It comprises rich underground apartments which yielded a splendid array of vases in alabaster, examples of the skill and workmanship attained by ancient craftsmen. Some cover the walls. One room is particularly interesting as it is adorned with three stelae framing a 'false door' showing the king conducting rites. Along the south side of the pyramid, the opening of the gallery is marked by a line of central pilasters which penetrate the same pyramid. It was excavated in Saïte times to permit the evacuation of materials which have crumbled with age and blocked the pit leading to the funerary chamber of Zoser.

North-side funerary temple The funerary temple annexed to the north side of the pyramid has, unfortunately, been reduced to ruins. However, the plan indicates the presence of double elements, such as two symmetrical internal courts and two areas for washing (all of which bring to mind the concept of Upper and Lower Egypt) in the temple. There is a passage, currently inaccessible, leading to the galleries of the pyramid. Beside the temple, slightly to the east and leaning against the face of the pyramid, lies the *serdab* (cellar), a small room containing a copy of the statue of Zoser (the original is now housed in the Cairo Museum). The *serdab* has two openings permitting the statue, which acted as a substitute for the person, to 'communicate' with the outside world.

The South Tomb A massive wall close to the southern side of the enclosing walls constitutes the cult area annexed to the South Tomb. The entire length of the east side is beautifully adorned with friezes of cobras evoking the goddess Uto, one of the two protecting divinities of the royalty. A deep pit leads to a granite-lined chamber and, towards the east, to an underground apartment with rooms embellished with blue tiles and three stelae with statues of the officiating king, much like the one in the pyramid. The South Tomb may have functioned as a second sepulchre, continuing the archaic tradition of constructing a double royal tomb, one in Saqqara for Lower Egypt and the other in Abydos for Upper Egypt, one being the true burial site and the other a cenotaph. The inclusion of the two tombs in a single complex in the immediate vicinity of the new capital underscored the idea of unified rule for Lower and Upper Egypt. According to widespread interpretation, the structures within Zoser's enclosures reproduced those of Memphis and represented royal schemes through symbolic models. The architecture of Zoser was followed by his successors, one of whom, Sekhemkhet, built a funerary monument south-west of the walls of Zoser. The complex was also believed to rise in 'steps' with enclosing walls, much like Zoser's, but this awaits full-scale excavation.

The pyramid of Unas Rising south of the funerary complex of Zoser is the almost-completely destroyed pyramid of Unas, the last king of the Fifth Dynasty. It was already in a bad state during the time of Ramesses II who assigned to his son Khaemwaset the task of restoring the pyramid. The funerary chambers of the Sixth Dynasty are covered with mortuary literature called the 'Pyramid Texts' which formed the basis for all subsequent funerary literature. The texts, in blue, vertically ordered, hieroglyphic characters, cover the end part of the corridor leading to the funerary apartment, the vestibule and the funerary chamber. The back walls and the extreme ends of the two side walls are lined with alabaster and decorated with the façade of the palace, forming the niche which contained the black basalt sarcophagus. The ceilings are decorated with stars. In front of the east face of the pyramid are the ruins of his funerary temple. The imposing remains of this majestic strip, over 700 metres (2,297 feet) in length, may be visited.

Originally, the inside walls were adorned with the bas-reliefs; the little that has survived is of high artistic value and shows descriptive scenes, such as the market with its goods, fish vendors, a vagabond with a monkey, and the stark figure of famine shown as a human reduced to a skeleton. Immediately south of the ramp, uncovered from a heap of rocks, were two large graves in the form of boats, one beside the other, approximately 40 metres (131 feet) in length with a covering of fine limestone. These follow the traditional practice of placing boats beside the sepulchre. At the south angle of the pyramid of Unas is a large pit, 25 metres (82 feet) in depth, providing access to the three tombs of the Persian era, those of the chief surgeon and healer Psammeticus, the admiral Thennehebu, and Padiesi, connected by a corridor to the modern part.

The *Mastaba* of Princess Idut Excavated along the external south walls of Zoser's complex was the *mastaba* of Princess Idut, the daughter of Unas, who lived between the end of the Fifth Dynasty and the beginning of the Sixth Dynasty. The tomb was originally constructed for a vizier and was usurped by the princess. It consists of ten rooms, some of which are embellished with very fine reliefs; others were used as stockrooms. The first two rooms are decorated with fishing scenes,

hippopotamus hunts, and a funeral scene depicting the transport of a statue to the tomb and the loading of offerings on boats. The last two rooms were used for the preparation of offerings.

Fifth–Sixth Dynasty tombs In the area north-east of the Pyramid of Zoser are mounds of stones which were once the pyramids of Userkaf (founder of the Fifth Dynasty) and of Teti (founder of the Sixth Dynasty). There is a considerable stretch of Fifth and Sixth Dynasty tombs, the largest and most famous of which is the *Mastaba* **of Mereruka**, a high functionary who took charge of various offices including that of vizier during the Sixth Dynasty. The *mastaba* is laid out on a very complex plan with over 32 rooms constituting the funerary apartments of Mereruka, his wife (a royal princess, daughter of Teti and high priestess of Hathor) and his son. In the magnificent pillared central hall, in a niche preceded by a flight of steps, stands a painted statue of the deceased. The themes on the reliefs are the usual ones of *mastabas* (scenes of life in the marshes of the delta, fishing, hunting in the desert, farming, arts and crafts), the most remarkable of which is the representation of goldsmiths at work. The central room shows scenes of mourning in the house of the deceased.

Moving east, one finds the *Mastaba* **of Kagemni**, another vizier of Teti and a minister of justice. This is adorned with reliefs of much more skilful execution compared to those of Mereruka. The structure is composed of five rooms and an inaccessible *serdab*, as well as numerous store rooms. The more interesting scenes depicted are those of sports and games, farming and a court hearing.

Further to the east is the so-called **Street of Tombs**. The *Mastaba* **of Ankhmahor**, also known as 'The Healer', shows scenes of circumcision and an operation on a foot.

The Serapeum This is one of the strangest sites in Egypt. It was once a temple in the middle of the sands, but only the long underground galleries, cut through the rocks, where the Apis bulls were buried, remain. Stripped of the Tura limestone covering with which it was finished, the Serapeum contains elements of non-traditional Egyptian designs, and may be explained by Ptolemy's attempts at syncretism (or reconciliation of beliefs), bringing the Greeks and Egyptians together in a common cult (Serapis was identified with the Greek god Dionysus). The Serapeum includes the underground graves of the Apis, the sacred bulls of Ptah, patron of Memphis. The principal gallery, inaugurated by Ptolemy I and used till the end of the Ptolemaic period, has a series of small anterooms lining its walls. Each of these contains a large monolithic sarcophagus in granite, basalt or limestone for the embalmed Apis. Of the 28 rooms, 24 still have sarcophagi, though these have been emptied of mummies. Another, smaller, corridor was originally lined with rooms containing wooden sarcophagi with the remains of 28 Apis. This was used from the time of Ramesses II until the Saïte era. One isolated tomb fortunately escaped the notice of looters, and magnificent jewellery bearing the name of Khamuase, now housed in the Louvre, was found here. To meet the needs of pilgrims who flocked to the renowned cult centre, an organized system of services and a network of religious buildings were developed in the vicinity of the Serapeum. Among the most recent finds in the site are the tombs and the temple of the mother of the Apis.

The *Mastaba* of Ti Further north of the Serapeum lies the *Mastaba* of Ti, one of the largest and most beautiful in Saqqara. Ti, who lived during the Fifth Dynasty, was a high dignitary of the court and assumed numerous offices, one of which was inspector of pyramids and solar temples of Neferirkare and Niuserre in Abusir. The most important areas of the structure are a spacious court marked by 12 pilasters, used specially for sacrifices or family reunions, and the chapel from which one can peer through three slots at a copy of the statue of Ti in the *serdab*. The original statue is in the Cairo Museum. This family tomb includes the graves of Ti's wife and one of his sons; its reliefs depict typical scenes of the preparation of food, wading cattle, arts and crafts, hippopotamus hunts, the presentation of offerings and the inspection of tombs in the territory administered by Ti.

Dahshur

A few kilometres south of Saqqara, is the area of Dahshur, which is marked by two very distinct pyramids. One is peculiarly bent and is attributed to Snofru whose name appears on two blocks inside the structure. However, the pyramid was abandoned because of stability problems. Another was erected for Snofru and was referred to as the 'obtuse pyramid', owing to the minimal inclination of its faces, and also as the 'red pyramid', because of the colour of the local limestone used. Another pyramid of Snofru rises in Medum, around 80 kilometres (50 miles) from Cairo. This was the subject of successive salvagings and is characterized by a typical 'tower' aspect.

Rulers of the Middle Kingdom, specifically the 12th Dynasty, also erected pyramids in Dahshur. Among them are Senusret III, Amenemhat II and Amenemhat III. The pyramids of Amenemhat I and Senusret I are situated in Lisht, 60 kilometres (37 miles) from Cairo. The Middle Kingdom pyramids of Dahshur were built with a different construction technique of stone frameworks and coverings

filled up with raw bricks — a quick and less costly method, but much less resistant. In fact, these monuments, after having been stripped of their coverings, were reduced to heaps of bricks.

Wadi el-Natrun

The Pyramids Road from Cairo towards Alexandria skirts the desert edges, passing Abu Rawash, site of the northernmost (unfinished) pyramid complex. Chosen by Djedefre, immediate successor of Khufu (Cheops), as his burial place, little remains here, but some fine sculptures can be seen in the Cairo Museum.

The Wadi el-Natrun is a desert depression, about 25 metres (82 feet) below sea level. It has about 25 lakes which dry up in spring, leaving rich deposits of sodium carbonate. In the early centuries AD, this was one of the major centres of monasticism, but only four monasteries are still occupied. The road to the largest monastery, St Makar (Deir Makaryus), lies some 89 kilometres (60 miles) north of Giza. Founded by St Makarios the Great (300–390), whose relics are preserved here, it has seen much restoration and new building in recent years, and has a large community of monks. Within the enclosure are several ancient churches containing many relics. The Qasr (fortress), a feature common to all Egyptain monasteries, is an imposing building with chapels inside. Some of the interesting early frescoes have recently been cleaned, and the main church has fine painted decoration in the apse.

The other monasteries are visited by the road from the Rest House further along the main Alexandria road, 103 kilometres (64 miles) from Giza. The two central monasteries are **Deir Amba Bishoi** (St Pshoi, a disciple of St Makarios), currently the residence of the Coptic Patriarch, Pope Shenouda III, and the **Deir el-Suryani** (Monastery of the Syrians). The already-old monastery was bought by Syrian merchants in the eighth century, for the use of Syrian monks. **Deir el-Baramus**, the Monastery of the Romans, is the most northerly in the *wadi* still occupied. A new road has made access quite easy. It is named after St Maximum and St Domitius, two brothers who served in the Roman army and later sought guidance from St Makarios. This is probably the oldest monastery in the *wadi*, and because of its remoteness and small size it conveys the spirit of desert retreat and prayer. The main church contains the relics of St Moses the Black and St Theodosios. It has fine woodwork, and the column of St Arsanious is a handsome Corinthian piece. Adjacent to the church are the ancient refectory with its stone table and benches, and the old oil and wine presses. The barrenness of the surroundings and the lushness of the cultivation within the walls, are best appreciated from the roof.

From Cairo to Luxor

The route up the Nile Valley from Cairo to Luxor can be made by road, with overnight stops at el-Minya and Nag Hammadi to allow time for visits to the most important sites, Beni Hasan, Tell el-Amarna and Abydos. Alternatively, you can take a Nile cruise, which is less tiring and more pleasant. The first stop on the bus route is at Lisht. About 12 kilometres (7.5 miles) south of Dahshur, but three kilometres (1.9 miles) off the road, are the ruins of the pyramids of Amenemhat I and Senusret I. Separated by a distance of one and a half kilometres (.93 miles), the pyramids are located on the site Amenemhat designated as his capital, after he had it moved from Thebes to enable him to govern Lower Egypt properly. Nothing much remains of these pyramids today; there are traces of two retaining walls around the pyramid of Senusret I, including some *mastabas* and small pyramids. On this site, ten statues of Senusret were discovered which are now in the Cairo Museum.

Medum

Upon arriving at **Rikka**, 80 kilometres (50 miles) from Cairo, the pyramid of Medum can be reached by taking the south-western road for about five kilometres (3.1 miles). The pyramid today looks like a tower with oblique sides, but it was once a regular pyramid with at least eight large steps covered with small blocks of limestone. The construction of the pyramid was begun by Huni and completed by Snofru, the founder of the Fourth Dynasty. Some exquisitely decorated tombs for princes were erected around the area of the pyramid. Among the more remarkable are the tombs of Nefermaat and his wife Atet, where the reliefs were filled with coloured paste, and that of Rahotep and his wife Nofret (whose statues are one of the main attractions of the Cairo Museum).

Beni Suef

Forty kilometres (25 miles) from Rikka, passing on the west the noteworthy area of el-Fayum, is Beni Suef. Lying on a vast plain, the area does not offer much in terms of sights for the tourist. The provincial capital city of Beni Suef is wedged between the Nile and the Libyan mountain chain and is an important commercial and agricultural centre.

el-Minya

About 120 kilometres (74.5 miles) further south is el-Minya, the chief town of the province of the same name. The town makes up for its lack of tourist attractions by providing a number of hotels which serve as ideal bases for trips to Beni Hasan, Hermopolis and Tell el-Amarna. There is also an airport here.

Beni Hasan

Beni Hasan is 23 kilometres (14.3 miles) south of el-Minya. It has a necropolis of the Middle Kingdom with 39 rock tombs, 12 of which are beautifully embellished with inscriptions. There are around 900 other tombs in the form of pits, belonging to high officials and functionaries of local princes, some of which date back to the Old Kingdom.

The Tombs of Beni Hasan From an architectural point of view, the tombs of Beni Hasan may be divided into three distinct groups. The first group is the biggest, laid out on simple plans of one or two rooms without columns. The next is characterized by banded columns crowned with lotus-form capitals aligned in such a way that they divide an enormous rectangular hall into two or three perpendicular aisles. The third group is distinguished by having a vestibule and fluted columns (conventionally defined as Proto-Doric), creating three longitudinal aisles in the room. The walls are plastered and intricately painted in tempera scenes which are arranged in horizontal order crosswise and depict much of the same figurative repertoire of the private tombs of the Old Kingdom — for example, the representation of agricultural and artisan activities. But, in fact, these tombs, unlike those of Giza and Saqqara, belonged to high officials of the royal court and local governors who acquired full powers over their territories during the First Intermediate Period and the Middle Kingdom. These sepulchres date back to the 11th–12th dynasties onwards, and only the four most important will be dealt with here.

The tomb of Amenemhat, also known as **Ameni**, belongs to the period of Senusret I. It is marked by an ante-portico with octagonal pilasters and a hall divided into three aisles by four Proto-Doric columns. A lengthy biographical text at the entrance informs the visitor of the deceased's honorary titles and various activities. The wall paintings depict diverse scenes such as culinary activities, hunting, combative sports like boxing and wrestling, a military exercise and the attack of an enemy's fortress, the navigation rituals of Abydos and Busiri (cities of Osiris), and the sacrifice and presentation of offerings to Ameni and his wife Hetepi.

The tomb of Khnumhotep III also belongs to the 12th Dynasty. It bears the same architectural features as that of Amenemhat. The basements of the chambers are richly embellished with 222 rows of hieroglyphs, narrating the life story of the deceased, considered today the most important document of the history of that particular epoch. This story emerged from the genealogy of Khnumhotep and from this history of his family who were endowed the provinces of Gazelle and Jackal by Amenemhat I and Senusret I. The paintings include a rare scene of dyeing and the celebrated 'Caravan of Asians' led by their chief Abisha, who arrived in Egypt in the sixth year of Senusret I.

The Tomb of Baqit, probably dating back to the 11th Dynasty, has no vestibule but does have a small chapel with two aisles flanked by lotus-form columns, the interior of which has seven covered pits. Among the paintings is an outstanding scene of a hunt in the desert showing fantastic animals such as a winged dragon, a four-headed serpent, a unicorn and an unidentified animal belonging to the god Seth. Elements of military life and training also appear here.

The Tomb of Khety (son of Baqit), though decoratively inferior to those of the other Beni Hasan tombs, is still full of interest. On the west wall, tiny men battle enormous fighting bulls, contrary to the usual practice in which large men do battle with rabbit-sized crocodiles and hippos. On the northern wall is the Old Kingdom motif of copulating animals. There are also elaborate wrestling scenes and a drawing of a mythological winged creature.

Speos Artemidos

A few kilometres south of the tombs, around 600 metres (656 yards) from the Nile into the interior of the great Arab tableland, is Speos Artemidos, the rock temple dedicated to the goddess Pakht, manifested with the head of a lioness and identified by the Greeks with Artemis. Its reliefs, which date back to the period of Hatshepsut, were removed by Thutmose III and subsequently replaced with the decorations of Sety I which, unfortunately, were never completed. A lengthy text above the entrance bears a eulogy of the queen with a listing of all the sanctuaries she had ordered reconstructed or expanded and a reference to the rule of the Hyksos in Lower Egypt. The Speos, which means 'cave' in Greek, is situated at the entrance of a *wadi* chosen by hermits as an abode for the ascetic life.

Antinoe

On the east bank of the Nile are the ruins of Antinoe, a city founded by Hadrian in memory of his favourite, Antinous, who drowned here

on 30 October AD 130. The city was built over the remains of an older
settlement, and archaeological excavations in the area have in fact
brought to light a Predynastic necropolis over which a temple
belonging to Ramesses II was constructed. The court and some
columns of the pillared hall still stand today. In its totality, the remains
of ancient Antinoe are composed of colonnaded streets, a triumphal
arch facing the Nile, a theatre, a hippodrome, and enclosure walls
around five kilometres (3.1 miles) in length which were almost entirely
destroyed and which today resemble a chain of low rocky hills.
Excavations of a vast necropolis at the foot of the mountain have
yielded Egyptian, Roman and Byzantine finds.

Ashmunein

The little village of Ashmunein, about ten kilometres (six miles) south
of Beni Hasan, was called Hermopolis by the ancient Greeks.
Ashmunein soared to great heights in antiquity as an important
religious centre where theological questions and ideas were discussed.
Its principal god was Thoth, identified with the Greek lunar god
Hermes, who took the form of an ibis or a baboon. Thoth is
accompanied by the eight primordial organizers of the world referred
to as the Ogdoad, which in Egyptian is translated as Khmunu (the
eight), the ancient name of Ashmunein. Ancient texts mention the site
as the place where the world was reputedly brought to order from the
din of creation and whence the first living being sprang forth.

Historically, the most interesting period of the city is placed
between the close of the Old Kingdom and the beginning of the Middle
Kingdom (Sixth – 12th dynasties), when princes believed to be
descendants of the sovereigns of the Sixth Dynasty ruled and exercised
full powers over the principality of 'the Hare'. Their tombs, some with
important historical provincial records, dot the right bank of the Nile
at Bersha. The ancient city of Ashmunein today has been reduced to a
sorry expanse of hillocks north of the newly formed, modern village. In
the vicinity of the sanctuary of Thoth, German excavations have
uncovered vestiges of buildings dating back to the Middle Kingdom,
among which is a chapel of Amenemhat II, marked by a monumental
doorway in stone. Nearby rises a temple of Sety II, characterized by
beautiful reliefs sculpted on the pillars. Countless fragments of reliefs
belonging to the temples were also excavated. At the entrance of the
sanctuary are two huge statues of Thoth represented as a baboon,
adorned with the cartouches of Amenhotep III. The largest and most
important of the ruins is the Agora of the Greek city contructed in
pink granite and marked by colonnades. The necropolis of this city is
located at Tunah el-Gebel, on the western desert confines.

Tunah el-Gebel

About two kilometres (1.25 miles) before Tunah el-Gebel, on the main road from Ashmunein, the famed '**Boundary-stelae**' of Akhetaten, mark the north-western territorial limits of Tell el-Amarna.

Most striking among the monuments of the vast necropolis of Tunah el-Gebel is the **tomb of Petosiris**, which dates back to around 300 BC. The reliefs on its walls, like its architectural inspirations, point to a deep-rooted and harmonious blend of Egyptian and Greek art forms. Actually, it served as a family tomb, distinguished by a vestibule for the cult of Petosiris, and a chapel dedicated to his father and brother. The façade, graced by four columns linked by screen walls, is adorned with representations of Petosiris making sacrifices to local gods. The interior walls of the vestibule are wonderfully covered with varied scenes of carpentry, enamel-working, age-old methods of preparing ointments, the harvesting of flax and wheat, threshing, cattle-breeding, grape-gathering and wine-making. The entrance of the chapel, on the other hand, is made beautiful by images of the deceased's sons and daughters, solemn ceremonies of an offertory, and the rituals of sacrifice. In the chapel marked by four stately pillars, the images portrayed are more in the traditional Egyptian style, dominated by religious or funerary themes highlighted by the workshop of divinities or a funeral march. The handsome wooden sarcophagus with hieroglyphics inlaid in various stones and vitreous wood pulp is preserved at the Cairo Museum. Behind the tomb of Petosiris stretches an entire city of tombs and dwelling places constructed with multiple chambers and floors. Most notable among these is the tomb of Isadora, a child who drowned in 120 BC.

North of this necropolis are three **cemeteries of sacred animals** where underground sepulchres of baboons and ibises have incredibly been preserved. The site has yielded *exvotos*, family archives with interesting papyri, among which were revealed the texts of an Egyptian civil code and a treatise on geometry and measurements. To the south is a grand *saqia* (water-wheel) linked to a well dating back to Roman times.

Mallawi

Further south of Tunah el-Gebel, the picturesque town of Mallawi is worth a visit for its cheerful local colour. Farmers, women and children can be seen busy at their daily activities presenting a real image of rural Egypt. A small museum holds interesting pieces from the surrounding rich archaeological areas: bronze statuettes, masks and sarcophagi from Tunah el-Gebel; small sarcophagi of ibises; mummies of workers and statuettes from Hermopolis; the beautiful sculpture of Pepy-Ankh-hor and his spouse, and other religious objects from Asyut and el-Qusiya.

On the opposite bank of the Nile is **Deir el-Bersha**, where there are the ruins of ten tombs. Only one, that of Djehutyhotep (the province's governor under Amenemhat II), is in good enough condition to justify a visit. There are interesting scenes of the daily life of the deceased while in charge of his office, and the transport of an enormous statue.

Tell el-Amarna

There may not be another period in ancient Egyptian history which has stirred so much interest and profound admiration, even beyond the esoteric circle of scholars and intellectuals, as the highly regarded Amarna age (1353–1335 BC). It must also be added that the engaging arguments which have sprung from the religious reforms of Akhenaten have not only stimulated a great number of our century's most illustrious thinkers, including Sigmund Freud and Thomas Mann, but have also been woven into the background of popular historical novels and adventure stories set in Egypt, an example of which is the bestseller *Sinuhe, the Egyptian* by Mika Waltari. For the readers of *Sinuhe*, the image of the plains of Tell el-Amarna, ten kilometres (six miles) south of Mallawi by boat and home of the ancient site of **Akhetaten (The Horizon of Aten)**, will never sufficiently satisfy their imagination. They may, however, recreate images from the scant remnants of houses and temples, mere shadows of ancient splendours, where life ceased a thousand years ago.

Destiny condemned the city of Akhetaten to eternal oblivion a few years after the demise of its king-god, Akhenaten. History, however, has left us traces of its age-old urban grid-system plan (the only one among countless other Egyptian cities to have been preserved). Sadly, of its once-magnificent palaces, grand depositories, houses and temples, only the foundations and a scattering of battered columns remain today. The delicately adorned walls of private tombs which dominate the living quarters of a forgotten time permit us to reconstruct an image of the architectural aspect of a great part of the city.

Excavations in the area of the ancient city of Tell el-Amarna began in the last years of the 19th century, spearheaded by the Germans with the operations of the Deutsche Orientgesellschaft conducted by Borchardt from 1907–14. From England came the team from Flinders Petrie and the excavation campaign of the Egypt Exploration Society in 1921–36. A large quantity of the treasures unearthed in el-Amarna

have made their way into the Cairo Museum, enriching its dazzling collection and prompting the setting up of a hall dedicated solely to the glories of the Amarna age, and to the Berlin Museums where the main body of Amarna treasures and works of art are divided between the Museums of East and West Berlin. Among the most valuable archaeological finds uncovered in the site are the Archives of Tell el-Amarna, a collection of clay tablets inscribed in Akkadian, the fruits of diplomatic correspondence with other courts of that period, particularly with the Hittite Kingdom.

To delimit the territory of the new city, Akhenaten ordered 14 boundary inscriptions to be carved into the cliffs on both sides of the river. Today, many are damaged and difficult to reach, but one, near the road at Tunah el-Gebel, is easily seen. The large stele has a scene of the royal family worshipping the sun-disk with, below, a long dedicatory inscription. Statues of the king, queen and some of their daughters are carved next to the stele.

The Necropolis The necropolis of Tell el-Amarna, which can be viewed from a distance against the mountainous cliffs which dominate the city, comprises two groups of rock tombs, the northern and the southern. Only those belonging to the northern group may easily be visited today. These include the sepulchres of Huya (number 1), Meryre II (number 2), Ahmose (number 3), Meryre I (number 4), Pentu (number 5) and Panehesy (number 6). The interiors of the tombs are laid out to a rather simple plan with three aligned rooms, one leading to the other. Their walls are richly decorated with scenes of Akhenaten and the royal family taking part in court life and the pomp and ceremony of divine worship in the time of Aten.

Of the southern group of tombs, the most important is that of Tutu (number 8), with its grand hall flanked by double colonnades — an excellent example of funerary architecture typical of that age. Another important tomb is that of Ay (number 25), a high official of the royal court who later assumed the position of sovereign. In the incisions on the doorjambs in the entrance to the tomb is the most complete text of the celebrated hymn to Aten (it is referred to by scholars as 'the lengthy version').

The Royal Tombs The royal tombs were erected upon the orders of Akhenaten himself, who made them larger so as to accommodate the rest of his family. They are located in a far flung *wadi* almost at the centre of a forbidding circle of mountains penetrating into the depths of the Arabian desert and are inaccessible as they are covered with sand.

El-Qusiya and Meir

About 23 kilometres (14.3 miles) from Tell el-Amarna, on the western bank, el-Qusiya is the base for a visit to the **Rock Tombs of Meir**, the necropolis of the ancient Cusae. Undoubtedly the most interesting tomb belongs to Ukhhotep, local prince and high priest of the cow-goddess Hathor. Singular scenes in the tomb, depicting *fellahin* and the prince's servants with all their physical imperfections, mark a departure from the popular tendency to idolize figures.

Asyut

Forty-five kilometres (28 miles) further south is Asyut, a crowded town with hotels and an airport. In the old town you can see craftsmen working on souvenirs to be sold in Cairo's bazaar. Forty per cent of Asyut's population is Christian. It was the chief town of the province, known in Graeco-Roman times as Lykopolis, after its chief deity, the wild dog Wepwawet. Four and a half kilometres (2.8 miles) south-west of the town are the remains of the necropolis of Asyut's princes, but this lies within a military zone and is difficult to visit. The most important tomb is that of Hep-Djefa, the local prince during the 12th Dynasty. It contains, among other objects, an interesting contract drawn up between the deceased and various priests who granted propitiatory offerings after the prince's death.

Sohag

Some 93 kilometres (58 miles) past Asyut is Sohag, a busy town engaged in cotton growing. Particularly interesting here are two Coptic convents, the **White Convent (Deir el-Abyad)** and the **Red Convent (Deir el-Ahmar)**. The first was built in the third century by St Shenuda with a donation from a Byzantine official. The precious manuscripts once kept here are now dispersed throughout Europe. The building was erected using material from the temples in the surrounding areas as shown by the hieroglyphs still visible on the nave and on other parts of the convent. The Red Convent is smaller and lies five kilometres (3.1 miles) north in a delightful little village. Its columns and capitals are more precious than the ones in the White Convent, where, despite its homogeneity, only second-hand materials were used.

Akhmim

Linked by a bridge to Sohag on the opposite side of the Nile, Akhmim was one of the most important towns in the Upper Egypt of ancient times. Characterized by a temple dedicated to Min (the god of fertility, represented with an erect phallus and later identified with the Greek god Pan), the town was always considered cheerful and lusty. Its attachment to unconstrained pagan customs, and an active school of sorcery, brought Akhmim cruel and bloody repression by the monks. The town was even the target of an iconoclastic crusade led by St Athanasius and St Shenuda.

Abydos

Abydos, 145 kilometres (90 miles) north of Luxor, was the chief seat of worship of Osiris, god of the underworld (*duat*). It is an obligatory stop on a full Nile cruise from Cairo to Luxor. Along with Saqqara, with which it is linked, Abydos was a funerary site from the earliest dynasties on record. During the Middle Kingdom, Abydos reached greater heights of religious importance. Its necropolis served other territories as well, and the archaeological materials gathered from here reveal much, not only of Sohag but also of outlying regions. There were so many funerary artifacts from the 11th and 12th dynasties, that most of the stelae in the museums come from this place. During this period, every Egyptian believer hoped to make the pilgrimage to Abydos at least once in his life, in order to visit the tomb of Osiris who took over from the local god Khenti-Amentiu, lord of the necropolis. Those who could not make their tombs near the burial place of Osiris had their mummies taken there by boat before entombment, or made the journey by proxy.

The myth of Osiris developed with particular importance in Abydos, spurred by a shrine believed to house the head of this god. Every believer harboured the wish to be buried near the tomb of Osiris, and the Egyptians soon developed a form of fictitious pilgrimage to Abydos. Countless cenotaphs were also erected by those from more distant areas to gain the favour of the god. The old city lies by the necropolis, now partially covered by the modern village of Beni Mansur. Once it probably lay on a low hill surrounded by a massive wall of raw bricks and stone, now mostly destroyed. The remains of a Predynastic allocation have been discovered in the south-east behind the Temple of Sety I, and probably in the north-west as well. The stratified debris of the town dates back to the Old Kingdom. Abydos was the royal necropolis of the First Dynasty and the first sovereigns of the Second, who resided in the cradle of the monarchy, the nearby town of Thinis.

The Temple of Sety I is the best-preserved among the ruins of Abydos, and was completed by his son Ramesses II. In front of the temple were two courtyards and a big pillar erected by Ramesses II, almost

completely ruined today and still subject to excavations. East of the courtyards, big storehouses made of raw bricks were found. At present, the façade of the temple is formed by the south-western arcade of the second courtyard and 12 rectangular pillars. On the bottom wall are carved scenes of the cult commissioned by Ramesses II for his father, and a long dedicatory inscription.

The temple is divided into seven parts: the two hypostyle rooms have seven doors leading to seven sanctuaries consecrated respectively to Amun-Ra at the centre, Osiris, Isis and Horus on the right and Harmakhis (Horus in the Horizon, solar divinity), Ptah and Sety I deified, on the left. The first hypostyle room, with two rows of 12 papyrus-shaped columns, has decorations of ritual subjects representing Ramesses II attending on the temple's divinities. The second room, with three rows of columns and transversally divided by a step, goes back to Sety I.

The chapels, apart from that of Sety I, contained the sacred boats of the gods to whom they were dedicated, and the painted reliefs which decorate them are among the best-preserved examples of Egyptian art. The chapel of Osiris leads to the bottom through two columned rooms, at the end of which are three chapels on each side. The three right chapels are dedicated to King Sety I, identified with Osiris, and to Isis and Horus. Carved on the right-hand side of the long passageway which connects the temple to the left wing is one of the famous royal lists or tables of Abydos, showing Sety offering incense to the names of 76 sovereigns, from Menes onwards. The left wing has three rooms, the first for boats used in processions, the second for sacrificial animals, and the third served as a storeroom.

Behind the big Temple of Sety I and on its axis is the **Osireion**, an interesting monument built to represent the primeval hill of the creation of the world. It is made of white limestone and reddish sandstone, with pillars and lintels in pink granite. A long corridor covered with funerary texts descends from the building, which is entirely dug into the mountain. In fact, it comprises a large pillared hall surrounded by 16 niches separated from the centre of the room by a moat. From the two shorter sides of the hall, two stairs lead to the water. In the centre, two niches seem to have contained a sarcophagus and a canopic set. An ample transversal hall with a very high ceiling complete the complex.

The dramatic stylistic difference between it and the temple of Sety, together with its apparently indifferent construction, suggest to many scholars that it was a much older building, a view supported by its superficial similarity to the valley temple of Chephren south of the Sphinx at Giza. Further study, however, shows that it differs in detail.

The Temple of Ramesses II, located several hundred metres north of the main temple, is only partially preserved. The lower part of the pillar is of pink granite as is the gate through which one enters into a courtyard of Osiris. The courtyard walls are decorated with liturgical scenes representing a pompous procession conducting 'the bull of the day of feast' for the divine offertory. Two hypostyle halls follow, encircled by chapels. In one of these chapels, a second king list, now in the British Museum, was found. The sanctuary, built with alabaster blocks, is divided into three chapels. In front of the central chapel is a badly damaged big alabaster stele and, in the interior, a group in grey granite representing five personages. Among the recognizable figures are Ramesses II and Sety I at the ends and, between them and Amun, two queens or goddesses. These temples are located in the southern part of the necropolis of Abydos among the tombs of the New Kingdom. To the north, on the left bank, are the central necropolis belonging to the end of the Old Kingdom and to the First Intermediate Period, and the northern necropolis with tombs of the Middle Kingdom.

Dendera

The ancient town of Dendera borders on the desert on the left bank of the Nile, 97 kilometres (60 miles) south of Abydos and 48 kilometres (30 miles) north of Luxor. Dendera was always an important town, and from earliest times its patron goddess was Hathor. Although Old Kingdom temples are known to have stood here, and remains of Middle and New Kingdom buildings have been found, these have been replaced by the Ptolemaic and Roman temple.

The Temple of Hathor was rebuilt by the Ptolemies from the second century BC, and its decoration continued until the Roman age (Antoninus Pius). The temple was originally accessible through a *dromos* (sacred avenue) which, starting from an entry kiosk, reached the monumental gate. The building, made of sandstone, like nearly all the Ptolemaic temples, had two main parts, the *pronaos* or hypostyle hall belonging to the Roman era, and the *naos*, the real sanctuary. After the completion of the hypostyle hall in the reign of Tiberius, major building work ceased, and the stone precinct wall, the first courtyard and the pylon were never added.

The temple's other rooms include crypts, (which were partially built into the thickness of the walls and partially subterranean, and were meant to keep the treasures of the temple and the insignia or the instruments for mysterious cults), the chapel of the New Year to the right of the sanctuary, and the tomb of Osiris on the balcony. The

Washing water buffalo, Asyut

Girl at Beni Hasan

Ox-driven water wheel, Qena

Pilgrim's home showing scenes from the Haj, Dendera

Hathoric columns are linked by low walls with scenes showing the sovereign consecrating the temple. The ceiling of the hypostyle room has an astronomic decoration with the symbolic representation of the sky. On the walls are scenes of the temple's foundation and consecration. Following the hypostyle room is a lobby surrounded by storerooms and laboratories: the first, on the left-hand side, was the laboratory where they prepared the ointments and oils to smear the statues; the second was the storeroom for agricultural products for the offerings. Next to the hypostyle room is the offertory room through which two stairways lead to the tomb of Osiris on the balcony and, through a passageway, to the chapel of the New Year. The sanctuary is preceded by another lobby and surrounded by 11 chapels.

The Tomb of Osiris The existence of this tomb on the roof of the temple has nothing to do with Hathor, but is concerned with the resurrection of Osiris. The tomb of Osiris was in the shrine and chapel where the expiatory ceremonies were celebrated, to commemorate his death and resurrection. The first room has a ceiling decorated with a circular zodiac. (It has been replaced here with a cast; the original is in the Louvre.) Inside the town walls, on the right are the Roman *mammisi*, the Coptic basilica built at the end of fifth century, the *mammisi* (birth-house) of Nectanebo I (the last Egyptian-born Pharaoh) and finally, the sanatorium which was built around a central bath of magic water (the only monument of its kind known up to this time). West of the big temple are badly damaged altars and the **Sacred Lake**, where, according to Herodotus, the passion of Osiris was re-enacted. Towards the south is the **Birth Shrine of Isis**, which leads directly to the town of Dendera.

The Dendera Triad The goddess of Dendara, Hathor, was later identified with Isis and with Aphrodite by the Greeks. At Dendera, a triad was formed with Hathor, Horus of Edfu and Ihy the 'musician'. The divine cult was celebrated every day in the Great Seat (sanctuary) and in the Room of the Offering. Furthermore, solemn feasts marked the most important moments of the year: the feast of the New Year, the mysteries of Osiris, the divine birth, and the feast of the inebriation.

Egyptian Feasts

The ancient Egyptians celebrated five main feasts within their liturgical year, which began with the flooding of the Nile in May. These were the Feast of the New Year, the Feast of the Living Falcon, the Feast of the Victory of Horus, the Sacred Wedding, and the Divine Birth. It was during the feasts that the Egyptian religion reached the masses, for the public had no part in the daily service to the gods, and access to the inner sanctuaries of temples was reserved for priests and kings.

Each temple had a calendar of feasts when the principal gods were taken in procession several times a month around the towns or to visit other temples. Some of the feasts were short, lasting only a few days, but the national ones, usually celebratory and sometimes orgiastic occasions, were prolonged and lasted for several weeks. Many of the feasts were connected with agriculture and the productivity of the land.

The Feast of the New Year corresponded with the beginning of the floods, and the ceremonies were held on the terrace of the Temple of Hathor at Dendera. It was only at the end of the celebrations that the disrobed statue of Hathor was exposed to the view of the waiting masses below. **The Feast of the Living Falcon**, which revolved around a specially-chosen falcon kept in the Sacred Aviary of the temple, included the ritual coronation of the bird in a small temple south of the main one.

The Feast of the Victory of Horus over the forces of evil, identified with Seth (represented as a hippopotamus struck with ten harpoons by Horus standing on a boat), was celebrated with the symbolic ritual of striking an effigy of a hippopotamus ten times. This ritual took place in the sacred lake of the Temple of Horus.

The Feast of the Sacred Wedding was celebrated before the flooding of the Nile when the statue of Hathor was taken from its sanctuary in Dendera and rowed upstream to Edfu, 160 kilometres (100 miles) away, for the wedding with Horus. The pilgrimage, calculated to arrive in Edfu at the same time as the rise of the new moon, attracted huge crowds. After protracted welcoming ceremonies, Hathor was placed with her consort Horus in the *mammisi* (birth-house) in front of the temple.

The Feast of the Divine Birth of Horus was celebrated in the *mammisi*. It followed a ritual inspired by royal birth: the union of the divine couple, the creation of the child by the potter-god, recognition of the child by the father, the nursing, and the investiture. According to the Egyptian concept of the universe, the annual rebirth of the god as well as the rites of the New Year and the Victory of Horus guaranteed the preservation of the world.

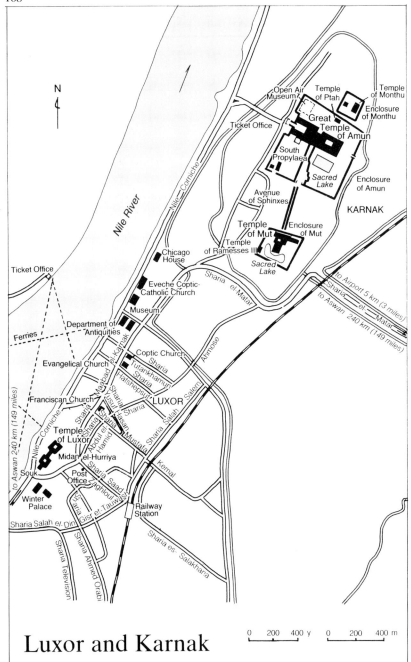

N

Temple of Ptah
Open Air Museum
Temple of Monthu
Enclosure of Monthu
Ticket Office
Great Temple of Amun
South Propylaea
Sacred Lake
Enclosure of Amun
KARNAK
Avenue of Sphinxes
Temple of Mut
Enclosure of Mut
Temple of Ramesses III
Sacred Lake

Nile River
Nile-Corniche

Chicago House
Eveche Coptic-Catholic Church
Museum
Ticket Office
Ferries
Department of Antiquities
Evangelical Church
Coptic Church
Franciscan Church
Sharia el-Karnak
Sharia Maabad el-Karnak
Sharia Tutankhamun
Sharia Hatshepsut
Sharia Yusif Hasan
Sharia Mustafa Kemal
Sharia Salah Salem
Sharia Ahmose
Sharia el-Matar

to Airport 5 km (3 miles)
to Aswan 240 km (149 miles)

LUXOR
Temple of Luxor
Midan el-Hurriya
Souk
Post Office
Winter Palace
Railway Station
Sharia Abdul el-Hamid
Sharia Saad Zaghloul
Sharia Gisr et-Tauwil
Sharia Salah el-Din
Sharia Television
Sharia Ahmed Orabi
Sharia es-Salakhana

to Aswan 240 km (149 miles)

0   200   400 y   0   200   400 m

Luxor and Karnak

Luxor and Karnak

The town of Luxor (in Arabic, el-Uqsur or 'the Palaces'), 676 kilometres (420 miles) south of Cairo, is the main tourist centre for the largest surviving concentration of ancient monuments in the Nile valley: the temples of Karnak and Luxor on the east bank, and the Theban necropolis on the west bank.

Many names have been given to this region during its history, but the most commonly used as a general term is Greek in origin, Thebes. Why the Greeks used the name Thebes is uncertain, but today it is used to refer to the whole of the area, both east and west banks. The original Egyptian name of the town was Waset, derived from the *was* sceptre, a symbol of divine power carried by the gods. In the later 18th Dynasty, the town was paralleled with Heliopolis (in Egyptian, Yunu) and called 'the Southern Yunu'. Biblical texts refer to it as No, or No-Ammon, from the Egyptian for 'City' and 'City of Amun', and in Ptolemaic-Roman times the name was Diospolis Magna. From the Middle Kingdom onwards one of the chief cities of Egypt, Thebes was a major residence city of the kings, as well as the burial place of the rulers of the 11th and 17th to 20th dynasties.

In the Old Kingdom, Thebes was a small town of little importance. Its rise to power began in the First Intermediate Period when the local princes extended their control over much of Upper Egypt and gradually northward against the rulers of Heracleopolis. After a civil war, Egypt was reunited by Nebhepetre-Menthuhotep I, who chose to be buried at Deir el-Bahari.

Although of Upper Egyptian origin, the 12th Dynasty kings chose the Memphis-Fayum region as their major power base and burial site. Their building works and endowments in the temple of Amun at Karnak established it as a shrine of national importance.

During the Second Intermediate Period, Thebes was ruled by princes who claimed descent from the 13th Dynasty kings, their control ranging over much of Upper Egypt. These were the rulers who began the campaigns against the Hyksos and the Kushites, most effectively under Kamose, and his younger brother and successor, Ahmose.

Ahmose's campaigns brought the whole of Egypt, and Nubia as far as the Second Cataract, back under the control of one king. His successors expanded Egypt's power even further afield, establishing her pre-eminence throughout the Near East, from the river Euphrates to the Fourth Cataract of the Nile. Although Memphis remained the major administrative city, the kings chose their native town of Thebes as their burial place and lavishly endowed the temples of its gods.

After Ramesses II made Piramesse in the delta his major residence, new building works at Karnak were much reduced in scale, although Thebes remained the royal burial place. The high priests of Amun and a group of noble families were the prime power during the Third Intermediate Period, the royal representatives being princesses who held the office of 'God's Wife of Amun'.

The last period of large-scale royal building activity was during the 25th Dynasty, whose kings were especially devoted to the worship of Amun. With their sisters and daughters serving as 'God's Wife', and with royal princes as High Priests of Amun and as mayors of Thebes, the 25th Dynasty had a strong presence in the city, which was of great importance to their empire which stretched from the Mediterranean to present-day Khartoum.

The Assyrian invasion of 664 BC, which drove Taharqo from Egypt, spelt disaster for Thebes. The city was sacked and looted of its treasure, a catastrophe which resounded throughout the world.

Restoration and building work continued throughout the late and Ptolemaic-Roman periods, but Thebes never regained its former importance. A rebellion, centred upon Thebes and encouraged by the priests of Amun, exacted the retribution of Ptolemy Soter II. Roman visitors, awed though they were by its monuments, found the city itself reduced to little more than a cluster of villages.

The Temples of Karnak

The temples lie some three kilometres (1.9 miles) north of Luxor. Although usually applied to the central enclosure, the temple of Amun, Karnak also embraces the southern enclosure of the goddess Mut and the northern enclosure of Monthu.

Karnak impresses the visitor less by the beauty and elegance of its buildings and sculptures (though these can be found), than by the vastness and complexity of the temples, and the massiveness of certain parts.

The temple of Amun was built, enlarged and rebuilt over more than 1,000 years, a process which is still imperfectly understood. Today, the three groups of temples, the enclosures of Amun, Mut and Monthu, are surrounded by enormous brick walls erected by Nectanebo I. In the New Kingdom, the Amun temple lay inside a far smaller precinct, with its wall still visible in places. The temple of Ptah, by the north gate, and the chapels of Osiris all originally lay outside the Amun precinct and within their own enclosures, probably along the roads of the city of Thebes which surrounded the Amun temple to the north and east.

In the Old Kingdom, the chief deity worshipped at Thebes was the solar and war god, Monthu. The earliest-known temples dedicated to Amun belong to the First Intermediate Period and the Middle Kingdom. The origins of Amun are obscure: in the earliest reliefs at Karnak, he is closely worshipped as an aspect of Min. Little remains *in situ* of these earliest temples at Karnak (see Middle Kingdom court, below), but many blocks and fragments of buildings and statuary have been recovered from the foundations of later works. Statues found here, of Senusret I as Osiris, and of Senusret III, are now in the Cairo and Luxor museums and in the Court of the Cachette. A good impression of the early building works is conveyed by the reconstructed chapels in the **Open Air Museum**, situated to the north of the first courtyard (the admission price of LE 1 is additional to the temple entrance fee).

The **White Chapel of Senusret I** was carefully dismantled and used as building material in the third pylon of Amenhotep III. A simple structure on a high platform with a peristyle of square pillars, the whole is covered in delicate low relief in the finest style of the Middle Kingdom. A ramp-staircase at both ends leads to the resting place for the statue or sacred barque. Built from hard white limestone, this small structure has a refined elegance lacking in many of the more massive monuments of the New Kingdom.

The building works of the early New Kingdom self-consciously continued Middle Kingdom artistic traditions. Amenhotep I had Senusret I's White Chapel copied, and the Middle Kingdom inheritance is clearly seen in the decoration of his own **Alabaster Barque Shrine**. The shrine, simple in design and with delicate relief (note the fine portraits of Amenhotep I) is made of alabaster from Hatnub in Middle Egypt. It originally had doors of wood and bronze, both brought from Asia. One of the outer faces was decorated by Thutmose I. The Barque Shrine was dismantled by Thutmose III who built an almost-identical shrine in the same place, the remains of which can be seen next to the seventh pylon (see below).

Whilst there is little earlier than the reign of Thutmose I *in situ* at Karnak, later constructions were also dismantled and used as building material. Many blocks were found in the third pylon of Amenhotep III (including parts of chapels he himself had built). One of the finest and most important of these works, the **Red Chapel of Hatshepsut**, is also housed in the Open Air Museum. Of hard red quartzite with a base of black granite, it is thought that the shrine was to have served as the main Sanctuary of Amun, although it may never have been completed. Hatshepsut included herself and Thutmose III in the decoration on the shrine, but after his accession as sole ruler Thutmose III seems to have attempted alterations to remove Hatshepsut's name and figures. This attempt was abandoned, perhaps because the hardness of the stone rendered the alterations unsightly, and the structure was replaced with a shrine of Thutmose's own. Most of Hatshepsut's figures and cartouches remain undamaged and the blocks have many interesting scenes, including one of the earliest depictions of the Opet Festival.

Also of interest in the museum is a relief of Amenhotep IV (Akhenaten) slaughtering his enemies. Originally decorating the gateway of the third pylon, this scene was carved before the change in artistic style and the emphasis upon worship of the Aten early in the reign. Many smaller architectural elements from buildings of the Middle Kingdom and early 18th Dynasty can also be seen, the earliest being a column of Antef II (with the earliest known reference to Amun from Karnak) found in the Middle Kingdom court. Stone lintels and the doorjambs with the names of Senusret I and III, Ahmose and Amenhotep I belong to other buildings which are now lost.

The Temple of Amun: the main axis

Any attempt to understand how Karnak developed should perhaps abandon the conventional (and practical) visitors' route from the first courtyard to the Sanctuary, and begin in the **Middle Kingdom Court** at the temple's heart.

This Court is actually the site of the Middle Kingdom temple, the plan of which (or its later replacement) is visible in the few foundation courses surviving. The temple was oriented east-west, with entrance towards the river. Its plan was simple, comprising sanctuary with side rooms and a hall in front. The relationship of the temple to the other Middle Kingdom buildings is very unclear, but in front of it, perhaps in the area of the third pylon and the junction with the southern courtyards, there may have been a 'Jubilee' court. It is certain that many of the Middle Kingdom monuments still stood until the mid-18th Dynasty.

Middle Kingdom houses have been excavated inside and outside the 30th Dynasty precinct wall, indicating that parts of the town then lay to the east where the Eastern Temple and Gate and the Osiris chapels now stand.

Few fragments of the building works of the 13th–17th dynasties have been recovered, but amongst them is one of Egypt's most important historical texts, the **Stele of Kamose**. Now in Luxor Museum, the stele was recovered from the foundations of the colossus ('Pinudjem') in the first courtyard, in 1954. One of at least two such monuments, the text is the second part of the account of Kamose's victories over the Hyksos at their delta capital of Avaris.

The 18th Dynasty and the New Kingdom are marked by the accession of Ahmose, Kamose's brother and successor, who finally drove the Hyksos from Egypt and reunited the country. Although he inaugurated the period of Karnak's greatest importance, Ahmose is represented here by only one fragmentary lintel (now in the Open Air Museum), which copies a monument of Senusret I.

Amenhotep I, a ruler later revered at Karnak and throughout the Theban region, certainly built many monuments to Amun, but again little survives *in situ*. A temple and gateway, oriented north-south, may have occupied the area of the Court of the Cachette. Here also may have stood the White Chapel of Senusret I, of which Amenhotep I commanded a limestone copy to be made. Further south still was the **Alabaster Barque Shrine** (now in the Open Air Museum) in which the god's sacred boat rested before being sailed on the Sacred Lake.

It is necessary to over-simplify the description of the Amun temple's expansion since many details are still uncertain, and it is not always possible to know whether the works of some individual rulers (e.g. Thutmose I and III) are the result of many additions and alterations during the reign, or part of a broader scheme extending over their whole reign. Indeed, just because a building carries the name of a king, does not mean that he founded it necessarily; he may have merely been responsible for the decoration of a predecessor's unfinished work.

Thutmose I enclosed the Middle Kingdom temple ('Court') within a circuit wall which extended to the west, creating a courtyard in front of the older building. The wall enclosed the area now occupied by the shrine of Philip Arrhidaeus and the rooms of Hatshepsut, its western limit being the sixth pylon. This court was probably lined with the colossal statues of the king as Osiris, which are now located in the halls between the fourth/fifth and fifth/sixth pylons. Thutmose I enclosed his building within a second circuit wall, creating a corridor around the northern, eastern and southern (where it is somewhat broader) sides. The temple was also extended further west with the construction of the fourth and fifth pylons and two narrow halls. Thutmose I may himself have had the Osiride statues removed to line these halls. The roof of the hall behind the fourth pylon was supported by a single line of columns, the foundations and bases of which are visible in excavated pits. The fourth pylon marked the main entrance to the temple, and continued to do so until the reign of Amenhotep III. Two obelisks of red granite were set up by Thutmose I before the gateway of his pylon, their points covered with electrum (a natural alloy of gold and silver). Both were still standing 200 years ago, but now only the southern obelisk remains, 19.5 metres (64 feet) high.

Hatshepsut's 22-year reign may well have seen the inauguration, or planning, of much of the work completed, decorated and dedicated in the name of Thutmose III. The monuments finished by her were either dismantled or altered by her successor. The magnificent barque shrine of Amun, the **Red Chapel** (now in the Open Air Museum), probably stood close to the present site of the **Sanctuary of Philip Arrhidaeus**, surrounded by the suite of rooms in red sandstone. The chambers which Hatshepsut built around the barque shrine abutted the Middle Kingdom temple on its western side. One wall has been removed from its original position to one of the side rooms, and although Hatshepsut's figures have been erased, the clear colour and handsome style of relief typical of this reign survive in the figures of Amun.

Hatshepsut removed the roof of the pillared hall of Thutmose I, between the fourth and firth pylons, in order to raise her two obelisks there. Brought into the hall from its northern side, they are of granite quarried at Aswan. Hatshepsut's own words record the event:

> *'My majesty began work on them in year 15; the 2nd month of winter, day 1, ending in year 16, 4th month of summer, last day, in total seven months of quarry work...'*

The northern obelisk stands intact, 29.5 metres (96.8 feet) high, but of its southern companion only the broken stump remains in place; its upper part now lies near the Sacred Lake. A block (now displayed in Luxor Museum) from the Red Chapel shows Hatshepsut presenting her two obelisks to Amun, having had the whole of their upper parts overlaid with electrum. Again, the event is recorded in her own words:

> *'I gave for them of the finest electrum. I measured it by the gallon like sacks of grain. My majesty summoned a quantity beyond what the Two Lands had yet seen. The ignorant and the wise know it...*
>
> *'Seen on the two sides of the river, their rays flood the Two Lands when the sun-disk rises between them at its appearance on the horizon of heaven.'*

Hatshepsut's other building works at Karnak extended the temple to the east, where a chapel with two more obelisks (their bases still visible) was later developed by Thutmose III (see the Eastern Temple, below). To the south, Hatshepsut elaborated the Southern Courtyards and the Processional Way to Luxor (see below).

The most striking feature of the bulding works of Thutmose III is that they enclose, develop within, and expand to the east and south of those of Thutmose I, but do not extend further to the west. Thutmose I's pylon (four) remained the main entrance to the temple, although

Thutmose III did set up his own pair of obelisks in front of those of his grandfather.

In the hall beween the fourth and fifth pylons, Thutmose III encased the obelisks of Hatshepsut in stone to the height of the roof, hiding them from view from within the temple. Here also he erected two rows of pillars where there had been one. Gates attached to both sides of the now-encased obelisks created a corridor between the fourth and fifth pylons. More gateways between the fifth and sixth pylons and walls in front of the Sanctuary turned the whole temple into a massive corridor with rooms to the north and the south. Immediately before the Sanctuary, Thutmose III set up the two square pillars of pink granite decorated in high relief with papyrus (north) and sedge-plant or lily (south), the symbols of Lower and Upper Egypt. The crispness of the carving and the simplicity of the design mark these as two of the most handsome of Egyptian pillars. The carvings on the new constructions in front of the Sanctuary record the king's victorious campaigns in Asia, and are consequently known as the **Hall of Annals**. Here Thutmose III presented to Amun the military successes which justified his rule. More material offerings are shown on the wall immediately to the north of the Sanctuary. A screen wall which masked the reliefs of Hatshepsut, now in the side-chamber, is rather awkward to view in this narrow space. Divided into registers, the wall has many different types of jewellery, chests and vessels offered by the king to Amun. In the narrow banks separating the registers are given the number of each type presented. Also included are two obelisks, and flag posts for the temple's gateway.

Abutting the east outer wall of Thutmose I, Thutmose III built the Akh-Menu, a complete temple related in design and function to the 'mortuary' temples of the kings (see below). Access to this temple was made by cutting a gateway in the Thutmose I wall, at the east end of the broad southern corridor. Further east still, the king constructed the Eastern Temple.

Thutmose III also made alterations to the southern courtyards and pylons (see below), dismantling some of the buildings of Amenhotep I. He also enlarged the Sacred Lake.

The main axis of the temple seems to have remained unaltered during the reigns of Amenhotep II and Thutmose IV, although buildings of theirs (many dismantled) are known. Thutmose IV added a porch (in wood) to the fourth pylon, which remained the main entrance to the temple.

It was Amenhotep III who began the expansion westward towards the river, removing whatever occupied the junction of the north-south and east-west axes. Immediately in front of the main entrance of

Thutmose I (pylon four), Amenhotep III built the vast, and now badly ruined, third pylon. Many earlier dismantled buildings were placed in this work, including blocks from his own temples. The gateway was decorated by Amenhotep IV in the early years of his reign (see Open Air Museum).

Amenhotep III may also have laid the foundations of the central colonnade of the **Great Hypostyle Hall**. The open papyrus columns, like those of the Luxor temple colonnade, would have been flanked by high walls, creating a dark corridor before the temple. It remains uncertain whether this is the case, but the king's other temples at north Karnak (the Monthu Temple), Luxor, and Soleb (in the Sudan) all have enclosed porticoes or colonnades of this type. Even if the foundations were laid, the work can have been little advanced at the time of the king's death, and Akhenaten soon abandoned work on the Amun temple. At some time in the late 18th–early 19th dynasties, the intention was altered to create a hypostyle hall. The names of Horemheb are to be found on the second pylon, itself filled with *talatat*, the dismantled blocks of Akhenaten's temples. The outer walls of the Hypostyle Hall were decorated by Sety I (north side) and Ramesses II, who completed and decorated the 134 columns.

Occupying an area 102 by 53 metres (335 by 174 feet) the hall has a central nave of 12 open-papyrus columns each 22 metres (72.2 feet) high, surrounded by avenues of bundle papyrus columns each nearly 15 metres (49.2 feet) high.

The Hypostyle Hall is best seen when it is deserted, very early in the morning, because only then can a true idea of its vastness be gained. A construction which is rather lacking in aesthetic charm, it needs silence and time to watch the light and shadow in this stone papyrus swamp. It is difficult to imagine this vast hall roofed in: the massive stone window panels with their narrow slits filtering shafts of sunlight into the central aisle and illuminating the colour on the reliefs (some traces remain on the underside of the architraves) and the many statues, their offering tables piled high with food and flowers.

The second pylon, called 'Illuminating Thebes', remained the main western entrance to Karnak for some 500 years. The great gateway is still flanked by royal statues, two striding figures of Ramesses II and the **Colossus of Pinudjem I**. Carved in pink granite, this rigid image of a ruler, his crook and flail crossed on his chest, is an impressive, but hardly beautiful, icon. Rather different is the graceful queen who stands on his feet and reaches just to his knee. The statue, carved probably for Ramesses II towards the end of his reign, was usurped by Ramesses VI and later by the High Priest of Amun, Pinudjem I. In front of it, the **Avenue of Sphinxes** stretched to the quay, and was surrounded by gardens. The sphinxes, each with a lion's body and a ram's head, protect figures of Ramesses II (usurped by Pinudjem I). Today the avenue runs only from the quay to the first pylon, and many of the sphinxes line the sides of the first courtyard. A large T-shaped harbour lay in front of the temple, with a canal (following the line of the modern road) connecting it to the Nile. The present quay was built by Ramesses II and has small obelisks of Sety II at the foot of the ramp (also notice here how much lower the level of the temple is compared to modern ground level). On the front (western side) of the quay are many important **Nile level texts**, recording the height of the river. The texts are a valuable addition to the historical sources as they give year dates for many of the kings. They can be seen from the wooden footbridge which connects the quay with the road, or by walking down into the cleared area around the quay. South of the avenue can be seen a series of ramps (25th Dynasty) which led down to the harbour and were used for collecting water for temple rituals.

The first stone building in these gardens in front of the temple was the **Barque Shrine of Sety II**, now contained within the first courtyard (north side). A resting place for the statues of Amun, Mut and Khonsu during the processional festivals, it contains three chapels decorated with scenes of the king making offerings to the sacred barques. Note also the niches in the easternmost chapel, which held statues of the king himself.

A second barque shrine of far more elaborate design was built on the southern side of the processional way in the 20th Dynasty. The **Temple of Ramesses III** is actually a complete miniature temple. A pylon entrance, flanked by statues of the king, gives on to the festival hall, a courtyard lined with a colonnade of square piers with Osiride statues of the king. A short stair leads to the terrace of the temple, with its portico, columned hall and sanctuary rooms. The courtyard has scenes of the processions of Amun (east wall) and Min (west wall), and the sanctuary decoration is quite well preserved. The outer western wall (access through a small door behind the colonnade) has a large scene of the river procession to Luxor. The whole gives a good idea of the basic 'classic' plan of a late New Kingdom temple (compare with the Khonsu temple).

The area of the first courtyard (103 metres by 84 metres, 336 by 276 feet) was enclosed with colonnades in the 22nd Dynasty, and between the Temple of Ramesses III and the second pylon, Shoshenq I built the **Bubastite Portal**, with, on its outer face, a scene of the king presenting captured Asiatic cities to Amun. Shoshenq I is often identified with 'Shishak, king of Egypt' who captured Jerusalem (I Kings 14: 25–26).

The final stage of the westward expansion of the temple occurred during the 25th Dynasty when the massive, and unfinished, first pylon was built (some scholars prefer a 30th Dynasty date for this). It flanked the existing gateway. (Its stones are dressed, but it is not bonded with the pylon's towers.) Note the brick ramps used in its construction against the southern tower. Although 113 metres (371 feet) wide, 15 metres thick (49.2 feet) and rising some 40 metres (131.3 feet) high, the impressiveness of the pylon is somewhat reduced by its unfinished state.

In the centre of the courtyard stand the ruins of the immense **Kiosk of Taharqo**. Ten open papyrus columns in two rows formed a great colonnade, probably unroofed, which flanked a huge altar of alabaster. The screen walls are a Ptolemaic addition. Today only one of the columns is complete, having been restored to its original height of 26 metres (85.3 feet).

The Temple of Amun: the Southern Courts and the Sacred Lake

At the junction of the north-south and east-west axes, where the third pylon now stands, there may have been a Middle Kingdom temple. Immediately to the south, there is thought to have been a temple of Amenhotep I, preceded by the White Chapel of Senusret I and Amenhotep I's limestone copy of it, and by the Alabaster Barque Shrine of Amenhotep I which led to the Sacred Lake. Hatshepsut and Thutmose III constructed pylons and courts in front of Amenhotep I's temple.

During the New Kingdom, a series of large courtyards and pylon gateways was built stretching south from the area in front of the fourth pylon towards the temple of the goddess Mut and the processional way to Luxor. Leaving the narrow court between the third and fourth pylons through the **Gate of Ramesses IX**, the first courtyard entered is the **Court of the Cachette** where, in 1902–9, a pit containing over 750 stone statues and stelae, and more than 17,000 bronze and wooden statues was excavated. Here the priests, probably in the early Ptolemaic period, had carefully buried some of the many, now surplus, dedications to the temple. The east and west walls of the courtyard, built in the 19th Dynasty, carry reliefs of Ramesses II (Treaty with the Hittites, west wall, outer side) and Merneptah (the king as a child protected by the ram-headed sphinx of Amun, east wall, inner side).

The seventh pylon, built by Thutmose III, forms the southern wall of the court. Here, against its northern face, are ranged some of the largest statues from the cache, of the Middle and early New Kingdom periods. Note, when passing through the gateway of the pylon, the two niches in the western side which were used for royal statues. The southern entrance to the pylon is flanked by the emplacements for two obelisks and colossal statues. These obelisks are probably the same as those represented in the offering scene of Thutmose III on the wall north of the Sanctuary of Philip Arrhidaeus (see above). The eastern obelisk is little more than a shattered fragment. Its western companion now stands in the Atmeidan in Istanbul. Made of red granite, its present height is 19.8 metres (65 feet), but probably one third of it is missing from the lower part. In the early fourth century AD, it was removed from Karnak (the earthworks can still be seen on the western side of the court) to Alexandria, in order to ship it to Constantinople. It eventually reached that city, and was raised on the *spina* of the Hippodrome in the reign of Theodosius (347–395). Visitors to Istanbul can examine the sculpted base, with its imperial inscriptions and scenes showing the obelisk aboard its barge, in the Hippodrome.

The remainder of the southern courts is presently inaccessible, being closed for restoration work carried out by the Centre Franco-Egyptien. It can be viewed, however, from the higher ground on the west side on the way to the temple of Khonsu (see below), and from the east side, where some interesting reliefs are on the outer walls.

Leave the courtyard between the seventh and eighth pylons through the gateway in the north-east corner of the courtyard. This leads into the **Barque Shrine of Thutmose III**, a small platform surrounded by a broken colonnade of square piers. In the centre are the lower parts of the alabaster shrine which Thutmose III built to replace the shrine of Amenhotep I (now in the Open Air Museum). Here, after having been carried from the Sanctuary, the barque of Amun rested before being sailed on the Sacred Lake. Now descend from the platform and turn right.

The outer wall of the courtyard, between the Barque Shrine and the door immediately north of the eighth pylon, carries three large and unusual scenes. These **reliefs of the High Priest Amenhotep** comprise two similar outer panels depicting the reward of the High Priest in front of a statue of Ramesses XI, and a central scene of the High Priest with the king. These reliefs are important in the history of Karnak and Egypt in the later 20th Dynasty as they mark the rising power of the High Priests, which culminated in Herihor's calling himself 'king' in the temple of Khonsu.

The eighth pylon is the work of Hatshepsut, but it was altered by Thutmose III and its decoration (south face) completed by Amenhotep II. The gateway is flanked by six colossal statues, the oldest being of Amenhotep I.

A view into the southernmost courtyard can also be gained. It is larger than the other courts, perhaps in order to bring the gateway opposite the entrance to the temple of Mut, and to include the chapel of Amenhotep II on its eastern side. The court is bounded on the north by the ninth pylon, which carries a dedication text of Horemheb and a copy of the Marriage Stele of Ramesses II (see also Abu Simbel). The stone pylon completed by Horemheb, and filled with *talatat* from the temples of Akhenaten, may have replaced an earlier brick gateway or pylon on the same site. Two colossi of Ramesses II flank the entrance. There are interesting reliefs of Horemheb in the southern part of the court, including a Nubian campaign, and the king with the chiefs of Punt. The eastern enclosure wall of the court incorporates the **Festival Chapel of Amenhotep II**, altered by Sety I to make it a resting place for the barque of Amun. Raised on a platform, the entrance façade is a long colonnade (more clearly seen from the western side, see below).

The southern gate of Karnak is the tenth pylon of Amenhotep III, its outer face and statues (which are worth visiting) can be inspected on the way to the temple of Mut. The inner face has two colossi of Horemheb, accompanied by small statues of his queen, Mutnodjemet, thought to be the sister of Nefertiti.

Turning towards the Sacred Lake, a view of the whole of the 18th Dynasty temple can be had, the southern courts of which lead to the junction with the main axis.

The **Sacred Lake** was originally much smaller, and the enclosure wall of the early 18th Dynasty probably came to where the seventh pylon now stands. The lake was enlarged by Thutmose III. On its southern edge, largely unexcavated mounds conceal many buildings, including the **Fowl Pens** where the geese of Amun were kept (the tunnel leading to the lake can still be seen). It is not recommended to walk in this area. On the far eastern side of the lake, beneath the seating stand for the sound and light show, are the **Houses of the Priests**. A street can be made out, with houses leading off. They seem to have occupied much of the area of the eastern part of the enclosure. Here also are remains of one of the earlier brick precinct walls. At the north-western corner of the lake is the **Granite Scarab of Amenhotep III**. Brought from the mortuary temple of the king (behind the Colossi of Memnon), the scarab is an image of the solar god Khepri. Nearby (next to the cafeteria) is the **Edifice of Taharqo**, a strange building with subterranean rooms which are inaccessible. Blocks from a building of Shabaqo are included in the building. Notice the fine relief head of the king wearing the white crown, rebuilt into an otherwise plain area of wall on the east side. The king wears the double *uraeus*, a feature of the 25th Dynasty, and often erased by later rulers.

The Temple of Amun: the Akh-Menu of Thutmose III, the Eastern and Northern Areas

On entering the columned hall behind the fourth pylon, turn right past the broken obelisk of Hatshepsut. Notice here the bases of the original single row of columns and the almost complete Osiride colossi of Thutmose I, as well as the lower part of a seated statue of queen Ahmose-Nefertari. At the south-east end of the hall, a doorway opens on to the corridor leading to the Akh-Menu. This door has a large relief of a processional statue of Amenhotep III (shown upon a rectangular base and a sledge with which to pull it). The corridor passes along the outer side of the rooms leading to the Sanctuary.

The entrance to the Akh-Menu was cut in the enclosure wall of Thutmose I, and is flanked by two broken standing statues of Thutmose III. The Akh-Menu is a complete temple which has much in common with the mortuary temples of the kings on the West Bank. The main entrance brings the visitor into a small vestibule. First turn right into a corridor opening into chambers. Half-way along this corridor are reliefs showing episodes from the *sed* festival ('jubilee') of Thutmose III. In one scene, the king wears the traditional short cloak, and in another shoots arrows, helped by the gods.

Return to the vestibule and enter the **Festival Hall**, oriented north-south. Immediately to the left are two small chambers, one of which contained the **Karnak Table of Kings**, showing Thutmose III making offerings to 61 of his predecessors. An important historical document, most of the blocks were removed to the Louvre and are now replaced by casts. The Festival Hall has a central nave of unusual 'tent-peg' columns which represent in stone the slim wooden poles used to support light constructions such as tents. Many traces of paint are preserved, giving a good idea of the original decoration. The nave is surrounded on all sides by square columns, indicating that although it was built as a hypostyle hall the room is actually conceived as an open courtyard. On the western side, the Middle Kingdom court is visible, due to the destruction of the side wall of the hall and the enclosures of Thutmose I. The far (north) end of the hall has three sanctuary rooms. In one of these is a large statue which gives the initial (deceptive) impression of a crucifix; it is actually a very fragmentary group showing the king between two deities. Other pieces lie around it.

On the eastern side of the hall are various suites of rooms. In a more conventionally planned temple, these suites would have surrounded the hypostyle hall, behind the court and before the sanctuary. The southernmost is the suite of Sokar-Osiris, deity of the underworld. Next to it, a small chamber with two chapels was

dedicated to the royal *ka*, and contained the cult images of the king.
North of the door on the axis of the main Amun temple is a suite with
a two-columned hall and two chapels, and from the north-east corner
of the Festival Hall a staircase leads to the chapel of Ra-Harakhty. The
main axis of the Amun temple has been used within the Akh-Menu,
and has a series of three rooms lying along it. From the second room,
turn right into a further two rooms, which were partially redecorated
by Alexander the Great. A modern wooden staircase leads into a suite
dedicated to Amun, the first hall of which is supported by elegant
sandstone columns. The columns are good examples of the mid-18th
Dynasty style. This room is known as the **Botanical Garden** because of
its delicate reliefs of the plants, animals and birds recorded by the
artist who accompanied the king on his Asiatic campaigns. As in the
Punt scenes at Deir el-Bahari, the artist has shown great interest and
skill in depicting the unusual and unfamiliar natural life of foreign
lands.

A second modern stair and bridge across the walls of the Akh-
Menu and the outer enclosure wall of Thutmose III lead to the
Eastern Temple.

Immediately visible is part of the **brick enclosure wall** which
encircled the Amun precinct in the reign of Thutmose III. Here, the
north corner and east wall create a court in front of the **Eastern
Temple**. Hatshepsut built a chapel here, probably in brick, with two
obelisks, the bases and some shattered fragments of which can still be
seen. A large alabaster statue of Hatshepsut with Amun which formed
the focus of this chapel now stands in the room to the south of the
shrine. Thutmose III's chapel comprises three chambers, in front of
which is a portico of square columns with Osiride statues of the king.
The small gateway opposite the central sanctuary room is of the reign
of the Emperor Domitian (AD 81–96). The focus of the chapel, the
shrine, is an enormous hollowed block of alabaster with seated figures
of the king with the goddess Amunet. About half of the block survives,
but even in this state it is impressive. The outer sides have delicately
carved reliefs of all the manifestations of Amun. Originally sealed with
wooden doors, this shrine is where Thutmose III was worshipped as
the intermediary with and manifestation of Amun.

Nectanebo I added two small chapels at the northern and southern
ends, which enclosed the bases of Hatshepsut's obelisks.

A courtyard, the 'Upper Court of Karnak', lay in front of the
temple, which was entered through the Eastern Gate from the town of
Thebes. Here Thutmose IV set up a single obelisk, and its
emplacement is still visible between the chapel of Thutmose III and the
temple of Ramesses II. The obelisk was quarried for Thutmose III at

Aswan, but it lay in the workshops of the Karnak temple for 35 years until Thutmose III's grandson completed the inscriptions and set it in place. The single obelisk designated this a solar court; the carved figures of Amun-Ra and Amun-Atum associated Amun with the morning and evening sun. The obelisk was removed from Karnak in the reign of Constantine, who wanted it to adorn Constantinople.

However, at the Emperor's death in 337, it was still at Alexandria. Diverted to Rome, it was set up in the Circus Maximus in 357 as a companion to an obelisk erected by Augustus. In 1588 it was re-discovered and erected in the square of St John Lateran, at the order of Pope Sixtus V. Today, at 32.18 metres (105.6 feet) high and weighing 455 tonnes, it is the largest of the standing obelisks.

Towards the east is the back of the Temple of Ramesses II. This temple, which was constructed in front of the Upper Court, served the same function as that of Thutmose III. The chapel itself comprised a pylon and a small hall with Osiride pillars of the king in the centre. The back wall had three doorways, which associated the king with Amun, Mut and Khonsu. Beyond lay a four-pillared hall, which effectively blocked direct access to the single obelisk and chapel of Thutmose III. Before the pylon lay a courtyard, extending probably as far as the huge **Eastern Gate** and brick *temenos* (a wall enclosing the whole area) of Nectanebo I. The temple was dedicated to 'Amun and Ramesses-who-hears-the-petitions-of-the-people'. In front of the pylon are the columns of the 25th Dynasty portico. Within this temple was discovered the magnificent black granite seated statue of Ramesses II, one of the most famous images of the king, now in the Museo Egizio in Turin.

To the north is the overgrown area between the 18th Dynasty and 30th Dynasty *temenos* walls. The several **Chapels of Osiris** here, which date to the 23rd−26th dynasties, originally lay within their own small enclosures along the streets of the city of Thebes. Of these chapels, that of **Osiris, 'Ruler of Eternity'** is the best preserved. This was originally a two-roomed chapel fronted by a brick walled courtyard, with its entrance on the northern side. A stone court was added to the chapel by the God's Wife of Amun, Amenirdis I, and her nephew, the 25th Dynasty king, Shebitqo. The reliefs are interesting for the regalia of the God's Wife and the king, which display Kushite influences. There is now a lake in front of the chapel, making entrance risky.

In the north-eastern corner of the *temenos* (not strictly accessible) are stored many blocks from a jubilee chapel of Thutmose III. With their well-preserved colour and elegant relief, they are interesting survivals of a reign whose monuments are rarely seen. The reliefs share much in common with the style of Amenhotep III.

Much of the area north of the main temple is unexcavated and overgrown with scrub. Cobras can be a problem here in certain seasons, and the ground can subside. Unaccompanied exploration is therefore not recommended. Here lay the Treasury of Shabaqo and other chapels.

Immediately to the north of the court between the third and fourth pylons lay the gate through the 18th Dynasty wall, and the northern entrance colonnade of the 25th Dynasty (called the Golden Hall of Shabaqo).

A well-defined path runs from the gate in the north wall of the Great Hypostyle Hall to the **North Gate** of the precinct. Here are more chapels of Osiris dedicated by the God's Wives of Amun, as well as the important **Temple of Ptah**.

Now wedged against the enclosure wall of Nectanebo I, the Temple of Ptah must originally have occupied a more spacious enclosure on the road leading from the north gate of the 18th Dynasty wall into the city. The chief interest of the temple proper, a small building of Thutmose III, is its complete state. The three chapels are roofed, and when the guardian closes the door, the headless cult image of Ptah, and the large granite statue of his consort, the lioness-headed Sakhmet, are eerily illuminated by single shafts of light from above. It is difficult elsewhere to achieve such an impression of an Egyptian sanctuary. In front of the temple stretches a series of six gateways built by the kings of the 25th and Ptolemaic dynasties.

The Temple of Khonsu

The Khonsu temple, situated on higher ground in the south-west corner of the Amun precinct, allows a good view of the southern courts. The seated colossi before the eighth pylon and the portico of the Amenhotep II jubilee chapel can be seen more clearly from here. The Temple of Khonsu is a good example of a well-preserved New Kingdom temple of the classic style. The temple is not included in the main tourist route, but it is often empty, and its quietness lends it a certain charm.

Built by Ramesses III, it contains a number of re-used blocks from the mortuary temple of Amenhotep III on the west bank. The decoration of the temple was completed by the later Ramessides and the High Priest Herihor, who adopted royal titles and cartouches.

The pylon leads to a colonnaded court (not lined with statues as in temples associated with the royal cult). A small hypostyle hall and the sanctuary rooms complete the building. In one of the eastern side-rooms, the painted relief is almost undamaged. Although it is forbidden, the guardian often allows visitors to climb to the temple roof from which fine views over the whole of Amun precinct are to be had.

As at many other places in Karnak, the 25th Dynasty kings built a many- columned portico in front of the pylon of the Khonsu temple. Little now remains but a few bases. More striking are the remains of the **Avenue of Rams**, which is punctuated by the precinct wall of Nectanebo I and the **Gate of Ptolemy Euergetes**. This is a fine example of a Ptolemaic gateway, with good reliefs depicting the king before the various forms of Khonsu. The Avenue of Rams can be seen through the (usually closed) modern gate bordering the modern road through Karnak village towards Luxor. Although it is often said to have connected with the processional way to Luxor, this avenue probably led to a landing stage and canal.

At right angles to the Khonsu temple, oriented east-west, is the unfinished Ptolemaic **Temple of Opet**, a hippopotamus goddess associated with childbirth, and here worshipped as the mother of Osiris.

Karnak: the Precincts of Monthu and Mut, and the Processional Way to Luxor

For those who have the time, a walk around the outside of Karnak temple and a visit to the other temple precincts is a worthwhile experience. For those who cannot complete the full circuit, the southern gate and avenue leading to the temple of the goddess Mut is the more rewarding part.

Instead of entering the Amun temple at the first pylon, turn left and follow the *temenos* wall of Nectanebo I to the north, to the village of el-Malqata. Continue following the precinct wall as it turns east, and walk to the outer side of the North Gate. Here the unnaturalness of the Nectanebo I precinct is most clearly appreciated. The massive brick walls of the Amun enclosure, with the temple of Ptah inside, come strangely close to the *temenos* of the northern group of temples, leaving only a narrow passage between. More extraordinary still is that the southern wall of the northern *temenos* is punctuated by the stone gateways of the temple of the goddess Maet and six chapels built by the God's Wives of Amun, all of which face directly on to the brick wall of the Amun temple. In ancient times there must have been a main road and perhaps a crossing here, with the small chapels lining the road to the north and the precinct of Ptah at the junction. To the north, an excavated area shows the complexity of the levels below the later wall. Here are a gateway of Thutmose I and some small chapels,

along with many brick buildings. A few fragments of stone buildings stand in the open space in front of the village. Follow the precinct wall to the east to the Ptolemaic gateway and remains of the avenue where the higher ground level allows a view of the **Temple of Monthu** (during the Old Kingdom, the chief god of Thebes). Little more than the foundations can be seen of this temple, which was founded by Amenhotep III and expanded by later rulers down to the Ptolemies. The avenue led to a quay, and the temple may at one time have been connected by canal with the temple of Monthu at Medamud, to the north.

A walk along the precinct wall to the east and then south provides a good view over the whole area. On the eastern side of the Monthu temple is a building dedicated to his son, Harpre. Along the same axis as the main temple with its entrance to the south is the temple of the goddess Maet, built by Ramesses II. Further to the east lie the excavated remains of the **Treasury of Thutmose I**.

Continue to follow the wall of the Amun temple as it turns south. There is little to see here, but the barrenness and desolation provide a stark contrast to the milling throngs inside the main enclosure. Half-way along the wall stands the Eastern Gate, with its bases of obelisks and statues of Ramesses II. For devotees of Akhenaten, a short detour should be made here. From the gateway, follow the track for a short distance due east to the bases of some of the colossi of Akhenaten, now in Cairo Museum. (Some of the heads are also in Luxor Museum.) Akhenaten built a temple here (one of perhaps four in the Karnak area), which he decorated with jubilee scenes. Like his other temples here, it was dismantled (probably by Horemheb) and used as building material in the second and ninth pylons.

Return to the East Gate and follow the wall first to the south and then west to the outside of the tenth pylon, the great southern gate of Karnak. Visitors with less time or inclination can follow the shorter and more direct route from the first pylon along the main road to the gateway of the temple of Khonsu, then continue west to this point.

The tenth pylon is badly ruined, except for its gateway. To the left are the lower parts of a colossus of Horemheb, and to the right the stupendous base and feet of the **Colossus of Amenhotep III**. This was probably the largest standing statue ever set up by the Egyptians and the remains are impressive not only for their size, but also for the loveliness of the sculpture. Fragments of the statue are ranged along the precinct wall. Note particularly the buckle of the king's belt which gives the name of the statue, 'Nebmaatre [Amenhotep III] is Monthu of the Rulers'. This statue, which must have reached to the same height as the top of the gateway, remained standing until the Roman period.

The tenth pylon marks the beginning of the **Processional Way to Luxor**. It is not known when this was established, but it was made considerably more elaborate by Hatshepsut, who built a number of chapels along its length. These way-stations, a room on a raised platform, with statues of Hatshepsut flanking each door, are depicted on the Red Chapel. It has been suggested that a canal originally ran between the two temples, and that this was later filled in and lined with ram-headed sphinxes. Behind each sphinx, or between them, was planted a tree. Today this shady avenue has taken on an eerie, almost lunar, appearance. The sandstone sphinxes, some shattered and eroded beyond recognition, are covered in drifts of sand. A few palms are the only vegetation.

At the beginning of the avenue are stored a number of sculptured blocks, including two from an early temple of Akhenaten, on which the Aten is shown as a falcon-headed god.

The South Gate faces the entrance to the precinct of Mut, a number of originally separate temples enclosed by Nectanebo I. Outside the entrance to the left (east) are the foundations, barely visible in the sand, of the **Temple of Kamutef**, the 'Bull of his mother', the fertility aspect of Amun. To the right, where the avenue turned, are the remains of the double **Barque Shrine**, built by Hatshepsut and extended by Thutmose III.

The main axis of the southern enclosure is occupied by the **Temple of Mut**, which is largely ruined. Thought to date from the reign of Amenhotep III, it has 25th Dynasty and Ptolemaic additions. Note the large reliefs of Bes in the Ptolemaic entrance. The area is overgrown with scrub and reeds and littered with black granite statues of the lioness-headed Sakhmet. Each statue has a different name, the whole forming a 'litany in stone' and an invocation of the different manifestations of this ferocious goddess. Some are standing, some seated; some whole, some broken. The lioness goddesses were believed to dwell within a crescent-shaped **sacred lake**, which can be seen at the back of the temple. Called Asheru, the lake gave its name to the goddess (Mut 'in Asheru') and to this region of Thebes. On the far side of the lake can be seen the **Temple of Ramesses III**, close by the continuation of the Processional Way.

To the east of the main entrance is the **Temple of Khonsu the Child**, built by Amenhotep III with additions by later rulers. Here, as in the *mammisi* of Ptolemaic temples, the birth of the god to the divine couple was celebrated. Amongst the few surviving reliefs is a circumcision scene. Broken statuary and a massive alabaster stele lie amongst the reeds. A little amusement can be had from the statue of Ramesses II, fallen on its face with its legs in the air.

On leaving the Mut enclosure, turn left and follow the precinct wall through a drift of powdered mud and sand, back to the main road. Fragments of the **Avenue of Sphinxes** are visible. It is not far to the junction with the main road from the airport, which will be followed the rest of the way into the city. First, however, look at the excavated section of the avenue in the right angle where the airport road turns east, and, a little further on, the area with excavated buildings, which were perhaps houses.

The Processional Way ends at the brick enclosure wall of Nectanebo I which creates a huge court in front of the Temple of Luxor. A well-preserved section of the avenue can be seen, but notice that here the sphinxes have human heads.

The Temple of Luxor

The Temple of Luxor is one of the most handsome in Egypt. Built of sandstone from the quarries of Gebel Silsila its great central court is particularly lovely at dusk when the stone deepens to orange. A late-afternoon visit has the advantages of seeing the building at sunset, as well as by the excellent lighting (without sound) which makes much of the relief easier to see.

Luxor was the venue of the feast of the Opet, one of Thebes' main festivals. Although a local, rather than national, festival, it was often attended by the king. Amun journeyed from Karnak to reside in Luxor, the 'Southern Opet' or Harem. Here he consummated his marriage and symbolically fathered the king. In the reign of Hatshepsut, the divine statues were probably carried along the Processional Way, but in the later 18th Dynasty they came to Luxor by river. The whole event was an occasion of rejoicing.

The main part of the temple was built by Amenhotep III, with the first courtyard and pylon completed and decorated by Ramesses II. The expansion of the temple northwards meant that several changes were made in its axis in order to line it up with the Processional Way to Karnak.

In front of the pylon is a large courtyard, created by the precinct wall. Here can be found the **Serapeum**, a small single-roomed chapel on a platform surrounded by a colonnade. This temple, inaugurated by the Emperor Hadrian on his birthday, 24 January 126, is built of brick, originally plastered and painted, with a stone doorway of typical Egyptian design. Inside is a Roman statue of the goddess Isis.

In front of the pylon are two seated colossi of Ramesses II, in black granite. Their four standing companions, in red granite, are in various states of restoration. Until 1831, two obelisks of red granite flanked the gateway. Now there is only one, 22.5 metres (73.8 feet) high and

weighing 227 tonnes. The second was given to France by Mohammed Ali. During the last century, the Temple of Luxor was occupied by part of the town, with streets running between the capitals of the columns (the ground level was much higher) and houses built throughout. The obelisk was lowered after the removal of 30 houses which surrounded it. In 1833 it was set up in the Place de la Concorde.

The western tower of the pylon has scenes of the Battle of Kadesh (best seen when lit in the evening) and, like the court beyond, it was probably built during the reign of Sety I, though decorated in the early years of Ramesses II.

Just through the gateway is the **Mosque of Abu'l Haggag**, the doorway of which is half-way up the wall, at the 19th-century ground level. Abu'l Haggag was a holy man whose relics are kept within the mosque, which is now used only for special services. His great feast, the time of which varies according to the lunar calendar, involves the towing of a boat around Luxor. Whatever its current symbolisn, this feast is surely derived from the Opet festival.

The **Court of Ramesses II** is lined by a double colonnade, with statues between the columns on the southern side. Not all of these were carved for Ramesses; some were the work of Amenhotep III. On the north-western side of the court is the **Shrine of Thutmose III**, consisting of three chapels with a granite portico. This, the earliest surviving building at Luxor, was rebuilt and re-carved when Ramesses II built the courtyard around it. The gate in the western wall of the court marks the old way to the temple quay. The gate in the eastern wall is the 'People's Gate', by which the ordinary people gained access to the courtyard in order to present their petitions to the royal statues, which then interceded with Amun on their behalf.

From the western gate, a fine procession moves south along the wall. The fat bulls are decorated for sacrifice; their hooves curve under their great weight, and between their horns, which have wooden hands attached to the ends, are the painted wooden heads of Asiatics or Nubians. The sacrifice of the cattle symbolizes the plundering of foreign lands. The Asiatic cattle have large humps over the shoulder whilst the Nubian ones have long, twisted horns. Some cattle have large tasselled earrings. The procession is led by some of the sons of Ramesses II to the pylon of the Temple of Luxor. This is one of quite few depictions of temples, and it is well-preserved. The pylon is shown with its flat-posts, and the six statues in front of it (viewed from the side); but the standing statues are shown wearing the double-crown. In reality, it is the white crown. An earlier, but less well-preserved, depiction of Luxor can be found on the back of the east tower of the pylon (in the corridor between the pylon and the mosque).

Two black granite seated statues of Ramesses II guard the entrance to the colonnade. The better-preserved statue is one of the finest surviving of the king. Particularly graceful is the figure of the queen at his side.

The colonnade, which was originally enclosed by high walls and lit only with shafts of light, had a small pylon entrance. This, and where it joins the wall of the Ramesside court, can best be seen from the central courtyard. Planned by Amenhotep III, the work was left unfinished at his death. Tutankhamun was responsible for the carving of the Opet scenes on the long walls, and Ay decorated the pylon, but the whole work was not finished and dedicated until the reign of Horemheb. For this reason, the names of Tutankhamun have everywhere been replaced by those of Horemheb. The western wall is the better preserved, depicting the Opet procession from Karnak to Luxor. The eastern wall has the return voyage to Karnak. The scenes are interesting for their content, and for their mixture of Amarna and classical styles. It is best seen when lit in the evening.

On the short entrance walls, Tutankhamun makes offerings to Amun. The figures are large and carved in lovely low relief. These, particularly on the north-western wall, are amongst the finest portraits of the young king. Marked by the return to a more classical style, they still show Amarna influence in the swelling stomach and large thighs. The figures of Amun, however, are dull and conventional.

The long wall begins with offerings made to the sacred barques inside the Temple of Karnak. Throughout the scenes the barque of Amun, shown on a larger scale higher up on the wall, has been lost, but the barques of Mut, Khonsu and the king himself can all be seen. The procession leaves the temple (it is unusual that the figures are shown superimposed upon the temple's pylon — the third pylon of Amenhotep III), with its knotted flagstaffs. Each barque is placed upon a river barge (a much larger, though almost identical vessel) and then rowed, while being towed by smaller barges. Soldiers help by pulling from the banks. It is obvious that this scene was designed and carved by artists who had been trained in the Amarna style, even to the technique used in carving the relief. Notice the tumblers, the Nubian drummers and stave fighters, the chantresses of Amun with their sistra, and the officials in their chariots. The arrival at Luxor is celebrated with offerings. (The small offering tables with their scenes of preparation are strikingly similar to reliefs in the tombs at Amarna, and from the Karnak *talatat*.) The short wall has a splended scene of the king dedicating offerings by extending his sceptre. Notice here the superbly carved royal hand, which is emphasised in deep relief as the focus of the scene.

The 14 columns with open-papyrus capitals, although not as massive as those of the Hypostyle Hall at Karnak, are somewhat more elegant. The effects created by the architecture must have been quite striking, as the procession of the sacred barques passed through this hall, lit only by narrow shafts of light from the windows high in the side walls, and emerged into the dazzling sunlight of the central courtyard.

The **Courtyard of Amenhotep III** is one of the great achievements of Egyptian architecture. It is lined on three sides by a double colonnade, and on the southern side by a deep portico. Unfortunately, some of the effect is lost due to the destruction of the side walls and of many of the roofing blocks of the colonnades. The portico, or **Hypostyle Hall**, is the entrance to Amenhotep III's original temple, which is distinguished by its being set upon a terrace (clearly visible from outside). The curving axes of the temple are easily seen from here. At the back of the hall (note in passing the altar dedicated to the Emperor Constantine) are the chapels used as resting places for the sacred barques of Mut and Khonsu.

Tomb of Ramesses VI, Valley of the Kings

The hall beyond the hypostyle is often, incorrectly, said to have been converted into a Christian church. Originally supported by eight columns, this room has two side chambers, probably used to keep the barque and portable statue of the king during the Opet festival. The doorway into the chamber beyond was turned into an apse in the later Roman period, and the reliefs were plastered over and painted. However, far from being a church, this was where the Roman

emperors were worshipped and Christians would have been forced to make sacrifices to them. The painting in the apse shows Diocletian (284–305) and Maximian with their two caesars, Constantius Chlorus and Galerius. Immediately to the left of the apse is an Egyptian artist's error. Two almost-identical scenes show Amenhotep III kneeling before Amun, who touches the back of his crown. Close examination of the lower scene shows that the artist put the wrong crown on this figure (though it is correct in the scene above). Traces of the alterations, which would have been disguised further with plaster and painting, are still visible.

A modern door has been cut in the apse, leading to the **Hall of Offerings**. The roof is almost complete, and a lot of paint survives on the splendid reliefs. Here Amenhotep III presents enormous offerings to Amun before being accepted by the god (on the south wall) and conducted into his presence in the sanctuary. Amenhotep III's sanctuary was supported by four columns, but this was replaced by the present **Shrine of Alexander the Great** (332–323 BC). Here Alexander, with all the regalia and attributes of an Egyptian Pharaoh, is shown being accepted by Amun.

Beyond the sanctuary is the suite of rooms where Amun resided during the Opet Feast. In one of the rooms to the east of the sanctuary is a badly damaged cycle of reliefs depicting the birth of Amenhotep III. Similar to the Hatshepsut cycle at Deir el-Bahari, Amun visits the king's mother, Queen Mutemwiya, the god Khnum forms the king on the potter's wheel, and the child is born and presented to the gods.

Around the temple are the remains of the Roman fort and later churches, although, due to the changing course of the river, some areas have been lost.

The Museum of Luxor

Inaugurated in 1975, the Museum of Luxor is situated on the way to Karnak. It contains documents from the Theban area, mostly of recent discovery, from great statuary to objects related to everyday life and domestic use, from prehistory to the Arab conquest. Besides the ceramic pottery and stone bases of the pre-dynastic and archaic epochs and the funerary ornaments of the Old Kingdom, the finds from the Middle Kingdom are also interesting. These include the foundation depository of Mentuhotep II's temple at Deir el-Bahari, an Osirian statue of Mentuhotep III from Monthu's temple at Armant, and a relief celebrating a king of the same dynasty in red granite from Amun's temple in Karnak. There are also two headless statues from the same temple of the king's vizier Mentuhotep portrayed as a scribe, a part of the famous treasure of Tod, silver objects of Syrian origin found in 1936 in Monthu's temple foundations at Tod and contained in coffers bearing Amenemhat II's name and a magnificent red granite head of Senusret III, from Amun's temple in Karnak.

An important historical document housed here is the great **stele of Kamose**, erected within Amun's temple to celebrate the king's victories over the Hyksos. A beautiful head in painted sandstone from Karnak portrays Amenhotep I, who ruled at the beginning of the 18th Dynasty and created the base for the strengthening of Egyptian international power.

A quartzite relief records the dedication of the two obelisks, cut in the Aswan caves and covered with gold leaf, by Hatshepsut to the god Amun. (One of these is still standing between the fourth and fifth pillars at Karnak; the other lies broken in the premises.)

Thutmose III is represented by a statue in extremely fine dark green stone, one of the New Kingdom masterpieces (from the cachette of Karnak in the seventh courtyard), and by a polychrome bas-relief from his temple in Deir el-Bahari.

A splendidly executed relief in red granite shows Amenhotep II's prowess as an archer. From a Theban tomb comes the wall decorating panel, recomposed in the museum, representing Amenhotep III on his throne. The same sovereign is also present in others here, including one showing the king in the company of Sobek, the crocodile-headed god, carved in calcite. His architect Amenhotep, son of Hapu (later deified because of his knowledge), is portrayed as a scribe in a splendid statue of exquisite black granite.

An exceptional find was that of the more than 40,000 talents (decorated slabs) in Amenhotep IV's buildings and re-used in Amun's temple in Karnak. Numerous slabs have been extracted from the ninth pylon permitting the reconstruction of nearly a full wall with everyday-life scenes and religious themes. Also from Karnak two monumental heads of Akhenaten form part of the king's Osiride pillars. The rich burial equipment of Tutankhamun is represented here by objects such as sandals, arrows, decorative rosettes in gilded bronze and a beautiful cow-head of the goddess Hathor in gilded wood. Funerary objects, statues, offering tables, stelae and reliefs complete the section of Egyptian civilization during the New Kingdom. Also interesting are some examples of funerary papyri from the 21st Dynasty, a mummy covering a casket and four canopic bases of the 22nd and 23rd dynasties.

The exhibition ends with examples from the Graeco-Roman, Coptic and Arab periods, found around the temple of Luxor and the Theban area.

Western Thebes

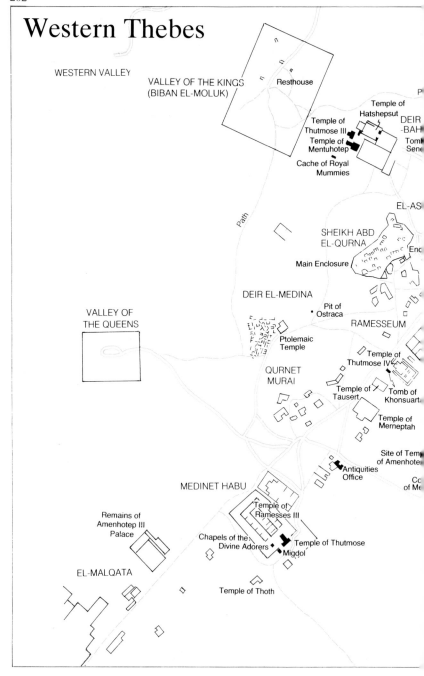

WESTERN VALLEY

VALLEY OF THE KINGS
(BIBAN EL-MOLUK)

Resthouse

P

WESTERN VALLEY

Temple of
Hatshepsut

DEIR
-BAH

Temple of
Thutmose III

Temple of
Mentuhotep

Tom
Sene

Cache of Royal
Mummies

EL-AS

Path

SHEIKH ABD
EL-QURNA

Enc

Main Enclosure

DEIR EL-MEDINA

Pit of
Ostraca

VALLEY OF
THE QUEENS

RAMESSEUM

Ptolemaic
Temple

Temple of
Thutmose IV

QURNET
MURAI

Temple of
Tausert

Tomb of
Khonsuart

Temple of
Merneptah

Site of Temp
of Amenhote

Antiquities
Office

Co
of Me

MEDINET HABU

Remains of
Amenhotep III
Palace

Temple of
Ramesses III

Chapels of the
Divine Adorers

Temple of Thutmose

Migdol

EL-MALQATA

Temple of Thoth

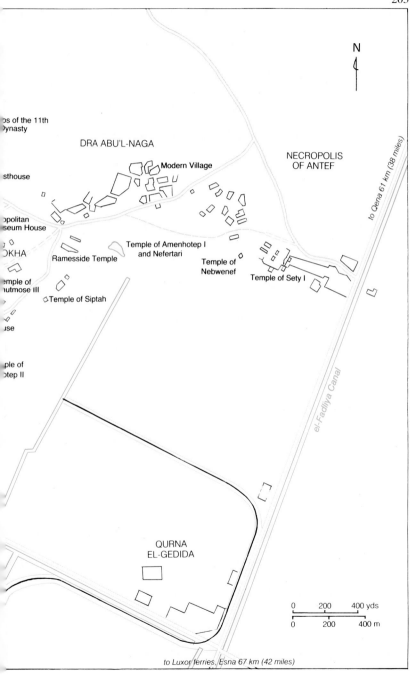

os of the 11th
Dynasty

DRA ABU'L-NAGA

NECROPOLIS
OF ANTEF

N

Modern Village

sthouse

opolitan
seum House

OKHA

Ramesside Temple

Temple of Amenhotep I
and Nefertari

Temple of
Nebwenef

Temple of Sety I

emple of
nutmose III

Temple of Siptah

use

ple of
otep II

to Qena 61 km (38 miles)

el-Fadliya Canal

QURNA
EL-GEDIDA

| 0 | 200 | 400 yds |
| 0 | 200 | 400 m |

to Luxor ferries, Esna 67 km (42 miles)

Thebes: The West Bank

The necropolis of Thebes lay on the west bank of the river, with the cliffs of the Western Desert providing a place for rock-cut tombs and a magnificent backdrop to the temples of the kings. The 'Mortuary Temples' of the rulers of the 18th−20th dynasties lay along the edge of the cultivation, the northernmost being that of Sety I, and the southernmost, that of Ramesses III (Medinet Habu) (see below). Many have been destroyed in ancient or more recent times and are known only from their foundations and fragments recovered by archaeologists. Behind the temples, in the hills beneath the natural pyramid of the Theban Peak (known locally as the Qurn), were the **tomb chapels of the nobles** of Thebes. Today these groups of tombs are named after the nearest village. From the 18th Dynasty onwards, the kings chose to be buried in remote desert *wadis* in an attempt to protect their tombs from robbery.

The necropolis of **Dra Abu'l-Naga** lies in the low slopes of the hills between the entrance to the Valley of the Kings and the bay of Deir el-Bahari. This was the site of the royal necropolis of the 17th Dynasty. Some 18th Dynasty nobles were buried here, but it was particularly popular in the 19th Dynasty (when several High Priests of Amun carved their tombs here), perhaps because it is opposite Karnak. The tombs here are rarely visited.

On the northern slopes of the bay of **Deir el-Bahari** are tombs of the Middle Kingdom, whilst those occupying its central plain, **el-Asasif**, are mainly of the 25th and 26th dynasties. Their massive brick superstructures (with pylons and gateways) are clearly visible from the terraces of Hatshepsut's temple. Montuemhat (Tomb 34), was the most powerful of the Theban officials of the late 25th Dynasty, being the Fourth Prophet of Amun, Mayor of Thebes and Governor of Upper Egypt. Pabasa (Tomb 279) and Aba (Tomb 36) served the God's Wife of Amun, Nitokris, daughter of Psamtik I. The fine reliefs in this group of tombs copy earlier tomb scenes from Thebes and elsewhere, and show the archaizing interest of artists of this period.

The hills on the southern side of Deir el-Bahari contain the cemetery of **el-Khokha**. The most notable tombs here are of the reign of Amenhotep III. The chapel of the sculptors Nebamun and Ipuki (Tomb 181), has fine painted decoration, but several other chapels are decorated in relief. The stone in which the Theban tombs are carved is not of the best quality for carved decoration, and so the usual method of decoration here was painting on plaster which gave a better surface. During the reign of Amenhotep III, however, the best bands of stone were sought out for the tombs of his most important Theban officials.

From the style and technique of the work it seems that they were decorated by artists brought from Memphis, where carved relief was usual. Amenemhet-Surero (Tomb 48) was the Steward of Amenhotep III at Thebes. His large and finely decorated tomb is unfinished. The figures of the owner are hacked out, indicating that he fell from office. Some of the loveliest low relief and most interesting scenes are to be found in the tomb of the Steward of Queen Tiye (wife of Amenhotep III), Kheruef (Tomb 192). These depict unusual episodes in the jubilee festivals of the king, including the setting up of the *djed*-pillar and the reward of the officials. Also decorated in low relief, and dating from the earliest years of Amenhotep IV-Akhenaten, is the tomb of the Steward, Parennefer (Tomb 188).

Sheikh Abd el-Qurna contains the largest and most important group of private tomb chapels. On the plain and the hill directly behind the Ramesseum are a number of easily accessible tombs which are always open to visitors. The largest of these is the **Tomb of Ramose** (Tomb 55). A broad staircase leads down to the forecourt (from which a second tomb chapel opens), with the smoothed façade of Ramose's tomb occupying the whole of the western side. Here the usual transverse hall has been expanded into a large chamber supported by four rows of eight columns (some of which are now restored). The finest series of reliefs is immediately to the left of the entrance. It shows the ritual banquet of Ramose's family, and includes people already deceased at the time of the tomb's decoration. Ramose, Vizier of Upper Egypt and Mayor of Thebes in the later years of Amenhotep III's reign, is shown with his wife and parents (his father had been Mayor of Memphis), his half-brother (the king's Chief Steward in Memphis) and a more distant relative (Amenhotep the son of Hapu, one of the king's most important officials). This scene is amongst the finest works of the 18th Dynasty, its appeal to modern eyes doubtless increased by its being unpainted. The southern wall has a painted funeral procession with a fine group of female mourners. Servants carrying the burial equipment are followed by a procession of highest officials, including the Viceroy of Nubia. A long sloping passage beneath this scene leads to the burial chamber, which is inaccessible. The back wall of the chamber is particularly interesting. The doorway leads to the second, ruined hall (supported by eight pillars) and the unfinished shrine beyond. Left of this doorway is a scene of the accession of Amenhotep IV (Akhenaten) in the 'classical' style. The king is seated on a dais under the triple canopy, with the goddess Maet behind him (compare this with the painting of Amenhotep III in Luxor Museum). To the right of the doorway is one of the earliest scenes in the Amarna style. Although much of the scene is uncarved, the line

drawing in black ink has great beauty. Akhenaten and Nefertiti are shown in the Window of Appearances, whilst Ramose is anointed with perfumes and rewarded with gold collars (compare this with the similar scene in the nearby tomb of Khaemhet). The figure of the vizier here is in striking contrast to those elsewhere in the tomb — Ramose is now shown with a long skull and jaw like the king. Also interesting is the 'action' drawing of Ramose prostrating himself in the royal presence (Khaemhet bows only from the waist). Notice also the representatives of the Asiatic and African states with which Egypt had contact, brought here to witness the power of the Pharaoh and the reward of loyal officials.

The **Tomb of Khaemhet** (Tomb 57), close by that of Ramose, is also decorated in delicate low relief. The scenes are interesting to compare with those in Ramose's tomb, which is almost contemporary. Khaemhet is shown being rewarded by Amenhotep III on the occasion of one of the jubilees. The other scenes, which are of agricultural activities, are of a type often found in painted tombs, and their treatment in the differing media can be usefully compared. The statues of the deceased and his family in this tomb are unusually well-preserved, both the large group in the transverse hall and the three highly polished groups in the shrine. Two fine relief heads of Amenhotep III from scenes in the transverse hall are now in the Berlin Museum (they have been replaced here with casts).

Almost adjacent is the **Tomb of Userhat** (Tomb 56), which is more typical of Theban tombs, being quite small and with lively painted scenes. The plan is a good example of the standard Theban type, with the doorway from the courtyard opening on to a narrow transverse hall, followed by a corridor-hall with a statue niche.

A steep climb up from this group of chapels leads first to the **Tomb of Rekhmire** (Tomb 100), who was vizier during the later years of Thutmose III. This is one of the most rewarding of the earlier 18th Dynasty chapels because of its fine painting and informative scenes. In plan it is typically Theban, with a transverse hall and corridor, but here the scale is greatly increased, with the roof of the corridor-hall sloping upwards to a great height. In the first hall, the presentation of the foreign 'tribute' to Thutmose III (left of the doorway to the corridor) is particularly notable. As is so often the case elsewhere, the Egyptian artist has skilfully captured the characteristics of unfamiliar animals: from Africa, an elegant giraffe is followed by vicious dogs, their teeth bared, and long-horned cattle; and from Syria, a bear and an elephant. In this same room is an unusual panel showing a hunt in the desert. The 'flying animals' in this scene show the influence of Aegean art (Aegean people are to be seen in the tribute scene). On the left side of

the corridor-hall are scenes of the workshops of the temple of Amun, depicting many fascinating details such as the fashioning of statues , the casting of bronze doors, leather-tanning and mud brick making. The large banqueting scene on the right wall can be compared with that in the tomb of Ramose. Here, at the peak of the early 18th Dynasty classical style, the continuation of Middle Kingdom traditions is still visible. The tall, slim, female figures are painted a creamy-yellow. Their tight-fitting white tunics and quite simple hair-styles seem austere when compared with the elaborate robes and coiffures of the later tomb. The whole style of decoration is more restrained, but equally delicate. Notice the servant girl shown (several times) with tresses hanging across her face, and once, unusually, from behind. In this delightful figure, the artist has broken with convention, and with great skill — except for the feet, which are unnaturally crossed. Between the banquet and the funerary scenes at the end of this hall, Rekhmire is shown being towed upon the lake in his formal garden. As well as the informative painted scenes in this tomb, one large text is especially significant. This records the appointment of Rekhmire by the king and the duties of the vizier. Not only does it tell the actual function of the office, it illuminates Egyptian morality.

A short distance further up is the **Tomb of Sennefer** (Tomb 96B), Mayor of Thebes in the reign of Amenhotep II. The tomb chapel is badly preserved and is now used as a storeroom, but a stairway leads to the burial chamber, one of the jewels of the Theban necropolis. The first small room has an unsmoothed ceiling decorated with vine trellises and painted bunches of grapes (hence the name given by early visitors, 'the tomb of the Vine'). A low door leads into the main chamber which is supported by four square pillars. The ceiling is decorated with abstract patterns and more vines. Although there is little that is striking in the content of the paintings, their clarity and execution are quite delightful. All the columns have large figures of Sennefer outlined in black and filled with flat washes of colour. Sometimes he is accompanied by his wife, Meryt. In nearly all of the scenes he wears the 'Gold of Honour', rewards from the king comprising necklaces of gold disk beads, double arm-bands and a heavy gold bracelet, its shape derived from an ivory ring. He also wears a double-heart amulet, one of gold and one of silver, which was a special favour from the king (whose names are sometimes written on it). In most scenes, Sennefer wears large gold earrings, which is unusual. (Men are often shown with pierced ears, but rarely with rings through them.) One of the loveliest column panels has Sennefer seated in front of a tree with Meryt (much smaller) at his side. The strength and simplicity of the painting, with its restful colour scheme, never fails to delight.

Behind the hill of Sheikh Abd el-Qurna, in a valley similar to, but not as grand as, Deir el-Bahari, King Mentuhotep II planned his temple and tomb. Little survives today, but opposite, in the back of the Qurna hill, lies the large **Tomb of Meket-re**, the king's chancellor. Although the fine reliefs are now little more than fragments, an undamaged statue chamber was excavated by the New York Metropolitan Museum of Art. Here many fine wooden models were discovered, three-dimensional versions of the painted tomb scenes found at Beni Hasan and el-Bersha. Now divided between the Cairo and New York museums, these models are a delightful and informative document for the study of the Middle Kingdom. Particularly fine is the elaborate group of the cattle census (Cairo Museum), with its wonderful spotted cows.

The most southerly part of the private necropolis is **Qurnet Murai**, a low hill between Deir el-Medina and the plain. The tombs here are of late-18th Dynasty to Ramesside date, and are rarely visited. The tomb of the Viceroy of Nubia, Merymose, who served under Amenhotep III, was occupied as a house earlier this century. It is now inaccessible, but a fine black granite anthropoid coffin from here is displayed in the British Museum, which possesses fragments of Merymose's two black granite sarcophagi. Close by is the **Tomb of Huy** (Tomb 40), the Viceroy of Nubia in the reign of Tutankhamun. This chapel is notable for its excellent paintings showing the appointment of Huy as viceroy, his arrival in Nubia, and the collection and presentation of 'tribute' to the king. Amongst the objects presented are foot-stools, fans and shields, which are very similar to examples found in the king's tomb. The Nubian princes are shown in all their finery, and a princess is brought in a chariot which is drawn by cattle.

In a small valley behind the Qurnet Murai hill lies the **village and cemetery of Deir el-Medina**. This was occupied by the workmen who carved and decorated the royal and private tombs, and, whilst in many ways not typical of ancient villages, it is one of few places where houses can be seen. At the northern end, a high brick wall surrounds the Ptolemaic temple. Raised over earlier New Kingdom buildings, this temple, dedicated to Hathor, is well preserved but unremarkable. In the New Kingdom, the chief deities of Deir el-Medina were Queen Ahmose-Nefertari and her son Amenhotep I, whose temple is just north of the Ptolemaic precinct. Adjacent is a Hathor chapel of Sety I and, opposite, are the remains of a temple of Amun built by Ramesses II.

The village can be entered from the north end. The main street is lined by terraces of houses, each long and narrow, running back to the village wall. The original 18th-Dynasty village was the length of this

main street. Where the street turns in a double bend is a later
extension. In the southern part, the house plans are not as regular.
Most houses follow much the same plan. A step goes down from the
street into the first room, which usually has an enclosed high brick
bench on one side. This was the place where women gave birth. A step
up leads into the main room of the house. This room was higher than
the others, and lit by windows just beneath the ceiling. A dais marks
the place where the owner and his wife sat, and often there is a stone
column base (the column being of wood). The wall often has a brick
'false door' and niche, which were used for the household cults,
offerings being presented to favourite deities and ancestors. The walls
were plastered (in some cases, patches survive) and the false door and
birth room would have been painted. Beyond the main room is the
master bedroom, and a corridor with stairs to the roof. At the back of
the house, against the village wall, was a courtyard, probably partly
covered. Here the cooking was done, and a deep shaft gave access to a
storage room for foodstuffs.

The cemetery lies on the steep hill surrounding the village. Two
tombs are usually accessible, and are the finest, although many others
have attractive and interesting paintings. The **Tomb of Sennedjem**
(Tomb 1) is surprising in the brightness and freshness of its colour. As
is typical of Deir el-Medina tombs, a steep staircase leads to a small
vaulted burial chamber. Although the subject matter is conventional,
the execution is superb. A rich palette, a fine hand, and perfect
preservation make this one of the most rewarding tombs to visit. The
coffins and other goods from this family tomb, which was cleared in
1886, are now displayed in Cairo Museum.

Adjacent to the chapel of Sennedjem, and almost as well-
preserved, is the **Tomb of Anherkau** (Tomb 359). A steep staircase
leads to small vaulted hall, which has good ceiling patterns (notice the
motif of a cow's head with a solar disk between its horns), and a badly
damaged scene of the tomb-owner making offerings to royal statues.
More steps lead into the burial chamber. Here the dominant colour is
gold. The painting is superb, and includes some unusual mythological
subjects: Anherkhau offering to the Bennu bird (the Egyptian
phoenix), a blue heron which was a symbol of the sun god; and the cat
of the sun god killing the evil serpent Apopis (notice here the stippling
on the cat's fur, also on the two lions on the horizon, opposite).

Dating from the late-18th−20th dynasties, these tombs have
yielded a vast quantity of information on the community of workmen
at Deir el-Medina. Families can be traced over many generations, and
their jobs and their connections with other families known. We
probably know more about the occupants of this village than any other
group in ancient Egypt.

The Valley of the Kings

A modern road runs northwards along the Dra Abu'l-Naga hills, past Carter's dig house, then twists and turns back south into the *wadi* leading to the secluded Valley of the Kings. The more energetic may climb the paths from the north side of the bay of Deir el-Bahari and over the mountain ridge into the valley (about 45 minutes to one hour), an effort amply repaid with splendid views of the Theban region.

The Valley of the Kings contains 62 excavated tombs but not all of these were royal; some belonged to privileged members of the nobility and were usually undecorated (these officials having tomb chapels in the main private necropolis). Several of these tombs have been discovered almost intact.

Changes in the plan and decoration of the royal tombs from the earliest, that of Thutmose I, to the latest, Ramesses XI, are quite clear. The earliest tombs have staircases, corridors and a right-angle bend, a plan which becomes simpler, until they are little more than huge sloping corridors.

The first of the tombs usually accessible is that of **Ramesses IX** (Tomb 6). This was never completed, the corridor beyond the four-pillared 'false burial chamber' being converted to serve as the king's resting place.

Between the Tomb of Ramesses IX and the Rest House lies the entrance to Tomb 55, one of the puzzles of Egyptology. Undecorated and now inaccessible, this tomb was excavated by Theodore Davis in 1907. Some of the contents are displayed in the Amarna room of the Cairo Museum. These include a wooden coffin inlaid with coloured stones and glass paste. Its gold mask had been ripped off in antiquity, and the names of the owner had been cut out of the inscriptions. Four alabaster canopic jars with superb female heads had been drilled to add a royal *uraeus* to the brow. Gilt-wooden panels from a funerary shrine made by Akhenaten for Queen Tiye blocked the corridor. The skeleton has, at different times over the years, been attributed to Akhenaten, Queen Tiye, and Smenkhkare who was once thought to have been the brother and short-lived successor of Akhenaten. More recently some scholars have suggested that Smenkhkare may actually be the name adopted by Nefertiti as Akhenaten's co-regent and successor. Another view has it that the burial was that of Kiya, the second wife of Akhenaten, and possibly mother of Tutankhamun. Whoever it was, this is a reburial, probably by Tutankhamun, of one or more members of Akhenaten's family.

Directly opposite is the entrance to the **Tomb of Tutankhamun** (Tomb 62), discovered by Howard Carter and Lord Carnarvon in 1922.

Most visitors leave wondering how the burial furniture was ever fitted into this cramped space. Probably carved not for the king, but for a high official (perhaps Ay), the rooms were hastily converted at Tutankhamun's early death. The paintings in the burial chamber are slightly unusual, including the dragging of the sarcophagus on a sledge by the high officials (notice the two viziers, with bald heads and loose white robes), and the Opening of the Mouth, performed by the king's successor, Ay.

Tutankhamun's tomb was concealed for many centuries beneath the mud brick houses of the workmen who cut the **Tomb of Ramesses VI**. This, one of the largest tombs in the valley, is a vast corridor sloping down to the false burial chamber with four square columns. From the floor of this room, the corridor descends further (note the large scene of the king offering to Osiris, over which the corridor continues) to the burial chamber proper. The tomb is decorated throughout with scenes from the books of the underworld. Decapitated figures marching along the walls, whole scenes which are upside down, and snakes with wings and human legs all contribute to the nightmarish vision. The burial chamber is dominated by the shattered remains of the massive granite sarcophagus, which is said to have been broken by thieves — but what sort of thieves have the means of destroying stone like this? The colonnade surrounding the chamber supports a vaulted ceiling, with its double figure of the goddess Nut in yellow against the dark sky. The sun can be seen passing through her body during the 12 hours of the night in the corresponding panels. The tomb has been open since Graeco-Roman times and there is much graffiti.

The decoration and layout of the royal tombs, seen in its ultimate form most clearly in the Tomb of Ramesses VI, actually dates back to the reign of Merneptah, the 13th son and successor of Ramesses II. The tomb of Merneptah, despite its badly damaged decoration, is worth visiting. The design is simplified, with far fewer side rooms along the corridors. The massive corridor plunges 80 metres (262.6 feet) steeply downwards to the cavernous burial chamber whose ruinous state makes it all the more impressive. An immense outer sarcophagus in the room preceding the burial chamber was never taken further down. The king's red granite anthropoid sarcophagus lies in the burial chamber. A third sarcophagus (now in the Cairo Museum) was appropriated by Psusennes I for his own burial at Tanis in the delta.

The **Tomb of Sety I** is the largest and most elaborate of the royal tombs. It is often closed because of rock falls and a lack of ventilation. Throughout the tomb, a delicate bas-relief which is characteristic of many of Sety's other monuments covers the walls with scenes from the *Book of What is in the Underworld* and the *Book of Gates*. The

corridor descends to a 'well room', a deep shaft (possibly to foil robbers, or trap rain-water) decorated with offering scenes. Beyond are two pillared halls, one a false burial chamber designed to deceive robbers. Here the decoration is unfinished, and the pillars have beautiful ink drawings of the king with various gods. To modern Western eyes, these are perhaps more satisfying than the finished, painted reliefs. The corridor descends further, from the floor of one of these chambers, passing over a second well, to an ante-room with the pillared burial chamber beyond. The king was destined to lie under the vault of heaven for eternity, its dark sky scattered with the constellations (note the pregnant hippopotamus). A number of decorated chambers surrounding this hall were used for storing the funerary furniture. Some large wooden statues of the king from here (similar to the black and gilt statues of Tutankhamun) are now in the British Museum. The tomb was first entered in modern times by Belzoni in 1817, and it was he who removed the alabaster sarcophagus and canopic chest, now in the John Soane Museum, London. A staircase descends a further 200 metres (656 feet) into the hill before being blocked by a rock fall.

Because of the brevity of his reign, the **Tomb of Ramesses I** is a single small chamber at the end of a steep corridor. It is, however, attractively painted with large figures of deities, brightly coloured on a blue-grey ground. The similarity of subject, style and colouring to the Tomb of Horemheb is striking, and the two tombs were certainly executed by the same artists.

The **Tomb of Horemheb** is transitional in its layout, from the right-angled plan of the earlier 18th Dynasty to the corridor of the 19th–20th dynasties. Not quite as elaborate as that of Sety I, it has many of the same features. Staircases and corridors lead steeply down to the well room, painted with figures of the king and gods on a blue-grey ground and almost identical to the burial chamber of Ramesses I. Beyond lie the false burial chambers. As usual, the staircase continues from the floor of one of these rooms to an ante-chamber, which duplicates the paintings of the well room above. The large pillared burial chamber is particularly interesting for its unfinished scenes. Here the Egyptian artist can be seen at work: the grid lines for laying out the design, the drawings and corrections in black and red ink, and various stages of the carving with figures abandoned half-cut. One of the small side-chambers has a handsome painted figure of Osiris.

The **Tomb of Ramesses III** was begun for his father, Sethnakht, but abandoned because the corridor cut into the adjacent tomb of Amenmesse. A small chamber allowed for the re-alignment of the axis and completion according to the typical 20th Dynasty layout. The finest and most interesting paintings are to be found in the small side-chambers near the tomb's entrance. Here are elaborate pieces of furniture, boats and Nile gods. The blind harpist (fifth room on the left) was first published by James Bruce who visited the tomb in 1769 (hence the name 'Bruce's Tomb' or the 'Harper's Tomb' given by early scholars). The large cartouche-shaped granite sarcophagus lid, removed by Belzoni, is now in the Fitzwilliam Museum in Cambridge. The king as Osiris, in very high relief, is flanked by the goddesses Isis and Nephthys. The box of the sarcophagus is in the Louvre.

Of those that can be visited, the **Tomb of Thutmose III** is the earliest, and certainly one of the most worthwhile. Situated at the end of one of the southern *wadis*, it can be reached by climbing a modern staircase, then passing through a short ravine to the entrance. The staircase and corridor, rough hewn and undecorated, lead to the well, a deep shaft now crossed by a short bridge. The ceiling is painted with stars, and the top of the walls with a simple ornamental frieze. The door into the rooms beyond would have been sealed and plastered over. The ante-chamber, supported by two square pillars, has walls covered with a textbook of 741 different divinities, its ceiling spangled with stars. Here the tomb takes a 90° turn, with the stairs to the burial chamber leading from one corner. Oval in shape, resembling a cartouche, this burial chamber is one of the loveliest in the whole valley. Far from grandiose, its decoration has an unrivalled elegance and simplicity. The painting is in the style of a funerary papyrus, with 'stick' figures in black. On one of the square columns (west pillar, north face), the king is shown with female members of his family, and in the scene below, sucking the breasts of the tree goddess. The whole is a delightful respite from the richness of the later tombs.

Situated at the southern end of another *wadi*, the **Tomb of Amenhotep II** is strikingly similar to his father's, but regularized. The ante-chamber was never painted, but the burial chamber is extremely fine. Rectangular rather than oval in shape, it is divided into two sections, the first supported by six square pillars, the furthest end of which is sunk to take the sarcophagus (*in situ*). The paintings again imitate papyrus, although within the rectangular shape of the chamber it is perhaps less effective than in the Tomb of Thutmose III. The pillars, unfinished, have large figures of the king with various deities. In many cases, only the headdress and a few details have been added in colour, but the ink drawing is elegant and its unfinished state appealing. (Compare with that of Sety I for differences in style.) Close inspection reveals some grid lines used in the layout, and occasional corrections to the figures. As in the Tomb of Thutmose III, four small chambers for the storage of funerary furniture open off the burial chamber. In the south-west chamber, Victor Loret found, in 1898, one of the caches of royal mummies. The seclusion of Amenhotep II's tomb caused it to be used by the officials who collected nine royal mummies for reburial here in the 22nd Dynasty. They included Thutmose IV, Amenhotep III, Siptah and Sety II. Amenhotep II was found still lying in his own sarcophagus.

The **Tomb of Sethnakht** is a grand ruin. In the entrance, the erased figures of Queen Tawosret, the tomb's original owner, can be seen. The burial chamber has a wrecked majesty, with the king's red granite sarcophagus lying amidst the rubble.

Several tombs belonging to officials were discovered more or less intact. Although undecorated and today inaccessible, their burial goods can be seen in the Cairo Museum. Maiherpra was a Nubian prince who was educated at the Egyptian court with the royal princes, under one of whom, Amenhotep II, he later held office. Yuya and Thuyu were the parents of Queen Tiye, the chief wife of Amenhotep III. Their tomb, discovered by Theodore Davis in 1905, contained many fine objects, including two chairs belonging to their granddaughter, the princess Sitamun.

Men and Women in Ancient Egypt

The ancient Egyptians appear to have approached life as a series of strict dichotomies. Examples of this can be seen in references to the rulers as the 'King of Upper and Lower Egypt' and their views of life and the after-life; these ideas also extended to their view of the relationship between men and women.

The role of women in Egypt can be interpreted from reliefs on tombs and the representations on statues which depicted the wife, and sometimes the mother, of the tomb-owner at the top of the familial hierarchy. The wife, usually elegantly dressed, is shown sitting at leisure with her husband accepting offerings, or accompanying him to the fields. There are statuettes of servant girls and women making bread and beer or weaving. The women are painted in yellow, (the men are a ruddy colour), suggesting they did not venture outside.

Reliefs from the early periods indicate that women generally stayed at home, although there are a few which show women playing music or performing acrobatic dances. The number of reliefs showing women increased during the New Kingdom (1570–1070 BC), perhaps because at this time they became more involved in social functions. Art from this age also shows them wearing more elaborate clothes than ever before.

However, women did not hold important titles in ancient Egypt; apart from queens and a few members of the royal family, they had little political say. Egypt's most famous queens were Hatshepsut (1498–1483 BC) and Cleopatra VII (51–30 BC).

Egyptian commoners were mainly monogamous despite the widespread notion that the men took more than one wife. However, kings and members of the royal family had many wives in addition to the 'Great Royal Wife'. Ramesses II (1279–1212 BC) is perhaps the best example; he is believed to have fathered no less than 186 children by his many wives and concubines.

Inheritance passed from father to child with no definite pattern. Women brought all their property into the marriage, but they could also make a will and leave their property to whomever they wished.

Marriage and divorce ceremonies appear to have been private affairs with no religious supervision or ritual celebration. Adultery was taboo. The main objective of marriage was to produce children who would help their parents, carry on the family line and, later, oversee their parents' mortuary cult, thus securing their passage in the after-life.

Very little is known about the exact nature of marriage customs, but it is evident that marriages to close blood relatives took place. In the royal families, there were some brother-sister and father-daughter marriages, such as those between Amenhotep III and his daughter Sat-Amun and between Ramesses II and three of his daughters, a practice carried out to enhance dynastic security.

The Valley of the Queens

The earliest tombs in the Valley of the Queens belong to the late-18th or early-19th Dynasty. The finest of the tombs, that of Nefertari, the chief wife of Ramesses II, is no longer open to visitors. Because of the rise in the water table in the Theban region, there has been extrusion of salts in the tomb, damaging the superb painted plaster.

The Valley is much smaller than the Valley of the Kings, but is ringed by impressive cliffs. Recent excavations have uncovered many previously unknown tombs, although most are undecorated or badly damaged. The accessible tombs belong to the 20th Dynasty.

The **Tomb of Queen Titi**, an otherwise unknown royal lady, has sunk relief in delicate colours, but not all of it is well preserved. One of the more interesting scenes shows Hathor as the goddess of the Western Mountain (i.e. the Theban necropolis) emerging from the hill. The golden cow, following Egyptian convention, is actually superimposed upon the hill, which is shown in bands of pink with stippling to represent the rock. The remainder of the tomb is decorated with mythological subjects and figures of the queen with various deities. In the first corridor, the figures are on a white background, but in the room beyond a richer effect is achieved with a golden ground.

The painted relief in the **Tomb of Prince Amenhirkhepeshef** is notable for its vivid colouring. Whilst bright and fresh, the palette lacks some of the subtlety of earlier work. Note the use of oranges, as well as very bright blues, turquoises and greens. The first chamber, the tomb's finest, has large figures of the prince being introduced to various gods by his father. Here the richly patterned and coloured robes of the prince and his father, Ramesses III, are well conveyed. Various scenes from the *Book of Gates* fill the corridor beyond. The burial chamber has an uninscribed granite sarcophagus.

The decoration of the **Tomb of Prince Sethirkhepeshef**, another son of Ramesses III, is very similar, but badly darkened by smoke. Also similar in decoration, though with a slightly more elaborate plan, is the **Tomb of Prince Khaemwaset**, Ramesses III's eldest son. The first corridor again has scenes of the king introducing his son to the gods, and the second scenes from the *Book of Gates*. Two small rooms lie off the first corridor. Here the prince is shown making offerings to the funerary goddesses, Isis, Nephthys, Selket and Neith, who are all painted a rather bright turquoise.

The Temple of Sety I at Qurna

East of the Valley of the Kings, along the edge of the cultivated plains at the foot of the rocky slope stood the cult sites neatly separated from the graves. Imposing ruins remain of these grandiose temples which were also referred to as the 'castles of a million years'.

The northernmost monument along the border of the Theban necropolis is the temple at Qurna dedicated to the Theban god Amun-Ra, which was begun by Sety I and completed by Ramesses II.

Access was originally through a walkway lined with sphinxes and included two courtyards, each preceded by a pylon. Of this part only a few traces remain, and the façade is now made up of the bottom porch of the second courtyard with nine papyrus-shaped columns. The reliefs in the interior of the porch represent Sety I and Ramesses II making offerings to the Theban triad and to other divinities. On the lower portion, a procession of the Nile's inhabitants offer the products of the provinces of the north and south to Ramesses II.

The interior of the temple is divided into three parts. The central area is formed by a hypostyle hall with six lotus-shaped columns decorated with offertory scenes and encircled by six small rooms with adoration, offertory and purification scenes, and a sanctuary (badly ruined) for the sacred boat. The right part includes a courtyard with two side porches and an altar for the sun cult in the centre. The left part, the more interesting, was consecrated by Sety I to his father Ramesses I, and was completed by Ramesses II. The hypostyle hall as well as the three rooms at the bottom are adorned with scenes of a religious character: the representation of the king to the gods, offering, worshipping and, in the central room designed for the sacred boat, Sety I offering incense to the boat of Amun.

Medinet Habu

The Royal Pavilion which constitutes the main entrance to Ramesses III's temple, is in fact a triumphal entrance gate in military style, imitating the Asian fortresses besieged by the sovereign. The building is made up of two towers, united in their upper parts, with small windows and crowned by half-circled battlements. Two sets of prisoners representing the populaces of the north and south are carved in relief on the base, and other scenes of a military character complete the decoration. The interior, divided into two floors, bears scenes from the king's harem. To the left, towards Ramesses III's temple, is the small **Temple of the God's Wives of Amun**, containing the funerary shrines of queens and princesses of the 25th and 26th dynasties. The sanctuary has a vaulted ceiling, the first-known example of a stonework vault. At the other end of the large courtyard of Medinet Habu is the **Temple of the 18th Dynasty**, enclosed by its own fence, but later included within the great enclosure of Ramesses III. Started by Amenhotep I and continued under Thutmose I, the temple was

enlarged by Thutmose II and later by Hatshepsut and Thutmose III. Expansion followed until the Ptolemaic and Roman epochs, ensuring the continuity of the temple through more than 15 centuries.

The most grandiose building in Medinet Habu, and one of the most important of all in Theban architecture, is the funerary **Temple of Ramesses III**. It has a harmonious unified plan, being planned and finished during the reign of the sovereign. The temple remained unaltered by subsequent rulers. Later, it was occupied by Copts until the Arab conquest. The temple, inspired by the Ramesseum, has two consecutive courtyards with Osiride pillared porticos both preceded by a pylon and a sanctuary with three hypostyle halls and the *naos*, all surrounded by chapels. The first bears military scenes depicting the victories of Ramesses III over the Sea Peoples (a confederation of peoples of the Mediterranean). The inner face of the pylon exhibits more military scenes: the bottom walls of the porticos on the northeast side are decorated with religious subjects, while the south-west side was once the façade of the royal palace. This was connected to the temple through three doors and a balcony or tribune from which the king was able to observe processions taking place in the first courtyard. The walls of this side are decorated with scenes of the massacre of prisoners, struggle, and horse racing. The façade of the second pylon is also consecrated to the military exploits of Ramesses III in a long commemorative text. The second courtyard pillars still maintain ample coloured areas, as well as ceilings decorated with images of the vulture goddess Nekhbet with spread wings, and the bas-reliefs of the fourth porches. Representations on the walls can be divided into two series. The first, military, shows a battle against the Sea Peoples, the counting of hands and genitals cut from dead enemies, the return of the king with troops and prisoners, and the offering of prisoners to the gods, with a text praising the king's valour. The second, religious, shows the procession and adoration of the sacred boat, and ceremonies in honour of the god Min. Only the lower portions of the columns in the great hypostyle hall are well-preserved. The rest of the temple is in a state of disrepair, having been used as a quarry for building materials. The surrounding rooms were in part designed as a repository for the treasures of the temple (to the left). Outside the temple, south-west of the first pylon, is a beautiful representation of wild ox hunting in the marshes. Scenes of a succession of expeditions by Ramesses III in the Upper Nile area and on the Mediterranean coast against the Sea Peoples can still be seen. On the north side is the famous battle between the Egyptians and the hostile fleet. There are also scenes with religious themes, such as the long procession of offering priests and the religious calendar, establishing the dates of feasts and holidays to be celebrated at the temple.

Deir el-Bahari

One of the most splendid examples of royal mortuary temples is certainly the **Temple of Queen Hatshepsut** which, due to its strategic position, its architectural plan and the high quality of its execution, is one of the most notable monuments of Egyptian architecture. The modern name of the site is 'the Convent of the North' after the Coptic monastery later built within the same temple.

The mountain range encircling the temple was consecrated to the goddess Hathor, often depicted as a cow with the typical crown formed by a solar-disk between two lyre-shaped horns, here coming out from the mountain to the west of Luxor, seat of the necropolis. The place had been chosen by the sovereigns of the 11th Dynasty for their burials, and the remains of a majestic temple erected for Nebhepetre-Mentuhotep are still visible on the south side of Hatshepsut's building. A pathway on the ridge links Deir el-Bahari to the Valley of the Kings. A path flanked by sphinxes leads to the ample courtyard of the temple which was divided into various terraces connected by ramps preceding a rock-cut shrine. The terraces, cut into the slopes of the mountain, rest on porticos the walls of which are decorated with high-quality reliefs showing various events which Hatshepsut felt were worthy of being recorded. Unfortunately, the reliefs have suffered extensive damage, both in ancient and more recent times. On the lower terrace (south side, far southern end) is a scene of the transportation of two obelisks from Aswan to Thebes on an enormous river-barge. The short south wall of the lower terrace (the northern side) has a large figure of Hatshepsut as a sphinx trampling her enemies, erased in ancient times, but still just visible. The reliefs of the main terrace are better preserved with, on the northern half, the divine conception and birth of Hatshepsut; Amun visiting Queen Ahmose; Khnum fashioning Hatshepsut on the potter's wheel; and a pregnant Queen Ahmose being conducted to the birth-couch by the frog-headed goddess Heket.

On the south side are depicted the expedition to the land of Punt, one of the most remarkable events of Hatshepsut's reign: the arrival of the Egyptian ships, the exchange of Egyptian handicrafts with local products, valuable materials, rare animals, resins, antimony for the eyes, gold, ivory, panther skins, monkeys, a giraffe and felines of various kinds for hunting. The Queen of Punt is depicted as being enormously obese, but opinion is divided about whether this is elephantiasis, or, as in many African countries, an indication of her wealth. The original block (here replaced with a cast) is in the Cairo Museum.

At the southern end is a rock-cut chapel dedicated to Hathor, with a hypostyle entrance with Hathorian pillars; that is, with capitals portraying the face of the goddess. The bas-reliefs are related to the feasts in honour of Hathor: parades of ships and soldiers, sacrificial, worship and offering scenes. The goddess is depicted as a cow nursing the queen. The architect Senenmut, designer of the entire temple, is himself represented by images hidden in various points of the numerous niches of the chapel. The portico of the third terrace is formed by pillars with the statues of the king as Osiris. This part of the temple suffered considerable damage at the hands of Thutmose III. The whole complex, on the other hand, has been restored, and many parts reconstructed to the south. From the courtyard of the third terrace there is access to the funerary chapel of Hatshepsut and of her father Thutmose I and, to the north, to a complex of buildings consecrated to the cult of the solar-god Ra-Harakhty. In the centre is the principal sanctuary, completed during the Ptolemaic age.

To the right of the avenue leading to the temple, in a depression used as a clay cave during the New Kingdom, the tomb of the architect Senenmut was discovered. It has a chamber whose ceiling has an astronomic decoration representing the various constellations (see the tomb of Sety I in the Valley of Kings). This tomb remained unfinished, perhaps because Senenmut fell from the queen's grace and was buried in another tomb, at Sheikh Abd el-Qurna. Between the upper terrace of Hatshepsut's temple and Mentuhotep's temple (11th Dynasty) are the ruins of a temple of Thutmose III. South-west of the circle of Deir el-Bahari is the hiding place of the royal mummies (now in Cairo Museum) discovered by Maspero in 1881; these were grouped within a deep *hypogeum* during the 21st Dynasty to protect them from pillagers.

A second discovery took place in 1891, east of the tomb of Senenmut, where the sarcophagi of the High Priests of Amon and Khonsu had been hidden.

The Ramesseum

The Ramesseum, the funerary temple of Ramesses II, stands about 500 metres (547 yards) from the necropolis of Sheikh Abd el-Qurna at the edge of the cultivated plains on the west bank of the Nile. Once one of the most beautiful temples of ancient Egypt it now lies in ruins with the colossus of Ramesses II strewn across its courtyard. The edifice is composed of two large courtyards each with a pylon, a big hypostyle hall or 'hall of appearances', three small hypostyle halls, a sanctuary surrounded by a series of small rooms, and crypts.

A part of the first pylon still stands and shows great military scenes relating Ramesses II's campaigns against the Syrians and Hittites, and the Battle of Kadesh. In front of the second pylon, to the left of the portal, lie the remains of the statue of Ramesses II. Its original height was probably about 17 metres (55.8 feet) and its weight more than 1,000 tonnes. It was one of the largest statues in Egypt and is perhaps the main attraction on the site, simply because of its size. The ear, for example, is 1.2 metres (3.9 feet) long.

The second courtyard, in a better state of preservation, had a double colonnade on its sides. The second pylon to the north inner face, reproduces the battle of Kadesh for the second time and, in the upper part, a countryside feast in honour of the god Min. The ample hypostyle hall has a central nave with bell-shaped columns and smaller papyrus-shaped columns on the sides. One of the walls bears decorations representing the siege and occupation of a Hittite fortress. Of the inner rooms, only two hypostyle halls remain: the first has a ceiling decorated with astronomic figures (divinities of the major constellations and stars), and walls depicting the transportation of Amun's boat. There is also a representation of the tree symbolizing the strength and duration of the royal family, with the gods Atum and Thoth on its sides, and the goddess of writing, Seshat, tracing the royal cartouche on the fruits, in the centre. Around the temple, on three sides, are the dependencies, buildings in unburnt bricks bearing the mark of Ramesses II's cartouches, designed as storerooms and for other services. The buildings were used as a school for scribes, shown by the *ostracas* and papyri with writing exercies on them.

The Colossi of Memnon

These two famous statues portraying King Amenhotep III once flanked the monumental entrance of the funerary temple of the Pharaoh. Carved from a single block of very compact sandstone, both statues stand 15.6 metres (51.2 feet) high on a base of 2.3 metres (7.5 feet). The upper portion of the northern statue underwent restorations, with the use of common sandstone, in the early third century AD. The throne is decorated on both sides with the figures of the two Niles of Lower and Upper Egypt and on both sides of the sovereigns's legs are the sculpted figures of his mother, Mutemuia, and his spouse, Tiye. The little that remains of the temple includes a stele in sandstone, broken in two and containing the act of consecration of the temple to Amun.

The two colossi enjoyed great fame in the ancient world, especially during the first two centuries AD. The Greeks identified them with Memnon, son of Titon and Dawn. Following the earthquake of AD 27 which probably destroyed the temple, the upper part of the north colossus broke into pieces, creating a strange acoustic phenomenon when the stone expanded under the hot morning sun. This in turn created interesting legends about the statue: Memnon, felled by Achilles according to the Homeric narration, was brought to life every morning by the sight of his mother, Dawn. The ancient Greek and Roman tourists, among whom were the Emperor Hadrian and the Empress Sabina, were attracted in large crowds by this peculiarity, as documented by the inscriptions on the same statue. The phenomenon ceased after the restoration ordered by the Roman emperor Settimius Severus.

UPPER EGYPT

Esna

Esna is a large village 54 kilometres (33.5 miles) south of Luxor on the west bank of the Nile. A large hypostyle room is all that remains of a temple started here by Ptolemy VI (170–164 BC) but completed under Emperor Claudius in the first century AD. Most of the Roman emperors contributed to the enrichment of the sanctuary. The temple is dedicated to Khnum, the ram-god, creator of the world. The walls and columns are completely covered with texts and figures of religious significance. Aside from a synthesis of past mythological traditions, there are hymns dedicated to Khnum, to rams and crocodiles, and numerous re-enactments of festive rituals. The first feast of Esna celebrated the creation of the universe by Khnum. In this version of creation, Khnum populated the earth with living beings thrown on a potter's wheel, established royalty and the god-Pharaohs, and finally gave the female being the power to bear life.

The archaeological site of **el-Kab** is situated on the east bank of the Nile, about 20 kilometres (12 miles) north of Edfu. An impressive wall made of mud bricks encloses the ruins of the ancient town and large temples. Inhabited since Palaeolithic times, the city of el-Kab was the major religious centre of the pre-dynastic age. It was sacred to the goddess Nekhbet, who was represented as a vulture and used as the symbol of Upper Egypt.

Among the other major monuments in the area are the rock tombs in the hills east of the city, belonging to high-ranking officials of the Second Intermediate Period and the beginning of the 18th Dynasty. In these tombs were found historical evidence of the military operations which guided the country to freedom from the Hyksos.

Edfu

Edfu which lies 100 kilometres (62 miles) south of Luxor is the site of one of the greatest and best-preserved temples of ancient Egypt. The temple, which is dedicated to Horus, was, until the middle of the last century, completely buried. It was only cleared of debris by Auguste Mariette in 1860. The **Temple of Horus**, completed during the Ptolemaic age (305–30 BC) on the site of an older sanctuary, is the second largest temple after that of Karnak. Its inscriptions have provided a wealth of information on the founding of similar temples and their construction as well as the use of daily rituals and myths of ancient origin. The great pylon, 36 metres (118 feet) high, contains rooms on four floors.

A stairway inside the pylon leads to the 'Balcony of Apparition' where the sacred falcon of Horus was presented to the crowd. Two statues made of black granite representing the holy bird stand by the sides of the gate, and two others stand in front of the entrance of the first hypostyle room.

Like most Ptolemaic temples, Edfu follows the 'classical' plan: a large porticoed courtyard, two hypostyle rooms, two lobbies, a sanctuary surrounded by chapels, and the entire complex is enclosed within a wall forming a narrow corridor around the temple. The decoration is also typical of Ptolemaic temples in that it is of an exclusively religious and mythological character. The columns surrounding the courtyard on three sides have different capitals, but are similar to those on the opposite side. The façade of the first hypostyle hall has six columns connected to each other by a wall on the lower half. The columns are decorated with scenes of offering on various registers. At the sides of the entrance are two chapels, one a vestry and the other a library.

The second hypostyle room with 12 columns, is connected by two doors to the corridor outside the sanctuary; one of the doors is for the solid food offerings, and the other is for the liquid offerings. A small room within the same hypostyle was used as a perfume laboratory, and its walls reveal lengthy formulae for the various ceremonial unguents. Next to this is the room of the offering, with two stairways leading to a terrace: at the north-western corner of this room was a kiosk where the god's statues were exposed to the rays of the sun during the New Year festivities. To the right of the room of the offerings is a courtyard with an altar and a chapel where the rituals for the consecration of the divine statues were performed. The sanctuary, preceded by another room, holds the monolithic *naos* of grey granite, four metres (13 feet) high, built by Nectanebo I (30th Dynasty). In the corridor around the sanctuary are ten rooms, one of which is the Room of the Fabric. The others are chapels dedicated to Osiris and other divinities, and the central one contained sacred emblems, including the golden *sistrum*, the symbol of the goddess Hathor. In the outer corridor, on the east side, a stairway leads to one of the many nilometers (built to measure the level of the Nile). The external walls of the temple and the internal walls of the boundary wall are covered with writings and paintings showing several feasts celebrated in Edfu. The Egyptian feasts were not commemorations of an event, but rather re-enactments of events that were believed necessary for the preservation of the world. These were carried out periodically because their beneficial effects were believed to diminish with the passing of time. The *mammisi* (birth-houses), also of the Ptolemaic age, face the temple.

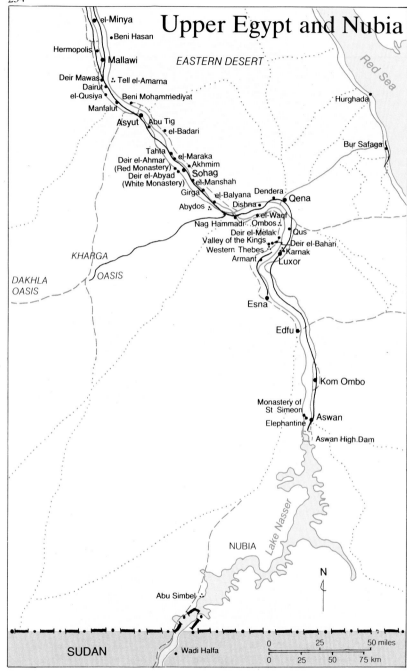

Upper Egypt and Nubia

EASTERN DESERT

Red Sea

el-Minya
Beni Hasan
Hermopolis
Mallawi
Deir Mawas
Dairut
Tell el-Amarna
el-Qusiya
Manfalut
Beni Mohammediyat
Hurghada
Asyut
Abu Tig
el-Badari
Bur Safaga
Tahta
el-Maraka
Deir el-Ahmar
(Red Monastery)
Akhmim
Deir el-Abyad
(White Monastery)
Sohag
el-Manshah
Girga
el-Balyana
Dendera
Abydos
Dishna
Qena
Nag Hammadi
el-Waqf
Ombos
KHARGA
OASIS
Deir el-Melak
Qus
Valley of the Kings
Deir el-Bahari
Western Thebes
Karnak
DAKHLA
OASIS
Armant
Luxor

Esna

Edfu

Kom Ombo

Monastery of
St Simeon
Aswan
Elephantine
Aswan High Dam

Lake Nasser

NUBIA

N

Abu Simbel

SUDAN
Wadi Halfa

0   25   50 miles

0   25   50   75 km

Five kilometres (3.1 miles) west of Edfu, tombs of local princes have been excavated. Underneath the present village lie the remains of the annexes around the main building: the chapels of the sacred falcon and other divinities, the sacred lake, the houses of the priests, storehouses, laboratories, shops, kitchens and stables.

Kom Ombo

Kom Ombo, 40 kilometres (25 miles) north of Aswan, has been since earliest times the exit point of caravan routes from Sudan through the Libyan and Arabian deserts. The town of Ombos gained administrative importance during the Ptolemaic age as it protected the southern border. In the Roman period it was a military station. Today at Kom Ombo one can visit the imposing remains of a temple built in the Ptolemaic-Roman age, situated on a promontory dominating the Nile. The temple has a double sanctuary and is dedicated to two divinities, Haroeris (Horus the Elder), and Sobek, the crocodile-god. The daily cult was celebrated simultaneously for the two divinities, while the calendar of the feasts gave more importance to Haroeris. The religious texts written on the walls define the sacred elements of the temple itself and the relations between the gods, especially in myths. Among the drawings, nearly all ritual, there is an interesting relief of surgical tools of the Roman age. Aside from the major temple in Kom Ombo, there are *mammisi*, a chapel to Hathor, and the remains of Coptic buildings and hydraulic installations used to fill a basin where the sacred crocodiles were kept. The official tombs of crocodiles and snakes were enclosed in the temple, but in the same area were also found cemeteries for falcons and ibises, sacred throughout Egypt, together with the mummies of several kinds of animals.

Today one can see mummified crocodiles piled up like logs of wood inside a small side chapel. Since the building of the Aswan dam in 1964, crocodiles are no longer found this far north.

Aswan

Aswan is situated at the gates of what was once Lower Nubia (now taken over by the vast basin of Lake Nasser which was created by the damming of the Nile). Aswan is believed to have been simply the market of a city which flourished on the island of Elephantine across the water, and its name does not appear in the texts until the 20th Dynasty. During the Persian era (27th Dynasty), it attained considerable importance and its name is mentioned repeatedly in the texts of Aramaic papyri from Elephantine. Scant vestiges of ancient Aswan stand in the southern section of the modern city, around the

Ptolemaic Temple of Isis. The sensational discovery in the surrounding area of three sandstone sarcophagi, adorned with Egyptian funerary representations with inscriptions in Aramaic, indicates links between the Jewish colony of Elephantine and this city. To the south are the renowned quarries of red and black granite. The famous Unfinished Obelisk, around 41.75 metres (137 feet) long and an estimated 1,168 tonnes which was abandoned because of a fissure in the stone, serves to illustrate how massive blocks were quarried. An interesting but much smaller obelisk of Sety I still lies today at its excavation site.

The High Dam completed in 1964, is a mammoth project aimed at controlling the flow of the Nile and its floods which, in the past, have determined whether there would be drowning of the crops or famine. The dam measures 42.7 billion cubic metres (1,508 billion cubic feet), a volume 16 times that of the Pyramid of Cheops at Giza. Lake Nasser, an artificial lake which was created by the waters behind it, has a maximum storage capacity of 157 billion cubic metres (5,545 billion cubic feet).

Though the project has succeeded in controlling the annual floods of the Nile and helped to provide work for the local population of Upper Egypt, it has had an adverse effect on the ecology of the area. Fertile silt, which once was deposited along the Nile's banks, is now gathering behind the lake, and rain has fallen in the area for the first time in centuries. The dam's worst threat, however, has been to ancient sites in the valley such as Abu Simbel and Philae, which would have been completely covered by water had they not been moved to new sites.

Elephantine

Elephantine was the name given by the Greeks to the island in front of Aswan, one of the largest in the Nile. In Egyptian, it is known as 'Abu' or the 'Land of the Elephant'. Situated at a strategic point north of the First Cataract along the southern frontier, an important city dating back to the Old Kingdom was established on the southernmost tip of the island over a prominent granite rock formation. It later became the capital of the first *nome* (or province) of Upper Egypt, and its *nomarchs* (or governors) came to be known as the 'Guardians of the Southern Gates'. The city was inhabited from prehistoric times up to the beginning of the Arab epoch. A vast number of archaeological treasures from this area were already being sent to museums as early as the last century, although thorough and serious excavations were begun only in the early 1900s following the discovery of Aramaic papyri. In 1946, the eminent Egyptologist Labib Habachi excavated

the temple of Heqaib, a deified monarch, uncovering stelae, statues and tombs, the inscriptions of which are a primary source of information about local history from the 11th to the 13th dynasties. Since 1969, the area has been entrusted to the German Archaeological Institute and the Swiss Institute of Cairo.

The New Kingdom saw Elephantine's rise as a religious centre. A number of rulers of the 18th and 19th dynasties erected temples or enlarged and embellished those already in existence. Two magnificent temples, one of Amenhotep III and the other of Ramesses II, were intact until the beginning of the 1800s, when they were demolished by a local governor. The presence of other edifices was revealed by the uncovering of the foundations of the Sanctuary of Satet. Elephantine retained its importance in later times when it took on the role of a frontier station and was the site of a Jewish court.

By the end of Pharaonic rule in the 30th Dynasty, the **Temple of Khnum**, the ram-headed god whom ancient Egyptians believed was responsible for the annual flooding of the Nile, had been entirely reconstructed. Khnum, the 'Lord of the Region of the Cataract', was accompanied by Satet, the 'Lady of Elephantine' (whose cults probably date back to prehistory) and by Anuket of Sehel (an island south of Elephantine). Since the annual floods rendered the land fertile, the priests of Khnum considered it their right and special privelege to partake of income from the annual harvests. Lavishly decorated tombs with gilded sarcophagi contained in huge cases of stone in a particular necropolis were reserved for the animals sacred to Khnum, particularly the rams.

Elephantine was one of the stations where the flood level was measured, the assessment of which defined the variable tax rates imposed on the citizens. A **nilometer**, connected with the sacred lake of the Temple of Khnum, was created for this purpose. The nilometer allowed experts to forecast the time and size of the impending floods of the Nile. The one here has a staircase of 90 steps descending into the Nile. Usually, the steps go below the water-level into a pit which has a graduated column to help determine how much the water would rise.

The island of Elephantine also houses the **Museum of Aswan**, which contains a small but interesting collection of local and Nubian treasures and artifacts. There are various plans and studies to organize a grand-scale museum of Nubia which, among other things, will document the feverish race against time to save the region's threatened archaeological monuments following the construction of the Aswan High Dam.

Along the west bank of the Nile are **rock tombs** of local governors or nomarchs and their high officials. These are important sources of

information spanning the years from the Sixth Dynasty until the Middle Kingdom and they reveal interesting texts describing commercial expeditions to Nubia, the import of valuable goods, and curious attractions such as a pygmy transported by Harkhuf for King Pepy II. There are also records of military expeditions for the conquest of Nubia which took place under Senusret III. The most important of these tombs are those of Sarenput I and II, Heqaib and Harkhuf.

On the eastern bank of the river rises the lovely **mausoleum of the Aga Khan**, built in pink sandstone and crowned by a small cupola. To the north is the majestic Monastery of St Simeon, one of Egypt's largest and most imposing Christian edifices. It is securely bordered by massive walls, creating an impregnable fortress. The church houses precious remnants of paintings dating back to the ninth century.

Kitchener Island, situated between Elephantine and the left bank of the Nile, has a wonderful collection of exotic plants and tropical flowers from Africa. Further to the south, dominating the First Cataract is the island of **Sehel**, which boasts granite rock formations covered with over 200 ancient inscriptions which record visits by royal functionaries and dignitaries. At a higher level is incised the so-called Stele of Famine, with a text dating back to the Ptolemaic era, referring to a famine during Zoser's reign. The famine was said to have been relieved by the prayers of the king to the god Khnum.

Nubia is the region extending between Aswan and Khartoum, capital of Sudan. It can be divided into Lower Nubia, the northern part up to Wadi Halfa, which is now completely submerged by the waters of the basin created by the High Dam, and Upper Nubia to the south. After the end of the Old Kingdom, Egyptians organized commercial expeditions to Nubia. Later, during the Middle Kingdom, it was occupied by the armies of Senusret I and III. Imposing fortresses were built, and Egyptian dominion lasted throughout the New Kingdom (except during the Hyksos period).

Many Egyptians settled in Nubia during these centuries, creating towns and villages (some of which were seats of administrative offices) at the outlet of the valleys, where there were particularly favourable conditions for agriculture and commercial exchanges with the Sahara oases and the Red Sea ports. In addition, the Nubian deserts were rich with gold mines and quarries for precious stones. After the New Kingdom, in about 1100 BC, Nubia ceased to be dependent on Egypt and broke up into two territories which were separated by a border passing through Maharakka.

The northern part of Nubia continued to be heavily influenced by the Egyptians until it was directly annexed to the Ptolemaic kingdom and, later, to the Roman Empire. Under the emperor Diocletian, the border was moved from Maharakka to Philae because of the increasingly frequent raids of the southern tribes (the Blemmyes and Nobates).

The southern territory became an autonomous monarchy from 750 BC, and at various times its sovereigns attempted to conquer Egypt. A culture with strong Egyptian influences, based on Napata and Meroe, developed in about 300 BC. Prosperous towns, Nubian in their basic structures but with Hellenic and Egyptian influences, flourished. The kingdom ended in about AD 350 because of the pressure exerted on it by the southern populations and the tribes of Blemmyes and Nobates from Nubia which had settled in the region around Aswan in 150.

Not far from the High Dam is the temple dedicated to the local god Mandulis, 40 kilometres (24.8 miles) south of its present location in **Kalabsha**. The complicated task of dismantling and reconstructing the temple was accomplished in 1970 by a German company with the financial support of the West German government. The temple is Roman, perhaps built on the site of a chapel of Amenhotep II. All the traditional elements of the Egyptian temple architecture are present: a pylon, porched courtyard, hypostyle hall and *naos*. The hypostyle hall included 12 columns with bell-shaped capitals richly decorated with floral patterns. On the column to the right of the entrance is a long Meroitic inscription, still undeciphered. A nearby text narrates the Nubian king Silko's expeditions against the nomadic tribes of the Blemmyes and the occupation of the region. The *naos*, transformed into a church towards the end of the fourth century BC comprises three successive chambers, and a staircase links the first of these to the terrace. The wall decoration shows Emperor Augustus making an offering to the Egyptian gods, among whom is the solar god Mandulis. In the last chamber, the sanctuary proper, the freshness of the relief has been preserved. A stone wall encircles the temple forming a sort of walkway; to the south are the remains of a nilometer in a good state of preservation.

On a small hill south of the temple rises the graceful **Kiosk of Kertassi**, originally located 30 kilometres (18.6 miles) south. Not far to the north-west, is the little rock temple of Beit el-Wali, 'the House of the Saint', erected by Ramesses II some 40 kilometres (24.8 miles) to the south and rebuilt at this location at the same time as the temple of Mandulis.

The temple includes a *naos*, re-used in the Christian epoch and decorated with religious subjects, preceded by a vestibule linked to an open courtyard, the walls of which are decorated with military scenes depicting Ramesses II's victories over Asians, Libyans and Nubians.

Philae

On the island of **Philae** ('Pearl of the Nile'), situated between the High Dam and the dam built last century, was the sacred complex of monuments built for the cults of Isis and Osiris. Philae was begun under the Ptolemies and finished in Roman times. It also incorporated some work done by Nectanebo. It is at Philae that the last-known inscription in hieroglyphs (dating back to AD 394) was found. The monuments of Philae suffered periodic and progressive submersions after the construction of the first dam in 1898 and would have been totally covered by waters from the High Dam but for action by UNESCO to raise the funds necessary to save the ruins. One by one the stones were removed to the nearby higher islands of Agilkia, where the area's original setting and orientation were recreated.

The Sanctuary, dating to the Ptolemaic age, was built on the site of an ancient chapel of Isis at the centre of the island and was later enlarged towards the south by the erection of a monumental *dromos* (sacred avenue) flanked by two arcades. The cult of Isis lasted in Philae until the Christian age. After the Edict of Constantine (AD 313), Philae became the most stable stronghold of paganism which was still widely practised in the Egyptian countryside. The strongest supporters of the pagan cult were the Blemmyes, nomadic inhabitants of the southern desert who frequently engaged in devastating raids into Upper Egypt. It was not until the middle of the fifth century that they were defeated by the Romans, with whom they concluded a 100-year truce allowing them to maintain their sanctuary in Philae. The pagan cult was crushed by the Byzantine emperor Justinian (527–65); and the temple was transformed into a church consecrated to St Stephen. During the following two centuries, other Coptic churches were erected on the island.

The dismantling of monuments in Philae brought to light a number of existing structures, the more remarkable of which date to the Saïte Age: a **Kiosk of Psamcik II**, discovered in the foundations of the wall on the western side of the Sanctuary and the stones of the temple of Amasis (570–525 BC), re-used in the construction of the pillars and the columns of the *pronaos*.

The **Kiosk of Nectanebo I** (378–360 BC), at the southern end of the island, is the only pre-Ptolemaic building still standing. It was probably relocated to its present position at the entrance of the *dromos* during the complete rearrangement of the area in the Roman age. The portal of the first pylon also goes back to the time of Nectanebo I. The *dromos* is flanked by two arcades, with column capitals decorated with various scenes. The eastern arcade is unfinished, while the western one, on the border of the balcony facing the river, has on the columns and the bottom wall scenes of the sovereigns making offerings to the divinities. The cartouches are of Augustus (the builder), Tiberius, Caligula, Claudius and Nero.

In front of the **Temple of Isis** is a first pylon, which shows the usual scene of the god-king subduing enemies. The king here is Ptolemy XII, and the gods are Isis, Horus of Edfu and Hathor. In front of the pylon stood two obelisks of Ptolemy II, later taken to England by the consul general Bankes in 1815. Two granite lions still guard the place. Inside the central portal, to the west, is a memorial inscription of the Napoleonic expedition. A secondary door, on the western side of the pylon, leads to the *mammisi* which encloses the courtyard of Isis' temple on one side.

On the other side of the courtyard is a building with six rooms fronted by an arcade with ten columns, the 'Annexes of Tiberius' (scrolls of Tiberius and Neos Dionysos) which probably served as a sacristy. Another room was set apart as a library. The temple has three rooms connected to each other, preceded by a *pronaos*; it is surrounded by an arcade to the north and to the east. It was started by Ptolemy II and completed under Tiberius. The pictures refer to the birth, childhood and education of Horus. Higher up, outside the eastern wall of the *pronaos*, are two bilingual inscriptions (in Hieroglyphic and Demotic characters), one of which is the reproduction of the decree carved on the famous Rosetta Stone. The second pylon of the Temple of Isis is not parallel to the first one; to its right a rock was incorporated, cut vertically to bring it to the level of the wall and engraved with a memorial inscription about a donation to the temple by Ptolemy VI. The *pronaos* follows, formed by a hypostyle room with ten columns, opening into a central courtyard. Astronomic, mythological and ritual pictures decorate the walls and columns. During the Christian age, this part of the temple was transformed into a church.

The *naos* consists of 12 rooms and a crypt decorated with scenes of offerings and liturgical pictures. In the sanctuary is an *aedicule* made of granite and a stairway leads from the balcony to the funerary chapel of Isis/Osiris.

West of the temple, at the same height as the second pylon, is the 'Gate of Hadrian and Marcus Aurelius' which, in the original site, faced the island of Biga.

In the middle, on the western side of the island, is a nilometer. To the north are the remains of Roman buildings which include a chapel of Augustus where the first trilingual stele (in Egyptian, Greek and Latin) was discovered. The stele which commemorates the first Roman military expedition to the Nile, is of Cornelius Gallus, the first prefect of Egypt under Augustus. To the east lies a small temple of Hathor with reliefs and texts of joyous subjects which include the picture of the god Bes (represented as a dwarf), symbols of joy and love, scenes with musicians, and a monkey playing the lute. To the south-east of this is the Kiosk of Trajan, a building composed of an arcade with 14 columns linked (apart from the two doors on the short sides) by partially decorated intercolumns. It was designed as a monumental entrance for the processions of Isis.

Abu Simbel

Abu Simbel, situated 240 kilometres (149 miles) south of Aswan in what was formerly almost trackless Nubian desert, is the last and mightiest site of a string of temples from the New Kingdom, most of which were built by Ramesses II. Before air travel, the only way to get to Abu Simbel was by steamer along the Nile or by camel. Today, you can get there by plane from Aswan in half an hour. What you see today, however, is the re-sited Temple of Abu Simbel, which, threatened by the waters of the High Dam, was cut out of the cliffs in manageable blocks and moved to higher ground. The five-year operation, which cost US$9 million, was completed in 1968.

The **South** or **Great Temple** was built in honour of Ramesses II during the 19th Dynasty. Cut in the rock and of gigantic proportions, the structure is a veritable *tour de force* commensurate with the megalomaniacal aspirations of Ramesses II. During this period, Egypt experienced a decline in her influence abroad as the Hittites became more powerful. In an effort to honour and celebrate the glory of Egypt, the kings of that period embarked on building programmes similar in scope and scale to the activity of the pyramid age.

Four colossal rock-cut statues of Ramesses II sit enthroned at the entrance to the temple with the façade shaped into a pylon. Running across the top of the pylon is a frieze of 24 seated baboons. In a niche above the entrance stands a large statue of the god Ra, the sun god with the head of a hawk. It was built on a strict east-west axis so that the morning sun actually reached the innermost sanctuary at dawn, illuminating the statues of Ptah, Amun, Ramesses II deified, and Ra-Horakhty.

The interior walls are completely covered with reliefs depicting religious and secular themes, the most interesting being the battle scene recording the victories of Ramesses II over a variety of foes and another version of the Battle of Kadesh. The nave ceiling is decorated with spread-winged vultures representing the goddess Nekhbet.

A stele between the two last pillars of the atrium dates back to the 35th year of Ramesses II's reign and lists all the buildings erected by the sovereign in honour of Ptah, patron of Memphis.

A vestibule in front of the sanctuary proper has four pillars decorated with images of the king protected by various divinities. The walls bear offertory and liturgical scenes. The sanctuary itself has an altar in the middle as well as four statues carved into the rock representing, respectively, Ra-Harakhty (Horus in the Horizon), a deified Ramesses II, Amun and Ptah. Eight other narrow and low-ceilinged rooms, unfinished, were used as storerooms for religious ornaments. On the exterior of the temple are many stelae carved into the rock, commemorating various episodes related to the king's life: the third from the south, called 'Marriage Stele', records Ramesses II's marriage to a Hittite princess following a treaty between the two sovereigns. Housed in the dome covering the back of the temple is an exhibition showing the various operations in the relocation of the temple complex.

Some 50 metres (55 yards) to the north is the **Temple of Hathor**, dedicated by Ramesses II to his wife Nefertari, whose physical features were adopted in the embodiment of the goddess. The temple, also carved into the rock, is smaller than that of Ramesses II. The façade has six niches containing statues of Ramesses II (four) and Nefertari (two), with a central doorway. The statues are ten metres (32.8 feet) high and the whole façade is shaped like a pylon. Dedicatory hieroglyphics cover the tapering buttresses and continue across the pylon, forming the frieze. The interior walls on the left and right of the door bear representations of the king defeating the enemies from the north and south; the other walls are decorated with offertory scenes. Three doors open to a vestibule leading to the sanctuary. The vestibule walls are also decorated with scenes depicting the king and queen making offerings to the gods.

In the sanctuary, a figure of Hathor represented as a cow and flanked by two Hathoric pillars juts out of the mountain, protecting the king's statue.

Lower Egypt

Alexandria and the Delta

There are two routes from Cairo to Alexandria. The first is the 218-kilometre (135-mile) delta route, which leaves Cairo by the north road, the Sharia Shubra, following the course of the Nile. Outside Cairo the road runs through ancient delta towns, the fields of Behna, colourful Tanta, Kafr Ez Zaiyat and Damanhur, until you reach Alexandria, entering along the course of the railway line.

The second is the 225-kilometre (140-mile) desert route which is also a recommended return route to Cairo, allowing you to see different places. From Cairo you drive to Giza, proceeding up the entire breadth of the Wadi el-Natrun, passing Deir Makaryus, Deir el-Baramus, Deir el-Suryani and Deir Amba Bishoi, until you reach Alexandria.

Buses leave Cairo via the desert route from Midan Saad Zaghloul; the booking office is near the Cecil Hotel. Alexandria and Cairo are also linked by rail, while Olympic Airways operates flights from Athens, and Egyptair from Cairo and Upper Egypt.

Alexandria is not strictly an ancient Egyptian city, for it was founded by Alexander the Great when he arrived in Egypt in 332 BC. Only 25 years old at the time, he had just won two battles, at the Dardanelles and in Asia Minor. He wanted a Greek city built to immortalize the best aspects of the civilization he so admired and to promote his pan-Hellenic ideals. He ordered his architect, Dinocrates, to build a great metropolis around the small Egyptian town of Rhakotis.·

Thus was born Alexandria, the capital of a new Egyptian kingdom which was to have everything: convenient access to the Nile, an ideal climate, a perfect harbour, fresh water, and limestone quarries. But Alexander never saw his city rise. He hurried on to fight other battles and to conquer other lands, and when he returned eight years later it was to be buried.

On Alexander's death, his empire was divided amongst his generals, and Egypt went to Ptolemy I who initiated grand projects and went on to fulfill Alexander's dreams. The Heptastadion, a causeway linking Alexandria with Pharos, was completed and fortified, and the Royal Palace was built. This enormous complex, which was both the seat of government and the royal residence, was comparable to the Imperial City at Beijing. The immense palace was connected to another grand complex, the Mouseion by a disciple of Aristotle, Demetrios of Phaleron. It became the cultural hub of the Mediterranean.

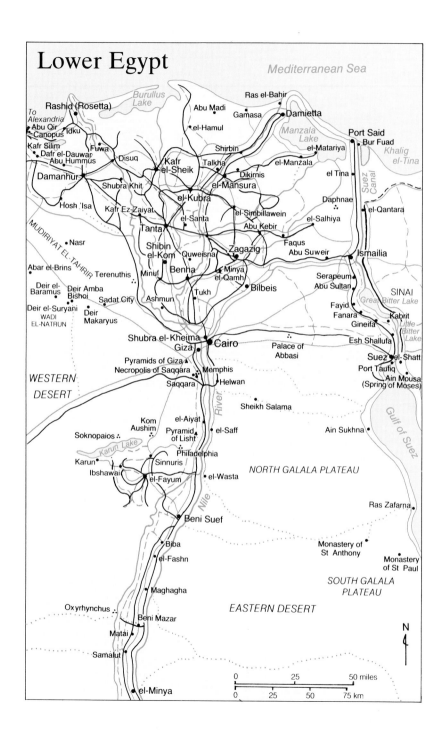

Lower Egypt

Mediterranean Sea

Burullus Lake

Ras el-Bahir

Rashid (Rosetta)

To Alexandria

Abu Qir

Canopus

Idku

Kafr Silim

Dafr el-Dauwar

Abu Hummus

Fuwa

Disuq

Abu Madi

Gamasa

Damietta

Port Said

Bur Fuad

Manzala Lake

el-Matariya

Khalig el-Tina

el-Hamul

Shirbin

Damanhur

Shubra Khit

Hosh 'Isa

Kafr Ez-Zaiyat

Kafr el-Sheik

Talkha

Dikirnis

el-Mansura

el-Kubra

el-Manzala

el Tina

Suez Canal

el-Qantara

Daphnae

el-Salhiya

MUDIRIYAT EL-TAHRIR

Nasr

Abar el-Brins

Terenuthis

Deir el-Baramus

Deir Amba Bishoi

Deir el-Suryani

Deir Makaryus

WADI EL-NATRUN

el-Santa

Tanta

Shibin el-Kom

Quweisna

Minuf

Sadat City

Ashmun

Benha

Tukh

Minya el-Qamh

el-Simbillawein

Abu Kebir

Zagazig

Faqus

Abu Suweir

Bilbeis

el-Salhiya

Ismailia

Serapeum

Abu Sultan

Fayid

Fanara

Gineifa

Esh Shallufa

SINAI

Great Bitter Lake

Kabrit

Little Bitter Lake

WESTERN DESERT

Shubra el-Kheima

Giza

Cairo

Pyramids of Giza

Necropolis of Saqqara

Memphis

Saqqara

Helwan

Palace of Abbasi

Suez

el-Shatt

Port Taufiq

Ain Mousa (Spring of Moses)

Sheikh Salama

Kom Aushim

Soknopaios

Karun

Ibshawai

Karun Lake

Sinnuris

el-Fayum

el-Aiyat

Pyramid of Lisht

Philadelphia

el-Saff

el-Wasta

NORTH GALALA PLATEAU

Ain Sukhna

Gulf of Suez

Ras Zafarna

Nile River

Beni Suef

Biba

el-Fashn

Monastery of St Anthony

Monastery of St Paul

SOUTH GALALA PLATEAU

Maghagha

EASTERN DESERT

Oxyrhynchus

Beni Mazar

Matai

Samalut

el-Minya

0		25		50 miles
0	25	50	75 km	

N

The finest expression of the Alexandrians' practical thinking and mathematical expertise, the **Great Lighthouse**, was built as a monument to be identified with the city, and one which would also guide sailors through the reefs along its shore. Sostratos, its architect, was a contemporary of Euclid, and the Great Lighthouse was included amongst the Seven Wonders of the Ancient World. The white marble tower stood over 100 metres (330 feet) high on the eastern side of the island of Pharos. Atop the tower, which was adorned with statues, resinous wood burned continuously, producing a bright light. A system of metal reflecting mirrors concentrated this light, making it highly visible over great distances. The name of the island, Pharos, extended to the tower, the first lighthouse in history, and to all lighthouses thereafter. Pharos was completely destroyed by the Mamelukes in 1302.

In a pantheistic world, it never crossed the minds of the Greeks and the Egyptians, who lived together in Alexandria, that one religion was true and another false. They believed that it was possible that the gods of other religions were their own gods by other names. So when Ptolemy Soter decided to create a god for Alexandria, he knew he was only giving material form to already existing sentiments. He mixed Osiris, whom the Greeks readily identified with Dionysus, with the bull-god Apis; the result was Serapis, the new god for the city, of ideal Egyptian origins, born with the features of Zeus and dressed in Greek garb. Serapis became popular immediately and his cult spread beyond Alexandria; his shrines rose all over the Mediterranean. The **Temple of Serapis (Serapeum)** at Alexandria stood on the old citadel of Rhakotis, today the site of Pompey's Pillar.

During the reign of Ptolemy II (285–247 BC), trade, sciences and the arts developed in Alexandria. The restoration of the old channel linking the Nile to the Red Sea made Egypt, particularly Alexandria, the centre of the world — the bridge between the Mediterranean Sea, Asia and Africa. Merchants readily took advantage of the new facilities, which replaced the long and dangerous transcontinental land routes. The city grew rich and crowded, while the rest of Egypt languished. Splendid edifices were built, such as the famous Library, which held more than a million precious manuscripts of ancient civilizations. Unfortunately, this magnificent phase of development lasted less than a century. One of the reasons for the decline was that the population of Alexandria itself was made up of a number of races who were always at odds with one another. Corruption was another major problem, but the *coup de grâce* for Alexandria was the interference of the priests in temporal matters and the incompetence of the last Ptolemies.

A few years before the birth of Christ, Egypt's last queen, **Cleopatra**, was crowned. The ambitious young queen vainly tried to lure Caesar into establishing an Egypto-Roman empire, but her scheme failed. Still determined, she tried again with Anthony. When the Roman general lost the battle against the legions of Octavius, Cleopatra committed suicide according to most accounts, by allowing herself to be bitten by a poisonous asp, and Octavius transformed Egypt into a Roman province. Despite numerous problems, the city remained the capital of Egypt and maintained its geographical importance. But in 639 when Amr, Lieutenant of Caliph Omar, invaded Egypt and converted it to Islam, Alexandria's importance waned. Cairo became the capital and Alexandria's population declined drastically.

The city of Alexandria was on the rise again in the 19th century, thanks to its port. During the campaign in 1798, Napoleon had brought with him a new wave of European scientific spirit. Benefiting from these ideas, Mohammed Ali undertook the modernization of Alexandria during the following decades. An arsenal was built, a canal (the Mahmudieh) was dug out for potable water, the Alexandria-Cairo railway was constructed, and cotton-growing was initiated in the delta countryside. The opening of the Suez Canal in 1869 restored to the city the importance it had once enjoyed and its promise of the good life attracted entrepreneurs, merchants and rich foreigners, as it had 2,000 years before. Thus Alexandria became a Mediterranean capital of the fasionable world. Casinos, night clubs and restaurants were opened and sumptuous villas were built on the seafront. Fortunes were made overnight by artists and intellectuals who came from abroad. But, in the areas outside Alexandria, just as in the time of the last Ptolemies, the people lived in misery. This fact was overlooked by King Farouk and his court, who were distracted by the amusements and worldliness of Alexandria. He was forced to abdicate after the revolution of 1952, which was led by Nasser.

Five years later, Nasser confiscated properties owned by foreigners, thereby prompting their flight. In the following years, the town quickly developed its industries, fuelled by the influx of people from the poorer areas of the country.

Alexandria Today: A Tour of the City

Today, Alexandria is a bustling city of about 2 million people and is still Egypt's main business centre. The city is a meeting point, a cultural hybrid of all the peoples of the Mediterranean, with only a few vestiges of its past. **Liberty Square** or **Midan el-Tahrir**, with the equestrian statue of Mohammed Ali, is the city's focal point. Around it are St Mark's Church, the Law Courts and the Stock Exchange, the oldest in the Arab world. Towards the Eastern Harbour, cross Midan Ahmed Orabi with its monument of Khedive Ismail, continue down the Sharia 26 July on the harbour, and make a right turn to Sharia Champollion with its Graeco-Roman **Museum of Antiquities**. The exhibits here provide a key to the successive cultural and religious transitions from pagan to Greek to Roman to Coptic Christian in Egypt.

The museum's 4,000 art treasures date back to pre-dynastic periods. Most of these treasures were unearthed while foundations were being dug for new buildings. The museum has recently been reorganized and, since the exhibits are constantly being moved, it is difficult to give a precise location for each. Amongst its most interesting exhibits are a statue of Nike, probably from Roman times, a cast of the famous Rosetta Stone with its trilingual inscriptions, a life-size black diorite statue of the Apis bull dating to the reign of Hadrian, a crocodile mummy found in el-Fayum, and a fine collection of objects including a group of vessels from the beginning of the third millenium BC and funerary masks of the Roman era. There is also a head of Julius Ceasar and in what is called the Treasure Room, a silver torso of Aphrodite and a silver gilt goblet with cupids gathering grapes.

Near the museum is **Kom el-Dik**, a small Roman ampitheatre with semicircular tiers of marble seats which could accommodate 800 people, discovered in 1964. From el-Hureya Avenue, you can take a left turn to Sharia Nebi Daniel, then go on to the train station and Sharia Bab Sidra where you will find **Pompey's Pillar**, which was probably erected in 302, in honour of the emperor Diocletian. This pillar of pink Aswan granite is all that remains of the great Ptolemaic sanctuary of Serapis, which was destroyed in 391 by the Bishop Theophilus, acting on orders of the emperor Theodosius I. Other remains include two pink granite sphinxes, several shafts of granite columns, a scarab of pink Aswan granite, and statues — all from the library which stood near the Serapeum. (This is not the great Imperial Library, which is situated elsewhere.) North of the pillar is an ancient water-basin.

Beyond the Sharia el-Nasriya, and along the path leading to **Kom es-Shugafa**, are the **catacombs** of the first and second century, which are among the most remarkable Roman tombs in Egypt. These catacombs wed the Egyptian taste in decorative mannerism with Graeco-Roman styles, often producing strange results, such as the god Anubis wearing a cuirass. There are three storeys linked by a flight of steps and an interior court with a spiral staircase leading to a rotunda. To the left is the Triclinium Funebre for funeral feasts. At the foot of the staircase are the vestibule and the antechamber.

The **Necropolis of Anfushi** is located along the course of the western harbour, its layout resembling that of the tombs of Kom es-Shugafa in the city centre. These Greek rock-cut tombs dating back to the second century BC are fine examples of the Graeco-Egyptian styles of the Ptolemaic period, in which one can see representations of Egyptian gods alongside Graeco-Roman mythological scenes. Nearby is the **Palace of Ras el-Tin**, built by Mohammed Ali, which was the official residence of the king of Egypt in Alexandria. It was here that King Farouk signed his abdication on 16 July 1952.

Behind the Palace of Ras el-Tin is the Turkish-style **Mohammed Karim Mosque**. Along the Sharia Qasr Ras el-Tin and past the Yacht Club is the **Museum of Hydrobiology**, which houses an interesting aquarium with marine life from the Nile, the Red Sea and the Mediterranean. There is also an exhibition of fishing implements, model boats and the skeleton of a 17-metre (56-foot) long whale, which was stranded near Rosetta in 1936. Not far away is the **Fort Qaitbay**, a fortress constructed in the 15th century on the site of the Lighthouse of Pharos by the sultan Ashraf Qaitbay, using the materials of an ancient structure. The enclosure walls form an irregular pentagon and provide a fine example of secular Islamic architecture. The fortress itself provides a view of the bay and the port.

Further south along the Eastern Harbour is the **Mosque of Abdul Abbas el-Mursi**. This masterpiece of Islamic architecture was built in 1767 on the site of the tomb of a pious Andalusian who lived in Alexandria in the 13th century. Further south still is the Ibrahim Tarbana Mosque, built in 1685.

The Alexandrian Hypogeum of Shatby is situated in the eastern part of the city, in the new Catholic cemetery. There is no indication of the owner of the tomb, but it must date from somewhere between the third and the first century BC. Some believe it was part of Sema, the family sepulchre of the Ptolemies, where Alexander the Great was laid to rest. Others believe it to be the Nemesion of Ceasar, where the head of Pompey was buried.

Excursions can be made to **Montazah Palace**, 17 kilometres (10.5 miles) away. The original structure has been altered since its construction in 1892; it was reconstructed in the neo-Byzantine style by the Italian architect Verracci. The buildings surrounding the palace were also built in the same style. The palace interiors have large frescoes which are imitations of those in the Vatican; in fact, much of the building was copied from famous edifices around the world. The private royal apartments are open as a museum. The palace affords a good view of the hanging gardens and the sea. The surrounding park covers an area of 150 hectares (370 acres), offering various sports

facilities and a good restaurant. To visit the palace, take bus No. 20 from either Midan Orabi or Midan Ramleh; or bus No. 28 from Midan Orabi or Misr Station.

City Strolls One of Alexandria's most charming attractions is the long corniche of the Eastern Harbour, Sharia 26 July, with its many small but excellent seafood restaurants. The shopping district revolves around Midan el-Tahrir and Midan Saad Zaghloul. Sharia Salah-Salem, the old Rue Cherif Pasha, is the most fasionable strip. Antique shops are located at Rue Attarine. Most of the airline offices and travel agencies are also located in this area. Cutting across this busy section in Sharia Nebi Daniel is the ancient street of Sema, Sharia Horreya; the street running east to west was the legendary Canopic way. This intersection was once the '**crossroads of the world**' having witnessed the traffic of 2,300 years of history.

Alexandria's major attractions may all be visited on foot. Unlike larger Egyptian cities, Alexandria has but fragmentary traces of its ancient glory. With no towering monuments to transport one back to those days, ancient Alexandria may be better appreciated by reading about it.

Sun and Sea Alexandria extends some 16 kilometres (ten miles) eastwards to seaside suburbs. Here are some of Egypt's best beach resorts, offering fine white sands, the azure Mediterranean and a sunny climate along a beautiful 30-kilometre (18.6-mile) stretch of shore. All of the beach resorts are on the No.20 bus route from Midan Orabi and Midan Ramleh. Among the most popular are Glim, Sidi Bishr, Stanley Beach, Cleopatra, Mamura and Montazah. On the western side are Hanoville and Agami.

About 50 kilometres (31 miles) south-west of Alexandria are the ruins of the ancient city of **Abu Mina**. To reach this important archaeological site, drive or take a train to Bahig, followed by a car ride north to Amirya on the road continuing west of the desert road; a 12-kilometre (7.5-mile) trail leads from here to the site.

In 1905, the German archaeologist Karl Maria Kaufmann discovered here the tomb of St Menas and a church, the most significant Coptic ruins so far uncovered. Excavations and research efforts were conducted in the following years and most finds are now housed in the museums of Cairo and Alexandria.

St Menas was born to a wealthy family in Phrygia. He joined the Roman army after the early deaths of his parents. During the Diocletian persecution, he deserted the army because he was a Christian, and was martyred in 296. There are many conflicting accounts of how his body was transported to Egypt. It is said that at a certain point the camels carrying his remains halted and refused to go any further. They were replaced with other camels who also refused to move. This was considered a sign, so he was buried on the spot. When the inhabitants of a nearby village came to know of the healing powers of the waters by the tomb of St Menas, they built an oratory with a small dome on the site. A century later, Abu Mina became a major pilgrimage centre; people came here to be healed from as far away as France. The pilgrims took home flasks of the miraculous waters; these became known as 'St Menas flasks' and were decorated with an image of the saint dressed as a Roman soldier, praying between two kneeling camels. According to recent tests, the water contains minerals which do have therapeutic effects. Abu Mina flourished in the late-fifth and early-sixth centuries. Four churches have been discovered here as well as two baptistries, two catacombs, baths, reservoirs and conduits, around which lie the remains of the old town.

East of Rosetta

The most convenient way to reach Abu Qir and Rosetta — site of the famous Rosetta Stone — is by private car. There are also buses to Abu Qir; No. 28 departs from Midan Orabi and No. 29 from Misr Station or Sidi Gabir. Sidi Gabir, Alexandria's second train station, serves Abu Qir and Rosetta.

Abu Qir Twenty-four kilometres (15 miles) east of Alexandria, Abu Qir is famous for its speciality seafood restaurants. The town is fast developing its tourist facilities and currently has two modest hotels. Abu Qir witnessed two great battles. The first, in 1798, was the Battle of the Nile, inaccurately named because Nelson stated that the 'engagement took place not far from the mouth of the Nile', although it actually took place in the bay of Abu Qir. Here Nelson surprised Napoleon's fleet and destroyed it in a matter of two days, cutting off Napoleon's sea link to France. A year later, in July, Napoleon himself commanded the second battle of Abu Qir. Turkey, prompted by England, declared war on France and landed 15,000 men at Abu Qir. Napoleon, accompanied by Murat and Kleber, rushed down from Cairo to defeat them. Most of the Turks were drowned and their encampment was taken by surprise.

The ruins of ancient **Canopus** lie around Fort Tewfikieh in Abu Qir. Little is left of the once-glorious city strategically positioned on the Canopic (western) mouth of the Nile, which has long since dried up. Ptolemy Soter built a temple for Serapis here, which became the most celebrated building in antiquity, a centre mysteriously linked to the occult and associated with licentiousness. Aside from the remains of the Temple of Serapis, there are fragments here of a granite temple where busts of Ramesses II were found, as well as baths and catacombs.

Idku The fishing town of Idku rises between the Mediterranean and Lake Idku. Red brick houses line its steep streets and its architecture is a simplified reflection of Rosetta's more elaborate lines.

Rosetta Sixty-three kilometres (39 miles) from Alexandria, Rosetta (Rashid) is today best known for the discovery here of the Rosetta Stone. The stone was discovered whilst Fort Rashid was being restored in 1799, and its importance was recognized by an officer of Napoleon's army. It was sent to Alexandria along with other antiquities, but was seized by the British and is now in the British Museum. It carries the same text written in three scripts, hieroglyphic, demotic and Greek. The inscriptions enabled rapid advances to be made in the deciphering of hieroglyphics by Champollion.

The town of Rosetta itself is interesting and offers some of the best examples of delta architecture. Rashid was founded in the ninth century and grew with the decline of Alexandria. In the 17th and 18th centuries, it was the most important port in Egypt. Charming houses of that period still grace the town's historic centre. Built in red and black brick, with façades decorated in the delta style, most of the houses incorporate stones and columns from older buildings. The **house of Ali el-Fatairi**, a 17th-century structure just off the main street, is one of the finest. Other examples are the early 19th-century el-Amaciali house and the 18th-century Arab Kerli, which is now a museum. The town's most important building, is the **Mosque of Zaghloul**, built with 300 columns from other edifices which were laboriously levelled.

Abusir Forty-eight kilometres (30 miles) from Alexandria, Abusir is the site of the Graeco-Roman town dedicated to the cult of Osiris, known as Taposiris Magna. The ruins of the Temple of Osiris are well preserved. North of this rather plain temple which has no inscriptions or decorative representations, are the remains of a Roman lighthouse which will give you an idea of how the Pharos of Alexandria must have looked.

El-Alamein Some, 110 kilometres (68 miles) from Alexandria, el-Alamein is the site of one of World War II's bloodiest battles. Rommel commanded the German and Italian forces here against the British Eighth Army under Montgomery. After this bitter struggle, the Allies assumed the offensive and later recaptured Libya and Tunisia from the Germans. War memorials and monuments were erected, and vast cemeteries spread all over el-Alamein. There is also a **Memorial**

Egyptian Hieroglyphs

The hieroglyphic script of ancient Egypt, an offshoot of pictorial art, is one of the world's oldest and most elaborate writing systems. It also has the longest documented history, starting from the fourth millenium BC and lasting until the end of the fourth century AD. Egyptian or Coptic script developed in the Middle Ages before it was overtaken by Arabic. The Coptic, however, contines to exist today in the liturgy of the Coptic Church.

The first hieroglyphs appeared in the late predynastic period in the form of short label-texts carved on stone and on ancient pottery objects dating back to between 3100 and 3000 BC. The most recent ones, which date back to AD 394, were found in a temple inscription in Philae. Originally, this script was used extensively; it was inscribed on temple walls, stelae, tombs and ivory tablets, but later it was restricted to official inscriptions on temple walls and for religious purposes.

The word 'hieroglyph' comes from the Greek words *hieros* (sacred) and *glupho* (sculptured). The signs of the script are mainly pictorial in character; most are recognizable depictions of natural or man-made objects, although a few are indeterminate. They are categorized as ideograms (sense-signs), which show the actual object they identify or refer to, and phonograms (sound signs), in which the pictorial words refer to something entirely different from their composition but which happen to have the same phonetic sound. For example, the name of Narmer, one of Egypt's first kings, was depicted as a fish for *n'r* and a chisel for *mr*. The system was never limited to a fixed number of hieroglyphs but expanded according to new requirements. This, however, did not follow a strict order; in some cases a new sign was developed, while in others they retained their original characters. So far, over 6,000 hieroglyphs have been deciphered and documented, but the number is misleading because most of these were found on walls of temples from the Graeco-Roman period where the number could have beeen deliberately increased for religious purposes. In earlier times, the number apparently did not exceed 1,000 signs.

A hieroglyph inscription was arranged either in columns or in horizontal lines with no punctuation marks to divide the words or sentences. The direction of the figures dictates which way the text is read and it is arranged within imaginary squares or rectangles to ensure a

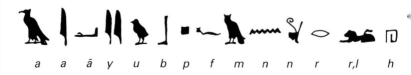

| a | a | ā | y | u | b | p | f | m | n | n | r | r,l | h |

harmonious arrangement. Words referring to entities of royal or high status were given precedence.

The hieroglyphs were used to promote the idea of an eternal existence for the objects or persons they depicted. A funerary formula, for instance, invoking benefits from a god, was enough to ensure that the owner of the tomb would receive those benefits, while the name of a person inscribed in hieroglyphs was believed to give an identity to that person. Without it, they believed, he was not guaranteed an existence in the after-life. Likewise, mutilating or wiping out a person's name amounted to depriving him of his identity, and even gods were vulnerable to this.

As time went by, another form of script known as hieratic (from the Greek word *hieratikos*), meaning priestly, was developed and used by priests during the New Kingdom. In the 25th Dynasty, demotic (from the Greek word *demotikos*), which means popular, became the normal form of script and continued to be used through the Roman period.

Because hieroglyphs were in continuous use for such a long time, it is important to outline the five linguistic stages of the language:

Old Egyptian is the language used in the Old Kingdom (2686–2181 BC), the time in which the first continuous text appeared.

Middle Egyptian is the classical form of the Egyptian language based on the script used in the First Intermediate Period and Middle Kingdom and which continued through to the Graeco-Roman period.

Late Egyptian is the everyday language of the New Kingdom and Third Intermediate Period, found in literary and monumental inscriptions. This language, which contains many foreign words, differed from the two earlier forms.

Demotic is the vernacular successor of Late Egyptian which began in the Late Period and lasted until late Roman times.

Coptic is the final evolution of the hieroglyphic language and was used from the third century onwards. It is the only stage of the language in which dialects became distinct. The language, used by the Christian descendants of the ancient Egyptians, used Greek characters supplemented by seven more taken from hieroglyphs. The language has two major dialects: *Sahidic*, which was the standard literary dialect until the tenth century, and *Bohairic*, the literary language of all Egypt, which originally had roots in the western delta. After the Arab Conquest in 639, Arabic gradually replaced Coptic as the main language.

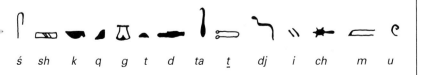

ś   sh   k   q   g   t   d   ta   <u>t</u>   dj   i   ch   m   u

Museum. El-Alamein offers some of the Mediterranean coast's best beaches. South of el-Alamein is the **Qattara Depression**, the site of a project of Pharaonic proportions. The plan includes excavation of a channel, 137 metres (450 feet) below sea level, which will link the depression with the Mediterranean Sea and render this desert area habitable.

Mersa Matruh Some 290 kilometres (180 miles) from Alexandria and only 230 kilometres (143 miles) from Libya, Mersa was once called Paraetonium. In fact, it has many historical associations with the Roman Empire . Alexander set off from here when he went to visit the Temple of Jupiter-Amun at Siwa. Just outside the town is the famous **Beach of Cleopatra**, also know as **Cleopatra's Bath**. It is a natural basin hollowed out of the rocks on the beach and filled with sea water.

Today, as in Alexander's time, Mersa Matruh is the ideal departure point for excursions to Siwa. And, as in Cleopatra's time, it is known for its superb white sand beaches and is a popular holiday resort. There are ten good hotels in the town. Most of the beach resorts are open only during the summer.

The 300-kilometre (186-mile) road from Alexandria to Mersa Matruh is well paved, following the coast with its superb views and excellent beaches. The train to Mersa Matruh is slow and rather uncomfortable, so it is best to travel there by car. It is also possible to drive from Cairo via the desert route to get on to this road.

The Delta Towns

Herodotus mentions seven branches of the Nile which irrigated the delta, one of Egypt's most important regions for agriculture. With its fields of cotton, wheat, maize, green cloves and rice, the delta is one of the world's most fertile and densely populated places. Most of the delta's ancient ruins and sites have not yet been explored because the swampy marshes have made the area practically inaccessible.

Sixty-five kilometres (40 miles) from Alexandria, **Damanhur** is the capital of the province of Behira, an important centre for cotton growing. It stands on the site of the ancient city of Horus, which the Romans called Hermopolis Parva.

Fifty-five kilometres (34 miles) from Damanhur, **Tanta** is the capital of the province of Gharbiya. The town's major tourist attractions are the *mulids*, religious festivals held each year in April and August in honour of Said the Bedouin, a Moroccan pilgrim from Fez who settled in Tanta in the 12th century on his way back from Mecca and who later became a Muslim saint. His mosque, with its three domes and two fine minarets, dominates the town. There are also several other mosques, a royal palace and colourful bazaars.

Some 65 kilometres (40 miles) further, past el-Mansura and Mendes is **Damietta (Dumyat)**. The town has very ancient origins, but came to be known only through its struggles against the Crusaders. Fortified by Saladin, Damietta was attacked continually by marauding Europeans who finally took the town in 1218. Today it is a rather sleepy town with some modest tourist facilities and a port to accommodate tourist boats. The popular resort of Ras el-Bahîr is 12 kilometres (7.5 miles) north.

The Suez Canal

Suez, which lies at the southernmost tip of the gulf to which it lends its name, has witnessed invasions of Hyksos, Assyrians, Persians and Arabs during its long history. Although it was not a popular tourist destination, it has, however, achieved importance since the opening of the canal linking the Mediterranean with the Red Sea in 1869.

The idea of opening a canal between the Mediterranean and the Red Sea dates back to 2100 BC. The earliest attempt to connect the Red Sea with the Nile, and thereby with the Mediterranean was undertaken by Necho during the 26th Dynasty. According to Herodotus, 120,000 men lost their lives in this ambitious project which was only abandoned when an oracle warned the king that invading barbarians, reportedly the Persians, would be the only ones to profit by it. In around 500 BC, Darius I completed the project. His canal ran from the Red Sea to the Great Bitter Lakes, and proceeded west to Bubastis, the modern-day Zagazig. The Ptolemies maintained it, and in AD 98 the Roman emperor Trajan improved it by adding a third course which reached Cairo. Even the Arab conqueror of Egypt, Amr, restored the canal in order to supply Arabia with corn. Unfortunately it was abandoned 100 years later in order to starve out Medina which had revolted against the Caliph. The canal then became unserviceable. The Venetians frequently contemplated constructing a canal through the isthmus to recover the trade they had lost when the new route around the Cape of Good Hope was discovered. In 1671, Leibniz recommended the construction of such a canal to Louis XIV. The idea obsessed, amongst others, Sultan Mustafa III, Ali Bey, the Mameluke prince, and Napoleon Bonaparte, who in 1798 undertook preliminary works, but as a result of a serious miscalculation by the chief engineer, Lepere, abandoned the project, thinking it was not feasible. A few decades later, the French Consul Ferdinand de Lesseps became convinced of the feasibility of the operation, but since neither Mohammed Ali nor his son Abbas gave permission for the work he had to wait for Ali's other son, Said Pasha, to be crowned. In 1854, the new ruler finally agreed to start the project. Work commenced in 1859 and was finished in November 1869. It was a magnificent inauguration, graced by a host of European princes and the Empress Eugenie herself. Giuseppe Verdi composed *Aida* for the occasion which was performed at the Cairo Opera Theatre.

Egypt's ruler, Khedive Ismail, had financed a third of the canal's construction, which contributed largely to his bankruptcy. In 1875, his shares were purchased by the British government. The canal then became a focal point in the fight for the independence of Egypt which started at the onset of the 20th century and ended in 1952 with Nasser's revolution. In July 1956, Nasser nationalized the Suez Canal Company in reaction to the continued control of Egypt by the West and with the intention of using its enormous proceeds to construct the High Dam at Aswan. Israel, France and Britain invaded Egypt three months later, which the world considered an outrage, forcing the invaders to retreat. The Six Day (Arab-Israeli) War in 1967 closed the canal for eight years. In 1975, President Anwar Sadat officially reopened it after a year spent clearing it of some 700,000 mines with the help of 5,000 American, French and British soldiers. Today, an average of 90 ships a day pass through the canal, transporting 14 per cent of the world's trade. Average transit time is 15 hours. The ships cross at Ballah and Bitter Lakes where the canal widens. The increasing amount of traffic requires that continuous improvements are made. The Suez Canal is now 173 kilometres (107.5 miles) long — originally, it was 161 kilometres (100 miles) long — and no less than 200 metres (656 feet) wide at water level. Depth is never less than 20 metres (66 feet). Since the Red Sea and the Mediterranean are at the same level no locks are necessary.

The Canal Towns

The Isthmus of Suez may be visited by ship on an interesting 171-kilometre (106-mile) cruise which departs from Suez and stops at Port Taufiq, Esh Shalluffa, Gineifa, Le Deversoir, Serapeum, Ismailia, el-Gisr, el-Fidan, el-Qantara and Port Said. The crossing can also be made by car or train on the western bank. Trains depart from the Midan Ramses Station in Cairo, and buses from Midan el Tahrir.

Ismailia From Cairo the fastest and most convenient way to Ismailia is the 128-kilometre (80-mile) route across the desert. A slow but fascinating route is by road through Bilbeis, along the course of the Ismailia Canal which offers glimpses of delta life. Ismailia is also accessible from Cairo by rail. Travel time is two hours and 40 minutes and trains depart twice daily. There are also buses to Ismailia at the el-Olali Terminal. An alternative would be the so-called collective taxi, which departs when all seats are taken.

The city derives its name from Khedive Ismail, the sovereign nephew of Mohammed Ali, remembered for his contributions to the achievement of the Suez Canal project. Today, Ismailia is one of the most pleasant of Egyptian cities, evoking a turn-of-the-century charm with its cool, tree-lined boulevards graced by fashionable *fin-de-siecle*, resort-inspired houses. Fortunately, the past wars have caused minimal damage, sparing its historic centre which sprawls along the shores of

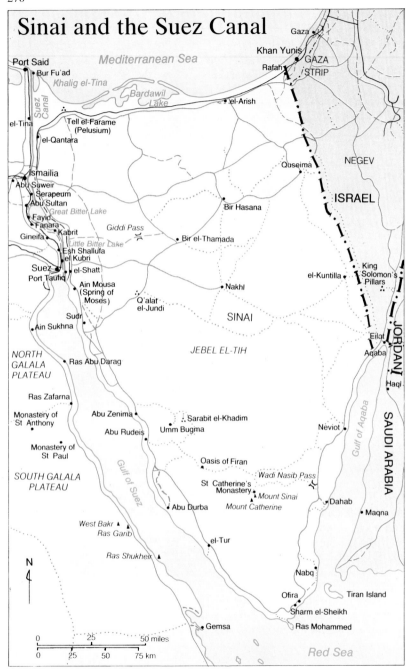

Sinai and the Suez Canal

Lake Timseh (also known as the Lake of the Crocodiles). During the closure of the canal, Ismailia lost half of its population, which diminished to a mere 200,000. With the resumption of canal traffic, Ismailia's population is expected to rise to a million by the end of the century. Situated in an area blessed with fertile soil, Ismailia is a promising tourist destination, already served by an array of hotels of varying categories.

The lake shore is dotted with well-kept public parks and lush gardens, among which is the famed **Garden of Stelae**, where remarkable finds from various archaeological excavations are to be found. Many of the excavated materials are attributed to Ramesses II. After years of closure to the public on account of war, **the Museum** has recently been reopened, displaying a wide collection of interesting treasures covering the long span of Egypt's past from prehistory to the Byzantine era. A stone sphinx guards the entrance of the museum.

There is a swimming club along the canal, offering refreshments, a sand beach and a good view of passing ships. North of the city are numerous resorts and clubs equipped with watersports facilities.

Port Said Established in 1859 as a base for the construction and operation of the canal, Port Said lies 80 kilometres (50 miles) north of Ismailia at the mouth of the Mediterranean, rising in the area of ancient Pelusium, from where the Holy Family was believed to have entered Egypt during the Biblical Flight. Six centuries later, Arab invaders began their conquest of the land from here. Named Port Said in honour of Said Pasha, the city occupies a strip of land between the Mediterranean and the vast, brackish lake of Manzala. Heavily damaged during the last Israeli attacks, Port Said was the focal point of grand-scale reconstruction until the re-opening of the canal. Today, the city is restored to peace and order. Its streets are laid out on a grid system, and its population is swelled by a large number of multinational technocrats, foreign consultants and businessmen.

Since 1975, the bustling city of Port Said has been a free port and thus provides a cornucopia of electronic products imported from Japan and Hong Kong. If you are planning to leave the country from here, remember that taxes have to be paid and this can cause long queues at customs. Adding to the bustle is the heavy traffic of passing ships loading and unloading passengers. These commercial and tourist leading passengers and unloadings. These commercial and tourist activities as well as the many hotels, restaurants, casinos, and entertainment spots, have made Port Said a vibrant, modern city. Sharia el Gumhuriyya, the principal thoroughfare, is shaded by trees and lined with banks. The New Corniche, on the other hand, is the tourist centre, with sparkling beaches, well-equipped resorts, casinos, and restaurants specializing in superb seafood.

Although the city is lacking in places of particular artistic or archaeological interest, it offers the best location for viewing the canal. A trip to the many islets which dot the Lake of Manzala — natural bird sanctuaries teeming with multifarious species, including fen birds, pelicans and flamingoes — is very rewarding. The city is served by hotels of varying categories, and its accommodation system is constantly being improved.

Suez Some 88 kilometres (55 miles) from Ismailia and 134 kilometres (83 miles) from Cairo, Suez (el-Suweis) is situated on the southern end of the canal. It was heavily damaged during the 1967 and 1973 wars which levelled three-quarters of the town. Suez is now an industrial centre producing petrochemicals, fertilizers and cement. These factories and industrial complexes are concentrated around Port Tanfiq. The small park situated along the canal affords excellent views of the Red Sea and Sinai. The Ataga Hills (Jebel Ataga) to the south-west are also scenic. Suez also offers very good views of the ships passing through the canal.

The Red Sea Coast

Ain Sukhna

Some 55 kilometres (34 miles) south of Suez is the town of Ain Sukhna, the nearest bathing resort to Cairo, once-famous for its silver-like sand and limpid water, rich with all types of fish and red coral. The landscape is partially disfigured by the immense cistern of a huge oil pipeline which carries raw material from the Red Sea to Alexandria. Here, you will find the only first-class hotel on Egypt's Red Sea coast and a camp-site. Apart from the bathing facilities, the hot thermal springs of the sulphuric type are also famous.

Ras Zafarna

A further 70 kilometres (43.5 miles) south on a narrow winding road overlooking the sea is Ras Zafarna, a small port with a lighthouse and a petrol station, situated at the headland of the same name, on the outlet of the modest Wadi Araba. A secondary road departs from Ras Zafarna along which, after about 30 kilometres (19 miles) on the left-hand side, you meet the crossroads of the **Monastery of St Anthony**, or **Deir Mar Antonius**.

After a further 14 kilometres (8.7 miles) of road, you will come to this most ancient monastery in Egypt, which rises from the foot of the grotto in which the saint spent his life (251–356) as an Anchorite, tormented, according to legend, by the flatteries and temptations of the devil.

St Anthony and St Pachomius were two of the first exponents of Christian monasticism, which originated in the Egyptian desert before spreading through the many orders to other Catholic countries. Initially the Anchorite saints lived in complete seclusion; they later organized themselves in small communities, but were still isolated from the rest of the world. Anchorites still exist in Egypt. They are monks from the small monasteries who have chosen seclusion and live in caves, following a vow of complete silence.

The Monastery of St Anthony, springing from the foot of the rocky hill, is surrounded by high walls, out of which some buildings have recently been erected for visitors. Women are not allowed entrance. The first buildings date back to the third century, but little of these remain except for the southern walls and the old church dedicated to St Anthony, built by his disciples, on the place where he was buried. Inside the walls are many churches, mainly from the tenth — 15th centuries, some of which are adorned with frescoes showing the holy knights in bright colours, and the hermits, the ascetics and the fathers of the church in dark, subdued colours. Walls enclose everything necessary to the monastery's life: a spring, a garden, an orchard, a mill and a library once full of books and ancient parchments, Arabic translations of sacred Coptic texts and other works. The Bedouins, who occupied and disfigured the monastery at the end of the 15th century, deliberately destroyed much of the library's contents by using it as fuel for their kitchens which they placed in the old church of St Anthony. After this invasion, the normal life of the monastery was resumed, but without its previous prosperity. About 30 monks live here today. The cave (*magharah*) of St Anthony can be visited by following a steep footpath climbing the mountain for about 400 metres (1,313 feet) above the monastery. The walk offers some excellent views of the valley.

Coming back from Ras Zafarna on the southern coastal road, after about 25 kilometres (15.5 miles) you will meet the crossroad which leads to the **Monastery of St Paul** or **Deir Mar Boulos**. After following an unasphalted road for about ten kilometres (6.2 miles) and crossing a steep ridge, you reach a monastery, similar to that of St Anthony, though smaller and less rich. St Paul of Thebes was a contemporary of St Anthony and though older was his disciple and friend. Coptic iconography often associates both saints, showing them with the raven which, according to tradition, brought St Paul his daily bread during his 60-year-long hermitage. (St Paul is believed to have lived from 228 to 342 AD.) The monastery has had few alterations through the centuries, thus keeping its homogeneous and ancient aspect, even though the frescoes adorning the church of St Paul were badly restored at the beginning of the 18th century. A number of subjects vary from the Coptic tradition; for example, the holy knights fight devils, not dragons. The church, built underground, was originally dug right in the cave where the saint lived and where his remains are kept.

There are other churches inside the monastery's walls. St Michael's is the biggest, built in the 17th century and containing a painting of the Virgin attributed to St Luke, the Evangelist, and dating back to AD 40. The library contains a few hundred old books. The monastery has a spring, mills, ovens, gardens and orchards, and tame animals live in the small town's narrow roads. One hundred metres from the walls is the spring of Miriam, Moses' sister, where she is believed to have washed herself during the Exodus. The monastery offers simple hospitality to both men and women. From the hill there is a panoramic view of the Red Sea down to the massive Mountain of Moses in the Sinai. The colours are fantastic, especially at sunset.

Another 80 kilometres (50 miles) along the well-surfaced coastal road, is the oil zone of **Ras Gharib**, surrounded by the massive Jebel

Gharib, a mountain range 1,740 metres (5,700 feet) high. There are 150 oilwells here. At Ras Gemsa, 330 kilometres (205 miles) from Suez, a headland marks the end of the Gulf of Suez. Opposite the headland, the small Tawila Islands face Ras Mohammed, the southermost part of Sinai. On the eastern slope of the plateau of Abu Sar el-Qibli, 55 kilometres (34 miles) from Ras Mohammed, are the ruins of ancient Myos Hormos, once an important harbour on the Red Sea. Much of it is now buried in sand. From here a rough road leads to Qena through 200 kilometres (124 miles) of stark desert along the eastern creek of the Nile.

Hurghada (el-Ghardaga)

Hurghada, is the major tourist destination on this part of the coast. Until a few years ago, this was a modest fishing village; today it boasts major oil installations, military posts and an airport with daily flights to Cairo. The outbreak of the war made the whole area temporarily inaccessible because of its great strategic and military importance, but the coastal road was reopened to authorized vehicles in 1976. The small town of Hurghada is not particularly attractive, consisting of low houses overlooked by minarets of small mosques and the governor's palace. Many small hotels have been established in the town, run mostly by families, offering warm and efficient service. These one- or two-star hotels are generally clean. Restaurants are located along the main road. Bicycles may be hired near the mosque. The **Institute of Hydrobiology** is very interesting. Do not miss the aquarium and museum with their complete collections of flora and fauna of the Red Sea. From here you can hire a boat for a trip to the coral reefs. The Red Sea's warm waters are an ideal habitat for rare species of fish and fascinating coral reefs which may be observed through the bottoms of these boats. The *ris* (captain) manouvres the *houri* (boat) expertly over the reefs and shallows. Hurghada offers full scuba-diving facilities as well as three- and four-star resort hotels.

Islands and aquasports activities off Hurghada

1. Shadwan Island: Diving, snorkelling, fishing. No swimming.
2. Shaab Abu Shiban: Diving from boat, snorkelling, swimming.
3. Shaab el-Erg: Diving from boat, all kinds of fishing, snorkelling.
4. Umm Gammar Island: Professional diving, snorkelling.
5. Shasb Saghir Umm Gammae: Diving.
6. Careless Reef: Diving.
7. Giftun el-Kabir Island: Beaches, snorkelling, diving, fishing, swimming.
8. Giftun el-Saghir Island: Beaches, snorkelling, diving, fishing, swimming.

9. Abu Ramada Island: Diving.
10. Shaab Abu Ramada: Fishing.
11. Dishet el-Dhaba: Beaches, swimming.
12. Shaab Abu Hashish: Diving, snorkelling, swimming, fishing, beach.
13. Sharm el-Arab: Diving, swimming, fishing.
14. Abu Minqar Island: Beaches, swimming.

From Hurghada you can arrange an excursion to **Mons Porphyrites**, the 'mountain of porphyry'. It is a 130-kilometre (81-mile) journey south, and includes a return trip which requires trekking through rough terrain. The Romans mined the 1,661-metre (5,451-foot) Jebel ed-Dukhan for porphyry. This beautiful purple-red stone was used in temples, baths, sarcophagi and statues in the imperial city. The emperor Hadrian erected a temple at the quarries as well as houses for the workers, most of which are now in total ruin.

Port Safaga (Bur Safaga)

Sixty kilometres (37 miles) from Hurghada (460 kilometres or 286 miles from Suez) is Port Safaga or Bur Safaga. This small port town has 7,000 inhabitants. It has a fine beach, faced by a small island. There is a scuba centre with instructors and a scuba equipment hire service; fishing boats may be hired for trips to the nearby islands and reefs. The most interesting excursion you can make from here, though, is to Mons Claudianus.

Mons Claudianus or 'Mountain of Claudius' can be reached by following a surfaced road up from Port Safaga to the turning on the right for the 'Roman Camp' in the Wadi Umm Husein. The round trip from Port Safaga is 95 kilometres (59 miles). Quartzy diorite, a high-quality granite, was quarried here during the Roman period. During the reign of Nero and in the time of Hadrian and Trajan, buildings in Imperial Rome were decorated with architectural elements hewn out of the granite. In Rome, one can still see them in the columns of the portico of the Pantheon, in Hadrian's Villa, in public baths built by Diocletian, and in the columns and floor fo the Temple of Venus, among other places. The site on Mons Claudianus has a Roman camp, dwellings, workshops, stables and a *dromos*. A temple erected by Trajan on a further elevated site has collapsed in ruins, but the remains of a staircase leading to it can still be seen. The camp was surrounded by a granite wall with defence towers at the corners. The entire site was well protected from Bedouin attacks. North-east of the camp was a bath and a temple, and there were walls all around the camp. In the

quarries, you can still see blocks of stones among unfinished flooring slabs, architraves and inscribed columns.

The new 175-kilometre (109-mile) long road from Port Safaga to **Qena** is well surfaced, running through the valleys in the Eastern Desert, where gold was mined and granite quarried during Pharaonic times. It is a very beautiful drive. From the Red Sea coast, the road to Qena is the best route for visiting the Nile Valley sites between Dendera and Luxor. In antiquity, the Eastern Desert routes between the Nile and the Red Sea were vital for trade with the seaports and the land of Punt (probably modern-day Somalia).

Qoseir

Eighty-five kilometres (53 miles) further on is the small port of Qoseir. Known as the 'White Harbour' during Ptolemaic times, Qoseir was the end of the desert route for caravans crossing the Wadi Hammamat. Later the town was fortified by Sultan Selim. Until the last century, it was the starting point for pilgrims travelling to Mecca. Today its narrow streets are lined with colourful bazaars with a distinct Bedouin flavour, and you can take boat trips from here to the long coral reef opposite the port. Qoseir is also an important port for the export of phosphate. A 220-kilometre (137 mile) road links the port town with Qena.

The road to **Quft**, 190 kilometres (118 miles) long, is generally smooth and crosses the desert through the famous **Wadi Hammamat**, the 'Rehenu' valley of the Egyptians, who quarried its hard dark stone for the statues and sarcophagi of the Pharaohs, particularly during the Old and Middle Kingdoms. This was the 'Niger' or 'Thebaicus Lapis' of the ancients. Layers of Nubian sandstone embedded with primary crystalline rocks rise to peaks of up to 2,000 metres (6,564 feet). During the Pharaonic period, these hard stones, breccia, carnelian, rock crystal, black and green basalt were intensively quarried. Qoseir was a busy port and ships from the Sinai Peninsula brought turquoise and malachite. There was also a great deal of trading activity with the legendary land of Punt. The caravan route across the desert ran from 'Leukos Limen' (Qoseir) on the Red Sea coast to Coptos (Quft) in the Nile Valley. After crossing the Wadi Adi Ambanga, the road continues along the Wadi Beida, and climbs the mountain to **el-Itema-Hokheben**, passing the Wadi Rosafa which is marked by a large well, and finally through the Wadi Abu Siran. The road now climbs to the top of a rugged pass. On the way down is **Bir Es Sidd**, where the Ababda Bedouins live near a spring. They were originally nomads belonging to the Baga Bedouin tribe, but have now settled here, raising goats, camels and sheep. Visitors are often invited to meals by these very hospitable people. Beyond Bir Es Sidd are the formidable Hammamat Mountains. Near Bir el-Hammamat, in an area settled during the Roman times, are interesting fragments of unfinished sarcophagi, and granite was also quarried here in ancient times. One of the earliest expeditions to Hammamat took place during the reign of King Isesi in the Fifth Dynasty. Later Mentuhotep III followed suit and sent his men to the quarry. Under Ramesses IV, more than 8,000 soldiers and labourers were employed to procure blocks of sandstone and granite for the Temple of Amun in Thebes. In the valleys, one can find rocks with inscriptions left by ancient expeditions describing their great undertakings, their prayers and thanks to the gods. There are representations of the sacred boat of Sokaris and stelae depicting the king in prayer. In the pass of Mutraq Es-Selam is a commemorative inscription of Amenhotep IV flanked by graffiti scrawled by travellers, quarrymen, soldiers and Bedouins. Further on, at Qasr el-Banat, are sandstone rocks with inscriptions in Greek, Arabic and Coptic. The Qasr el-Banat is actually a rock eroded to the shape of a tower, whence the name of the place meaning 'castle of maidens' is derived. The road passes the ruins of a Roman watering station and arrives at Laqueita, a village of the Ababda Bedouins. The Roman road, Via Publica, which linked Coptos (Quft) and Berenike, once crossed here. There is a fragmentary inscription bearing the name of Tiberius near the principal well. The road continues on to Quft. From here one can reach Qena by following the line of ruined semaphore towers built by Mohammed Ali and used as signalling towers for transmitting messages. Because the road from Qoseir and Mersa Alam is rather bad, make sure your vehicle is in excellent running condition and take along an extra supply of petrol and plenty of drinking water.

Further along this road is the small fishing port of **Mersa Mubarak**. At the end of the *wadi*, seven kilometres (4.4 miles) away, are the ancient gold mines of Umm Rus. Further along the coast is Mersa Alam.

The small port of **Mersa Alam** boasts an ideal fishing centre with organized trips for anglers. Sharks, lobsters, turtles and muraena are among the great catches. There is a rest house at the port.

From Mersa Alam, 230 kilometres (143 miles) of desert road leads to Edfu. This road goes through Wadi Abu Karalia to Bir Besah. From this area, beautifully encircled by mountains, the road passes the ruins of ancient mines, then proceeds to Wadi Barramiya and finally into the **Wadi Miah** and the **Temple of el-Kanayis**.

Discovered in 1816 by Frederic Cailliaud, the Temple of el-Kanayis in Wadi Miah was built by Sety I near an ancient watering station and was dedicated to the god, Amun-Ra. The vestibule is built of sandstone blocks with four papyrus columns adorned with bud-capitals. The central span of the ceiling is decorated with vultures. Reliefs on the walls depict scenes of the king's victories over Nubians and Asiatics. The next chamber was hewn out of rock, with four square pillars and reliefs on the walls recording the sinking of the wells, the building of the temple and the king's offering to the gods. In the rear wall there are three niches. The central niche was dedicated to Amun, the left one to Sety, and the one on the right to Ra-Harakhty. This sanctuary is similar to those in the Ramesside rock temples in Nubia. The king founded this temple in around 1300 BC. To the east, on an adjoining rock, are three stelae. The first has an Asiatic goddess on horseback; the second has a dedication of the official in charge of the sinking of the well; and the third shows Yuny, viceroy of Nubia, kneeling before the king. On a higher rock, is an inscription of an earlier viceroy, Merymose, dating from the time of Amenhotep III.

The coastal road from Mersa Alam to the Sudanese border is bad; 145 kilometres (90 miles) from Mersa Alam is Berenike, the last Egyptian town before the border crossing.

Berenike

Situated on the bay of Ras Benas, Berenike was built on coral and founded by Ptolemy II Philadelphus in about 275 BC. He named the town after his mother, establishing it as an important entrepôt for trading with the ports on the eastern shore of the Red Sea and those in the Indian Ocean. Berenike was then as vital as Myos Hormos as a port town. However, the ruins of a temple of Serapis, built by Trajan and Tiberius, are all that is left of its ancient glory. A representation on the external wall shows Emperor Tiberius before the god Min, and another depicts offerings to the tutelary deity of the Green Mine. In fact, just north of Berenike, in the desert near Wadi Sakeit, are the remains of ancient emerald mines which were worked until the Middle Ages. Today Berenike is famous for its fishing, and has some of Egypt's best health spas. Berenike is accessible by bus from Luxor, Hurghada, Safaga and Qena. Beyond Berenike, a track leads to Halayib, on the border of Sudan. You can also reach this point by way of a desert road from Kom Ombo.

Sinai

In antiquity, Sinai was referred to as the 'Land of Enchantments', and it is, in fact, one of the most interesting areas of Egypt. The Sinai Peninsula is a rugged but enticing triangle of desert and mountain wedged between Africa and Asia, dividing Islamic Egypt from Israel and offering a Christian monastery as its major tourist attraction.

This mystical land has many connections with Biblical events. It has also exerted compelling influences upon ancient Egyptian myths and legends. Isis came here in search of the scattered remains of her spouse, Osiris, slain by his brother, Seth. The Pharaohs, on the other hand, came in search of gold, malachite, copper and turquoise. They crowned the goddess Hathor 'Lady of the Land of Turquoise'. She became the guardian of labourers in the turquoise and copper mines, where the first written alphabet in history, the 'Protosemitic Inscriptions of Sinai', was discovered.

Throughout history, Sinai has been rocked by turbulence. Being a meeting point, melting pot and battleground of the great Middle Eastern civilizations, it has witnessed the passage of the Egyptians, Hittites, Phoenicians, Arabs, Mamelukes, the Napoleonic French and the Israelis, who relinquished it only in 1982 having annexed it during the Six-Day War of 1967. Only the nomadic Bedouins and a few ascetic monks have remained in the desert, enduring its climate and overcoming its barren, unyielding soil. Today its population is only 20,000.

Sinai remains a land of inaccessible mountains rising to over 2,600 metres (8,530 feet), of rough rocks and boulders. In some areas, the endless stretches of sand dunes are tempered by rare oases with palms, acacias, tamarisk and patches of grass. The peninsula, where temperatures reach 42°C (107°F) in the summer, offers some of the finest unspoilt beaches of the Red Sea and the Mediterranean.

The wealth of Sinai once lay in its marble quarries, turquoise, porphyry and copper mines, all of which have been exhausted and abandoned. Today, promising oil-fields have taken their place. The areas of Abu Rudeis and el-Arish are rich in oil deposits and the near future should see a considerable increase of population as new installations are established.

Refreshed by the Mediterranean Sea and the gulfs of Aqaba and Suez, the peninsula offers fine sandy beaches. The northern coast is studded with tall, shady palms, while the shores facing the gulfs of Aqaba and Suez are flat and sandy in some parts, and rocky and treeless in others. A marvellous wealth of animal life is found on both coasts. With the increasing growth of tourism in the area of Aqaba, small resorts are slowly being established along the Egyptian coasts, particularly around Sharm el-Sheikh.

Access to the Sinai is facilitated by the **tunnel of Ahmed Hamdi**, the martyr, which runs beneath the canal from an opening along the road to Ismailia, 17 kilometres (10.6 miles) north of Suez. In the near future, an aqueduct will run across this tunnel, encouraging agriculture and farming in this vast, arid region and, it is hoped, bringing with it a portion of the fast-growing urban population.

The Mediterranean Coast

Aside from the underground passage between Suez and Ismailia (to which three other points are destined to be linked in the near future), the canal may be crossed at Ismailia, el-Firdan, el-Qantara and Port Said. Arriving from any of these points through the east coastal road of the canal, it is possible to proceed north to el-Qantara along the Mediterranean coast, winding through miles of desert interspersed with indented coves.

El-Arish It is difficult to encounter a traveller until el-Arish, a sea resort town providing ample facilities and comforts. There are a number of small, clean hotels along Sharia 26 July. Several resort complexes have also opened, as well as good restaurants. The palm-dotted beaches have fine white sands, and the sparkling sea makes for excellent swimming. A grand-scale industrial and agricultural development programme for the interior of el-Arish has been put into effect for completion by the end of the 1980s. Another possible road from the canal to el-Arish is through the heartland, penetrating the hilly area of Shushet el-Mughara.

Along the Gulf of Suez Intersected by roads from other cities in the canal zone, the road beyond Sudr leads to Abu Rudeis. At this point, the road departs from the coast and only approaches it again 80 kilometres (50 miles) further on at Abu Zenima. This entire stretch crosses oil-fields and mining zones (a diversion road leads to Ras Matarma, along the coast, finally arriving at Asl). About 127 kilometres (79 miles) from Suez, turning right from the main road, is a track leading to the gypsum mines of el-Gharandel. The area is characterized by rocky hills and gorges crossed by numerous *wadis* which form interesting valleys.

The road winds towards the sea, and then connects again with the main road until it arrives at **Abu Zenima**, a minor port which deals mainly in the transport of oil. 164 kilometres (102 miles) from Suez, it was once an important port centre for the area's manganese mining industry. Before the war, there was a rest-house and a filling station. Constructions and other projects to re-open various tourist facilities are in progress. The oasis of Firan and the Monastery of St Catherine are accessible by way of a road off to the left from the main road.

The next stop along the main road running along the coastline, eight kilometres (five miles) from Abu Zenima, is the ancient port city of **Markha**, which, 3,500 years ago, was the main outlet for the transport and export of turquoise from the mines of Maghara. At the entrance of these turquoise caves were stelae listing the names of Pharaohs who led the mining work. There appeared the names of Cheops and Snofru, dating back to the Old Kingdom, and Hatshepsut, Thutmose III and a host of others until Ramesses III, representing the New Kingdom. At the end of the Old Kingdom, the area fell to foreign invaders and Bedouins and was not recovered by Egypt until a few centuries later. The mines were well-organized, providing workers with decent lodgings surrounded by defensive walls to keep away robbers and looters. Nearby, the remains of a foundry annexed to the copper mines of Serabit el-Khadem have been found. Rising beside the remains is a small temple dedicated to the goddess Hathor, guardian and patroness of the miners. Already in practice at that time was the custom of leaving *ex-votos* in the small chapels in the area. The celebrated Protosemitic Texts of Sinai were also discovered here. A great part of the finds are currently housed at the Cairo Museum.

Seventeen kilometres (10.6 miles) down the road is **Abu Rudeis**, the site of Sinai's most important oil wells. A few kilometres further along on the right is a road continuing on to the coast and the oil wells of Abu Durba. To the left is a road leading to the oasis of Firan. The main road proceeds to **el-Tur** back to the sea coast.

In the area of el-Tur, 100 kilometres (62 miles) south of Abu Zenima, begins an immense coral barrier reef which extends up to Ras Mohammed on the southern tip of the Sinai in the vicinity of Sharm el-Sheikh. Once a Christian city, el-Tur's major attraction is the charming Greek Orthodox church of St George. Today, a small mosque dominates the few houses in the area.

Sharm el-Sheikh, on the southernmost tip of Sinai, is one of the most accessible destinations on the peninsula and is linked to Cairo by efficient public transport. At Naama Beach, eight kilometres (five miles) away, there are a couple of three-star hotels and a campsite. **Ras Mohammed** provides a commanding view of Asia on the left and Africa on the right. Once an important city, Ras Mohammed was the point of arrival for pilgrims heading for Mecca. Further down the coastal road is Nabq. Here, a sparkling stretch of beach is refreshed by

mangroves. Nearby you can see the exotic colours of a Bedouin encampment shimmering in the sun. The **fort of Nasrani**, within the same area, offers panoramic vistas of the islets of Tiran, scattered at the mouth of the Gulf of Aqaba.

Dahab Further on lies Dahab, another 'pearl' of the gulf which has become the focus of tourism development plans. Swaying palms, fine sands, and an extraordinary underwater landscape are the major attractions. Snorkelling is a popular sport here. A few kilometres beyond, towards the Israeli border, is the Island of Coral, marked by the ruins of a fort built by the Crusaders. Boat trips can be arranged. The coastal road is relaxing and beautiful, winding through long stretches of beach, coves and deserted rocky promontories. Dahab has a three-star hotel.

Nuweiba, 92 kilometres (57 miles) north of Sharm el-Sheikh, is another good place for underwater fun. You will see both the imposing mountains of the Sinai and green oases along palm-fringed beaches. Nuweiba has a three-star hotel.

Further up the western coast of the Gulf of Aqaba is **Taba**, right next to the Israeli port of Eilat. The resort town boasts the luxurious Sonesta Beach Hotel.

These towns dotted along the coast of the Gulf of Aqaba offer some of the world's best scuba diving.

Biblical Sinai

The most famous historical event in Sinai is the Exodus of the Hebrews led by Moses. In about 1200 BC, under the reign of the Pharaoh Meneptah, son of Ramesses II, the sons of Israel fled from Egypt in quest of the promised land. A host of miraculous events occurred during their arduous journey. Foremost was the parting of the Red Sea, permitting their passage into the forbidding Sinai Peninsula which was bereft of life and vegetation. Heavenly manna, however, rained on them, appeasing their hunger. The final divine gesture was manifested when, after having reached the heights of Jebel Mousa, also known as the Mountain of Moses or Mount Sinai, the chosen people received the Ten Commandments, bestowed upon Moses.

Sinai was the birthplace of the deep-rooted Judaeo-Christian tradition. Many of the places here are mentioned in Biblical stories and are still identifiable today in the stark mysterious landscape. The miracles and mysteries of Sinai do not end with the story of Moses. The mangled remains of St Catherine, the martyred Christian from Alexandria, are believed to have been transported by angels to Mt

Catherine or Jebel Katerin, along the slopes of which rises the celebrated monastery of the same name.

Thirty-seven kilometres (23 miles) from Suez is **el-Shatt**, which faces the industrial zone of Port Taufiq. Eight kilometres (five miles) beyond, a road on the right takes you a kilometre further to the **Spring of Moses (Ain Mousa)**. Twelve springs of water irrigate the small but luxuriantly verdant oasis. The southernmost spring is believed to have been born from a rock Moses struck with his stick.

The **Oasis of Firan** lies 208 kilometres (129 miles) from Suez and is the largest and most fertile on the peninsula. Date trees, tamarisk, maize and other cereals grow here. There is a small monastery — the **Monastery of Firan** — by the spring at the centre of the oasis, rising on the site where the Hebrews, headed by Joshua, defeated the Amalekites. The oasis is situated at the foot of Mt Horeb (Jebel Serbal), 2,078 metres (6,820 feet) high, where Moses spoke with God. It was also here that Aaron and Hur supported Moses during the battle against the Amalekites. On a road to the right is a hermitage belonging to the Monastery of St Catherine. This is one of the two hermitages the monastery has kept for the poor and needy.

The oasis extends for over four kilometres (2.5 miles) and is inhabited by Bedouins who live in houses made of sun-baked mud surrounded by walls of the same material, enclosing precious patches of palm-shaded gardens. The small town of Firan dates back to the second century. It was once the seat of an Episcopal community until Muslims expelled the monks. The ruins of a basilica, a church, houses, a fortified wall and some rock tombs may still be seen.

From the Oasis of Firan, the road passes through valleys and gorges, before rising in a succession of hair-pin bends over an area covered with tamarisk and manna trees, named after the Biblical manna. After crossing the rugged pass of el-Buweid, one enters the Wadi Sheikh. Here is the tomb of Nebi Saleh, where Bedouin pilgrims flock annually. Twelve kilometres (7.5 miles) on is the Mosque of Sheikh Harun and the Golden Calf Chapel. From Wadi Sheikh, a six-kilometre (3.7 mile) track leads to the Monastery of St Catherine, situated at the foot of Mt Sinai (Jebel Mousa).

The **Monastery of St Catherine** stands in a valley surrounded by Jebel Safsaga, Jebel Katerin, Jebel Moneiga and Jebel Mousa. In 342, Empress Helen, the mother of Constantine the Great, ordered a chapel built here on the site where the Hebrew people had heard the voice of God and where God revealed himself to Moses in the form of the burning bush. The monastery was officially founded in 527 by Emperor Justinian I, the builder of the Cathedral of St Sophia in Constantinople.

A veritable fortress with rampart walls, the monastery successfully protected monks throughout history from marauding Bedouins. Hermits and pilgrims met here to re-trace the path of the Exodus, safe from attack by soldiers. The monastery has preserved its special character. The thick walls are 12 to 15 metres (40 to 50 feet) high, and the corners coincide exactly with the cardinal points. The door which now serves as the entrance was built at a much later period. Initially, there was only a little door nine metres (30 feet) off the ground from where provisions necessary to the monks' survival were lifted in through a system of pulleys. The monks, in turn, often fed nomads who rested outside the walls. Inside the great walls are buildings from different eras, with small yards, kitchen gardens and stairs crossed by narrow climbing streets. Curiously, in this centre of Christian faith (Greek-Orthodox), there is a mosque, probably built in the 11th century for the Bedouins working in the convent, or according to another version, to prevent Islamic warriors from attacking it. In the mosque are a wooden throne with Kufic inscriptions (a form of Arabic script) and a *minbar* of the Fatimid period. Both items date from the reign of the seventh Fatimid Caliph, el-Mustali, who ruled from 1094 to 1101.

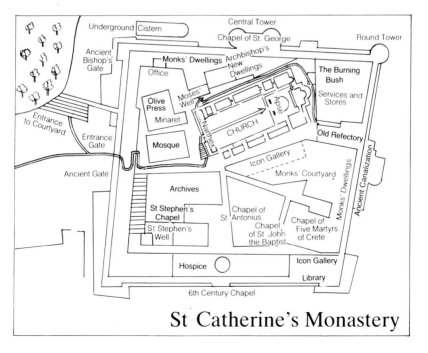

St Catherine's Monastery

A Fatimid-style 11th-century gate leads to the long arcaded porch of **the Basilica**, and then to a sixth-century Byzantine gateway. Beyond is the narthex. The floor is of white marble and porphyry. Twelve granite columns with black rock capitals, representing the 12 months of the year, divide the church interior into three aisles. On the left are the chapels of St Cosmas, St Damian and St Simeon, and on the right are those of St Marisa, St Constantine and St Helen. Gifts are laid on both sides of the 13th-century iconostasis. In the apse is a sixth-century Byzantine mosaic, and the splendid wood altar with mother-of-pearl inlay was a gift from Damascus. The relics of St Catherine are preserved in a marble reliquary, to the right of the altar, beneath a canopy. Two silver reliquaries inlaid with precious stones stand behind iconostaries. One was donated by Czar Alexander II in the 19th century, and the other was a gift of Empress Catherine of Russia in the 17th century.

Immediately behind the chancel is the monastery's most celebrated and holiest place, the **Chapel of the Burning Bush**, thought to be the actual site of the Biblical event. Before entering, visitors must remove their shoes just as God instructed Moses to do.

Another pride of the monastery is its rich library, containing some 3,500 manuscripts in Greek, Coptic, Arabic, Armenian, Hebrew, Slavic and other languages. The extensive collection of manuscripts is said to rank second only to that of the Vatican. Between 1844 and 1859, the German scholar Konstantin Tischendorf discovered a Biblical manuscript, the 'Codex Sinaiticus' from the fourth century. This precious document is now preserved in the British Museum in London.

Two thousand icons dating from the period of iconoclasm in the sixth century to the end of the Byzantine period in the 15th century are housed in the **museum**. There are also fascinating paintings on wax from the fifth and sixth centuries. Other treasures include fine sacerdotal ornaments. In the garden is the charnel-house or ossuary. The last remains of the monks lie in two crypts. In a separate box are the remains of St Stephen of Eilat. The monks celebrate the main daily service between 4.30 and 7.30 pm.

The Holy Mountains

Mount Moses or the 'Holy Peak' is a three-hour walk from the monastery, entailing a climb up 3,750 steps carved out of hard granite by monks who had made a vow to accomplish this task. This is the mountain where God gave Moses the Ten Commandments. It is probable that the Mountain of the Law, known as Mt Horeb in the Old Testament, was in fact Jebel Serbal. Nonetheless, pre-Christian Nabatean inscriptions refer to Mt Sinai as a sacred mountain. Islam also considers the mountain sacred. Here Mohammed's horse, Boraq, touched the stone steps when he ascended to heaven. The steps pass the fountain of Moses, a small chapel of the Virgin, and two arches, the Gates of St Stephen and the Gate of the Law. On the summit is the Chapel of the Holy Trinity, built in 1934 on the site of a smaller chapel dating back to the fourth century.

The ascent of **Mt Moneiga** takes about an hour and follows the path at the beginning of the climb to Mt Moses, before turning left on to another path leading to the top. Here, a small chapel is dedicated to the Mother of God. From the summit there is a very good view of the Monastery of St Catherine.

The ascent of **Mt Catherine** takes five hours, but follows a very interesting route. On the way up, you pass the Chapel of Aaron, the monastery of the garden convent of the Holy Apostles, a pavilion built by King Fuad, and the Monastery of the Forty Martyrs. The chapel of St Catherine, built by the monk Callistes, is at the peak.

It is believed that the headless body of the martyred saint was transported by angels and laid on the summit of this mountain. Nearby is Jebel Sebir, which takes about 25 minutes to climb from Mt Catherine. On its summit stands an observatory of the Smith Institute of Metereology of California. Solar radiation was first measured here between 1933 and 1938.

The Egyptian Oases

The Egyptian oases, even in their diversity, have some common characteristics. First , one must work hard to get to them, as they are off the beaten tracks of organized tourism and are quite inaccessible. The exception is **Kharga** which has an airport.

It is appropriate to use the word 'oasis' for anything meaning quietness, like the calm after a storm. Time does not exist in the oases. The oases — and their inhabitants — are, like the desert, quite different from others, seemingly unchangeable, indifferent and self-sufficient. The best advice for travellers visiting the oases is to be flexible and ready to experience a totally different landscape.

One cannot describe the excitement one feels when, from the immense ocean of sand, 'something' emerges. The desert is like the sea; it is indifferent to man and dangerous. Today there are jeeps, radios and sophisticated equipment, and the risk of getting lost in the desert is greatly reduced. But the adventure of the desert remains deeply interesting to man. A little wind can, in a few minutes, erase tracks and even the asphalted roads.

The Oasis of el-Fayum

The Oasis of Fayum, the largest and most famous in Egypt, is situated 80 kilometres (50 miles) south of Cairo on the west bank of the Nile. The oasis can be reached from Cairo by both a direct asphalted road across the desert and a road some 74 kilometres (46 miles) outside Cairo on the main artery to Aswan. Those arriving by car from the south will find a good asphalted road on the left of Beni Suef.

The great **Lake Karun**, which has shrunk over the ages, closes the oasis on the northern side, the place being in a depression once filled by the waters of the lake. El-Fayum, circular-shaped, has a diameter of about 50 kilometres (31 miles) and is densely populated and cultivated. The oasis, known, loved and attended through thousands of years, resembles an immense palette of colours surrounded by the desert. This is the place from which the most beautiful flowers of Egypt come and it has been the hunting and fishing reserve of Egyptian sovereigns from the Pharaohs of the 11th Dynasty to King Farouk. The brackish waters of the lake swarm with fish, some of which are nearly two metres (6.6 feet) long and gastronomically highly-prized.

The oasis of Fayum is the first place in the world, according to current historical knowledge, where water conveyance and regulation projects to protect the fields from the unpredictable flooding of the Nile were carried out 4,000 years ago. Today one can see the remnants

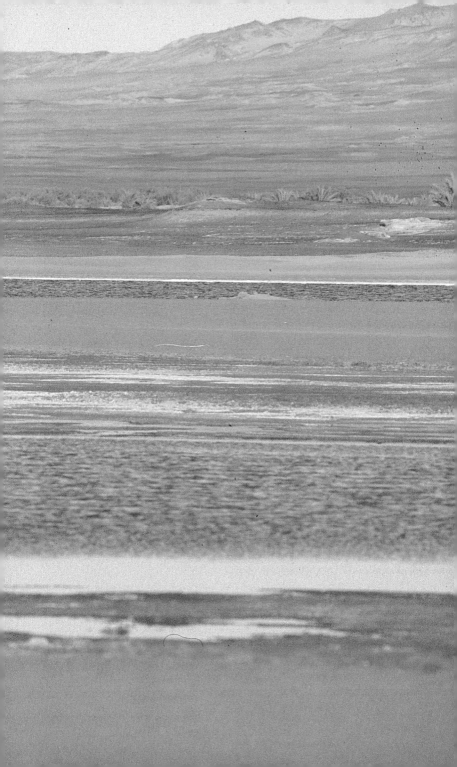

of the Pharaonic system of dams and canals north of **Medinet el-Fayum**, the chief town of the region. The processing of terracotta also first occurred here.

Medinet el-Fayum is an extremely lively and active city, producing in abundance the fresh fruit and vegetable supplies for Cairo. The numerous markets, rich with colours and scents, vie for the attention of the tourists, who may find themselves caught up in a joyful frenzy. Medinet el-Fayum lies where Shedit, the city of crocodiles, once stood. It was re-named Crocodilopolis during the Greek domination. North of the city are several remains, among which is the temple of the crocodile-god Sobek; already very ancient at that time, it was rebuilt by Ramesses II during his reign. In the neighbourhood, remains of finely built Graeco-Roman thermal plants were recently discovered. Most of these have been stolen, apart from a few pieces in the local museum in Kom Aushim, or those that are now in the Cairo Museum.

Medinet el-Fayum can provide only very basic accommodation. It is thus better to spend the night in Shakshuk, on the lake, or in Fedimin, halfway between Medinet el-Fayum and Shakshuk. The Auberge du Lac, once the summer residence of King Farouk, is currently being developed into a hotel school. The oasis people are very kind and hospitable, more simple and spontaneous than the inhabitants of the big cities, and communicating with them is easy despite language problems. The roads in the oasis, not in good condition, lead to wonderful places like **Qasr Karun**, the ancient **Dionysias**, where there are two temples. One, restored in 1957, is a sanctuary belonging to later periods, where a corridor flanked by 14 rooms leads to three small chapels with wonderful frescoes (partially damaged), showing the king worshipping Sobek. The area is full of archaeological remains from different epochs and in varying states of preservation.

The only problem in reaching Qasr Karun is the road which is passable until Ibshawai where it becomes a track until el-Shawashna, where it becomes worse. Only cars in good condition can reach Qasr Karun. There is, however, a better road which begins at Medinet el-Fayum to Beni Suef and along which you will find, after about eight kilometres (five miles), the **Pyramid of Hawara**. The pyramid, in mud bricks, is in a bad state. Nearby are, the remains of the one of the most splendid buildings of ancient Egypt, the funerary temple of the pyramid, called 'the Labyrinth' by the Greeks because it had 3,000 rooms, half of which were underground. Unfortunately, the years saw the dismantling of the magnificent structure for its stones — a precious type of limestone — which were utilized for other buildings.

Also at Hawara, a large Roman period cemetery was discovered. The usual type of mummy mask was here replaced by a thin wooden panel carrying a portrait of the deceased painted in wax. The best collection of these 'Fayum Portraits' can be seen in the Cairo Museum, and the British Museum in London. Some of the faces are painted in a naive style, with large staring eyes, but others are remarkably realistic. The technique employed, called encaustic painting, and the styles, are Hellenistic, although often the panels are attached to coffins decorated with traditional Egyptian religious motifs. The people represented are the mixed Greek-Egyptian middle class, whose lives are well-documented in the hundreds of letters and official records discovered in the excavations of Fayum towns. A few kilometres further south is **el-Lahun**, a large village on the Bahr Yusuf, the river feeding the irrigation system of the oasis, where the Pharaohs built a lock.

One and a half kilometres (0.93 miles) from the village, the small pyramid of Senusret II is slowly being eroded. Here, archaeologists discovered a wonderful sarcophagus made of red granite. In one of the four funerary wells, extraordinary royal jewels were discovered, among which a diadem stands out. Today, these are on exhibition in the Museum of Cairo.

Another interesting trip, is to the ruins of **Medinet Madi**, 30 kilometres (19 miles) from Medinet el-Fayum. The temple there is small, but is the best-preserved of those of the Middle Kingdom. Medinet Madi is the centre of a monumental religious complex, with a course for processions flanked by sphinxes and lions. The Oasis of Fayum does not offer the visitor much in the way of nightlife or sports facilities, but it is possible to find guides with whom one can safely venture into the desert.

The Oasis of Baharia

This oasis, in the middle of the Libyan Desert, is accessible from Cairo along a recently-built 334-kilometre (207.5-mile) road which is often covered with sand. The oasis is small and quiet with about 10,000 inhabitants who live in four villages: Bawiti, Zabu, Mandisha and el-Qasr. In Bawiti and el-Qasr there are some hot springs, where one can bathe even in winter. The major product of the oasis is dates, which are also exported. Another favourite product is the local beverage, a fermented sap extracted from date-palms which tastes like a mixture of cider and wine. The principal centre, Bawiti, is extremely picturesque, with small multi-coloured houses and narrow streets. The inhabitants of the oasis, who are discreet and shy, have descended from Bedouin tribes. The oasis has temples from the 26th Dynasty, a

Roman triumphal arch, the Temple of Alexander, a Roman necropolis and the Tomb of Amenhotep. It is advisable to set off for the oasis in a car in perfect condition and with enough petrol for the return trip.

The Oasis of Dakhla

This oasis which covers 1,125 square kilometres (434 square miles) and has 35,000 people, is the second-largest Egyptian oasis. You reach the oasis along a road from Kharga to the east. As soon as you arrive, you must go to the police station with your passport. All archaeological sites can only be visited with authorized guides. The oasis has about ten villages where fruit-growing, particularly of mangoes and apricots, is the main trade. The oldest remains are close to the village of Balat, a Neolithic village with ruins from the Old and Middle Kingdoms and a necropolis with huge pyramidal tombs. Spread throughout the oasis are remains from various periods: of these do not miss the **tomb of Medounefer**, the governor of the oasis during the Sixth Dynasty, discovered in 1979 in Mut, the chief town in the oasis. The medieval capital of the oasis, el-Qasr, lies along the road leading to the Oasis of Farafra, 30 kilometres (19 miles) away. The area's major attraction, the **temple of Amun**, which was probably restored during the Roman period, lies 13 kilometres (eight miles) further south. The temple is built from sandstone and has three chapels, a lobby and a hypostyle hall, all of which are surrounded by a brick wall. Along the boundaries of the oasis is a thermal spring with sulphurous hot waters which has been famous since Roman times.

The Oasis of Farafra

Farafra is the smallest of the Egyptian oases, with just 1,000 inhabitants and very few resources. It is reached along a 180-kilometre (112-mile) long road from Baharia. Here, there is just a village, el-Qasr, which is surrounded by a fortified wall. This oasis might appeal to those who are are looking for absolute peace rather than traces of ages past.

The Oasis of Firan

Firan in Sinai is reached along a track between Abu Zenima and Bir el-Safra. Only four kilometres (2.5 miles) long, it is populated by Bedouins who grow mainly cereals and dates (see Sinai).

The Oasis of Kharga

Of all Egyptian oases, Kharga is the easiest to get to as it is linked to Asyut by road and has an airport with flights to Cairo and Aswan. There is also a bus service and taxis to and from Cairo. The reason behind these transport facilities is a desert land reclamation project, launched in 1959 and named 'New Valley', which saw the building of hundreds of wells allowing the cultivation of larger areas for the benefit of homeless people and inhabitants of Nubian villages flooded because of the Lake Nasser projects. The experiment has succeeded, though its concrete buildings have marred the scenery.

Along the Asyut-Kharga road are three police checkpoints with obligatory passport controls. Archaeological sites can only be visited with authorized guides. The area's main attraction is the Temple of Amun in the town of Hibis which lies a couple of kilometres north-west of Kharga's centre. The temple, 42 metres (138 feet) long and 20 metres (66 feet) wide, was built by the emperor Darius in the first Persian occupation (525−404 BC). It was enlarged by Nectanebo II in about 360 BC and then by the Ptolemies and the Romans.

About 90 kilometres (56 miles) south of Kharga is a necropolis dating back to the Ptolemaic period (third-fifth centuries) and where the discovery of several mummies, completely covered with gold leaf, stirred excitement because in ancient times only high-ranking persons were given such treatment. Near the necropolis is a Roman temple of Serapis and Isis.

The Oasis of Siwa

This oasis lies in the extreme west of Egypt close to the border with Libya, and is difficult to get to because of dangerous tracks which link it to Mersa Matruh on the Mediterranean coast. You need a permit from military authorities to get there because of its proximity to Libya, with which Egypt has no diplomatic relations. There is also no chance of finding petrol, tourist or hotel accommodation. One kilometre (0.6 miles) east of the town of **Siwa** stands the Temple of Amun of the Oracle, which attracted sovereigns and generals like Croesus, Alexander and Hannibal. The temple is now completely ruined and other edifices in Siwa are in equally poor condition. All told, the place is for those seeking adventure. It is advisable to take two jeeps, petrol supplies and enough food and drinks to last the entire trip.

Useful Addresses

Airlines (in Cairo)

Aeroflot
8 Qasr el-Nil, tel. 753386

Air Canada
26 Sharia Mahmoud Bassiouni, tel. 758939

Air France
2 Sharia Talaat Harb, tel. 743300, 743516

Air India
1 Sharia Talaat Harb, tel, 742592, 754864,
754873, 754875

Air Sinai
Nile Hilton, tel. 760948

Alitalia
Nile Hilton, tel. 767109, 743488

Qantas
13 Sharia Talaat Harb, tel. 742755, 752699

British Airways
1 Sharia Abdel-Salam Aref, Midan el-
Tahrir, tel. 762914, 759977, 772981

British Caledonian
26 Sharia Mahmoud Bassiouni, tel.758939,
743336

Cathay Pacific
26 Sharia Mahmoud Bassiouni, tel 758939,
760071

Egypt Air
6 Sharia Adly, tel. 922444, 920999
12 Qasr el-Nil, tel. 59915
Nile Hilton, tel. 765200, 759703

El Al
5 Sharia el-Maqrizi, Zamalek,
tel. 3411620, 3411429, 3411795,
340912

Japan Airlines
Nile Hilton, tel. 740809, 740621, 740999,
779845

KLM
11 Qasr el-Nil, tel. 740999, 747747,
740650, 662226

Lufthansa
9 Sharia Talaat Harb, tel. 750343, 750425,
750534, 750366
6 Sharia el-Sheikh el-Mersaffi, Zamalek,
tel. 3420471

Pan American Airlines
2 Sharia Talaat Harb, tel. 747399, 747007,
747302

Qantas-Gsa
1 Qasr el-Nil, tel. 749900, 760300

TransAmerica Airlines
3 Behler Passage, Qasr el-Nil, tel. 754277,
754122

TWA
1 Qasr el-Nil, tel. 749900, 960300

United Airlines
16 Sharia Adly, tel. 911104, 938874, 938964
2 Sharia Moustafa Kemal, Maadi,
tel. 3501240, 3501241
25 Sharia Ibrahim Lakani, Heliopolis,
tel. 2591954, 2591311

Banks (in Cairo)

Arab International Bank
35 Sharia Abdel-Khalek Sarwat,
tel. 916120, 911893

Banque du Caire
22 Sharia Adly Pasha, tel. 746727, 746616

Central Bank of Egypt
31 Qasr el-Nil, tel. 741752, 751738, 751529

American Express
15 Qasr el-Nil, tel. 750892, 753142
Nile Hilton, tel. 743383
Meridien Hotel, tel. 844017
4 Sharia Ibn Zanki, Zamalek, tel. 3405351

Bank of America
106 Sharia Qasr el-Aini, tel. 3547788,
3541051;

Bank of Tokyo Ltd.
Nile Hilton Annex, tel. 766318 ext. 247

Chase Manhattan Bank NA
21/23 Sharia el-Ahram, tel. 728485,
728419

Chase National Bank (Egypt) SAE
10 Sharia el-Mansour Mohamed,
Zamalek, tel. 3404722, 3412970

Citibank NA
4 Sharia Ahmed Pasha, Garden City,
tel. 3551873

Car Hire

Amercar (Hertz)
15 Sharia el-Nabatat, Garden City,
tel. 23203
Avis
16 Maamal el-Sukkar, Garden City,
tel. 28698, 845444
Meridien Hotel, tel. 845444
Nile Hilton Hotel, tel. 766432
Cairo International Airport, tel. 667711
Cairo International Hotel, tel. 731817
Sheraton Heliopolis, tel. 665500, 667700
Jolie Ville Hotel, Giza, tel. 855510,
855977
Movenpick Hotel, Heliopolis, tel. 664242
Budget (Rent A Car)
5 Sharia el-Maqrizi, Zamalek,
tel. 3409474, 3400070
Mena House Oberoi, tel. 855444, 855532
ext. 0663
Navotel Cairo Hotel, tel. 661330
Heliopolis, tel. 666027
International Airport, tel. 667721
ext. 4223
Europcar
15 Sharia Mahmoud Bassiouni,
tel. 753130, 746169
Hertz
Central reservations in Cairo, tel. 814172
Ramses Hilton Hotel, tel. 758000
el-Salam Hyatt, tel. 2455155
Sonesta Hotel, tel. 609444
President Hotel, tel. 3416751
International Airport, tel. 667788
ext. 3629
Osiris Travel
Atlas Hotel, tel. 938411, 918311
PAN Arab Tours
55 Sharia el-Gumhuriyya, tel. 938880,
902133

Embassies and Consulates

Australia
Cairo Plaza, Nile Corniche, Bulaq,
tel. 777900, 777489
Canada
6 Sharia Mohamed Fahmy el-Sayed,
Garden City, tel. 3543110, 3543119,
3543158/9, 3546415

China
14 Sharia Baghat Ali, Zamalek,
tel. 3411219
France
29 Sharia el-Ahram, tel. 728649
6 el-Dokki, Dokki, tel. 711955
5 Sharia el-Fadi, tel. 754322, 754534
Germany (D.R.)
141 Sharia el-Tahrir, Dokki, tel. 3484500
8 Saleh Ayoub, Zamalek, tel. 3401804
11 Sharia Amer, Dokki, tel. 3484603
Germany (F.R.)
8 Hassan Sabri, Zamalek, tel. 3403687,
3406017
Israel
6 Ibn Malek, Giza, tel. 727706, 726000
Norway
24 Sharia Hassan Asem, Zamalek,
tel. 3408046, 3403340
Sweden
13 Sharia Mohamed Mazhar, Zamalek,
tel. 3414132, 3411484
Switzerland
10 Sharia Abdel-Khalek Sarwat,
tel. 758133, 758284
United Kingdom
Sharia Ahmed Ragheb, Garden City,
tel. 3540852/9
United States of America
5 America el-Latineya, Garden City,
tel. 3548211/9
USSR
95 Sharia el-Giza, tel. 984841, 984996
35 Sharia Mohamed, Mazhar, Zamalek,
tel. 698191
8 Midan el-Saad el-Ali, Dokki, tel. 706942

Hotels
Cairo

Five-star hotels

Cairo Sheraton
Galaa Bridge, Sharia el-Ahram,
tel. 3488600, 3488700; tlx: 92041, 22382
SHUN
Heliopolis Sheraton
Airport Road, Heliopolis, tel. 665500,
667700; tlx: 93300, 93350 HELSH UN
Mariott
Sharia Saray el-Gezira, Zamalek,
tel. 3408888; tlx. 93464, 93465 Mar UN

Meridien
Nile Corniche, tel. 845444; tlx. 93918,
22325 HOMER UN
Nile Hilton
Midan el-Tahrir, tel. 740777, 750666;
tlx. 92222

Four-star hotels

el Borg
Sharia el-Gezira, Zamalek, tel. 3406179,
3409978; tlx: 94148 BORGHT UN
el-Nil
12 Sharia Ahmed Ragheb, Garden City,
tel. 3542800, 3542805; tlx. 93284 NITEL
UN
el-Salaam Hyatt
61 Sharia Abdel-Hamid Badawi,
Heliopolis, tel. 2455155; tlx. 92184
President
22 Sharia Taha Hussein, Zamalek,
tel. 3416751, 3418021, 3413195;
tlx. 93655 PRES UN
Shepheards
Nile Corniche, tel. 33800, 33900
Mena House Oberoi
Sharia el-Ahram, Giza, tel. 855174,
857999, 855444; tlx. 92316, 93096 OBHTL
UN
Green Pyramids
Off Sharia el-Ahram, Giza, tel. 852600,
856786, 856778; tlx. 93701 GPHOT UN

Luxor

Five-star hotels

Etap
Nile Corniche, tel. 82160, 82011;
tlx. 92080 ETAPX UN
Winter Palace
Nile Corniche, tel. 755216, 774116;
tlx. 92160 WINTER UN

Four-star hotels

Luxor Hotel
Near Luxor Temple, tel. 82400, 82405;
tlx. 24126 UN
Savoy
Nile Corniche, tel. 2200; tlx. 92160
WINTER UN

Aswan

Five-star hotels

Aswan Oberoi
Elephantine Island, tel. 23455; tlx. 92120
OBEROI UN
New Cataract
Sharia Abtal el-Tahrir, tel. 767395, 22016;
tlx. 92720 ASCTE UN

Four-star hotels

Amoun
Amoun Island, tel. 22555, 22816;
tlx. 92720 ASCTE UN
Amoun Sheraton Village
Sahara City, tel. 24826
Old Cataract
Sharia Abtal el-Tahrir, tel. 23510, 22233;
tlx. 92720 ASCTE UN

Alexandria

Five-star hotels

Alamein
Sidi Abdel-Rahman, tel. 5863580, 5863586
Montazah Sheraton
Corniche Road, Montazah, tel. 969220,
968550; tlx. 54706 MONSH UN
Ramada Renaissance
Corniche Road, Sidi Bishr, tel. 866111;
tlx. 54177 RAREA UN

Four-star hotels

San Stefano
Sharia Abdel-Salam Aref, San Stefano,
tel. 5863589, 5861184; tlx. 54201 SANTEL
Cecil
16 Midan Saad Zaghloul, tel. 802546,
807055; tlx. 54358

Ismailia

Four-star hotel

Etap Hotel
Forsan Island, tel. 22220, 22274, 22250;
tlx. 63038 ETAPI UN

308

Port Said

Four-star hotel

Etap Motel
Corniche Road, tel. 8823

Two-star hotel

Abu Simbel
15 Sharia Gumhuriyya, tel. 23802

Suez

Red Sea
Sharia Riad, Port Taufiq, tel: 23334;
tlx. 66074 RDSEA UN

Sinai

Booking arrangements can be made in
Cairo through a travel agency: **el-Urba
Hotel**, el-Arish, **Dahab Tourist Village**,
Dahab, **Isis Guest House** (within St
Catherine's Monastery).
Marina Hotel, Sharm el-Sheikh, **Nuweiba
Tourist Village**, Nuweiba

Restaurants
Cairo
International and Continental

Aladin
26 Sharia Sherif, Immobilia Building,
tel. 755694
Caravan
Nile Corniche, Shepheard's Hotel,
Garden City, tel. 3553900, 3553800
Citadel Grill
1115 Nile Corniche, Ramses Hilton,
Garden City, tel. 758000, 777444 ext. 3228
Fontana
Nile Corniche, Meridien Hotel, Garden
City, tel. 845444
La Belle Epoque
Nile Corniche, Meridien Hotel, Garden
City, tel. 845444
La Patisserie
Ramses Hilton, 1115 Nile Corniche,
Garden City, tel. 758000, 777444 ext. 3185

Manial Palace
Sayala Bridge, Roda Island, tel. 846014
Terrace Cafe
1115 Nile Corniche, Ramses Hilton,
Garden City, tel. 758000, 777444 ext. 3222

Egyptian and Oriental

Abou Shakra
69 Sharia Qasr el-Aini, Garden City,
tel. 848711
el Americain
26 Sharia 26 July, tel. 919666
Excelsior
35 Sharia Talaat Harb, tel. 745002
Falafel
1115 Nile Corniche, Ramses Hilton,
Garden City, tel. 777444, 758000 ext 3171
Qasr el-Rachid
Nile Corniche, Meridien Hotel, Garden
City, tel. 845444

Chinese and Far Eastern

Kowloon
11 Sharia Modiriet el-Tahrir, Garden City,
tel. 3540128
Fu Ching
28 Sharia Talaat Harb, tel. 756184

French

Caf Fontana
Nile Corniche, Shepheard's Hotel,
Garden City, tel. 845444
La Palme D'or
Meridien Hotel, Nile Corniche,
Garden City, tel. 845444

Heliopolis
International and Continental

el Zahraa
Sharia Uruba, Heliopolis Sheraton Hotel,
tel. 667700, 665500
Bierstube
Sharia Uruba, Heliopolis Sheraton Hotel,
tel. 667700, 665500
Groppi's
9 Sharia el-Ahram, tel. 2585099

Le Baron
Sharia Uruba, Heliopolis Sheraton Hotel,
tel. 667700, 665500
Terrace
Sharia Maahad el-Sahara, Le Baron
Hotel, tel. 2915757,2912467 ext. 2022

Egyptian and Oriental

Lebanese Restaurant
57 Sharia Beirut, tel. 662347
Oriental Tent
Sharia Uruba, Heliopolis Sheraton Hotel,
tel. 667700, 665500
Chinese Restaurant
57 Sharia Beirut, tel. 662347
Seoul House Korean Restaurant
4 Sharia Said Abd el-Wahed, Roxi,
tel. 2581515

French

el-Sarraya
el-Horria, Movenpick Hotel, Cairo
Airport, tel. 679797, 679787, 664977
Le Jardin d'Heliopolis
Novotel Hotel, Cairo Airport, tel. 661330,
678080

Italian

Alfredo
Sharia Uruba, Heliopolis Sheraton Hotel,
tel. 667700, 665500
Il Giardino
el-Horria, Movenpick Hotel, Cairo
Airport, tel. 679797, 679787, 664977
La Gondola
4 Sharia el-Tayaran, Sonesta Hotel,
tel. 609444, 611066 ext. 286
Mama Mia
Egyptel Hotel, tel. 662258, 662304

Indian and Pakistani

Chicken Tikka
5 Sharia Said Abd el-Wahed, Roxi
Tikka Grill
7 Sharia Sayed Abd el-Wahed

Patisseries

Le Café
4 Sharia el-Tayaran, Sonesta Hotel,
tel. 609444, 611066 ext. 815
Pastry Shop
Sharia Maahad el-Sahara, Le Baron
Hotel, tel. 2915757, 2912467
Vienna Cafe
Sharia Uruba, Heliopolis Sheraton Hotel,
tel. 667700, 665500

Maadi
International and Continental

Lola
15, Road 9B, tel. 3515587, 3515465
Pub 13
Road 13, tel. 3504544
Sea Horse
Nile Corniche (across the Salaam
Hospital), tel. 988499

Egyptian and Oriental

Good Shot
Nile Corniche, tel. 3503327

Italian

Fouquets
Sharia el-Nasr, New Maadi, tel. 3523450
Petit Suisse Chalet
151, Road 9, tel. 3518328

Mexican

Happy Joe's
67 Road 9, tel. 3501526
Mermaid
77 Road 9, tel. 3503964

Giza
International and Continental

Abu Nawas Nightclub
Sharia el-Ahram, Mena House Oberoi,
Giza, tel. 855444, 857999 ext. 500

el-Boddega
Sharia el-Ahram, Green Pyramids Hotel,
tel. 855778, 856887
el-Hambra Nightclub
Cairo Sheraton, 23rd Floor, Giza,
tel. 3488600, 348700 ext. 175
Arrous el-Nil
Cairo Sheraton, Ground Floor, Giza,
tel. 3488600, 3488700
Blow Up Disco
287 Sharia el-Ahram, Vendome Hotel,
Pyramids, tel. 850977
Golden Club
Alexandria Desert Road, Ramada
Renaissance Hotel, tel. 538111
Habiba Nightclub
Ramada Renaissance Hotel, Alexandria
Desert Road, tel. 538111
Khan el-Khalili
Sharia el-Ahram, Mena House Oberoi,
Giza, tel. 855444, 857999 ext. 330
Oasis Nightclub
Sharia el-Ahram, Mena House Oberoi,
Giza, tel. 538111
Oasis Nightclub
Sharia el-Ahram, Mena House Oberoi,
Giza, tel. 855444, 857999 ext. 700
The Greenery
Sharia el-Ahram, Mena House Oberoi,
Giza, tel. 855444, 857999 ext. 545
The Grill
el-Gezirah Sheraton Hotel, Giza,
tel. 411333, 411555 ext. 5250
The Rubayyat
Sharia el-Ahram, Mena House Oberoi,
Giza, tel. 855444, 857999
Vendome Coffee Shop
287 Sharia el-Ahram, tel. 850977

Egyptian and Oriental

Aageba Restaurant
113 Sharia el-Manial, el-Helbawe, Giza,
tel. 3632856
Kebabgy El Gezirah
el-Gezirah Sheraton Hotel, Giza,
tel. 411333, 411555 ext. 5190
Lebanese Restaurant
287 Sharia el-Ahram, Vendome Hotel,
Pyramids, tel. 850977

Chinese and Far Eastern

Korean Restaurant
287 Sharia el-Ahram, Pyramids,
tel. 850977
The Moghul Room
Sharia el-Ahram, Mena House Oberoi,
Giza, tel. 855444, 857999 ext. 661

Italian

La Fontana Del Nilo
el-Gezirah Sheraton Hotel, Giza,
tel. 411333, 411555 ext. 5289
el-Gondool
el-Gezirah Sheraton Hotel, Giza,
tel. 411333, 411555 ext. 5184
el-Sultan Lounge
Sharia el-Ahram, Mena House Oberoi,
Giza, tel. 855444, 857999
Mameluke Bar
Sharia el-Ahram, Mena House Oberoi,
Giza, tel. 855444, 857999 ext. 400
Oasis Bar
Cairo Sheraton, Ground Floor, Giza,
tel. 3488600, 3488700

Zamalek
International and Continental

Almaz Nightclub
Sharia Gezira, Cairo Marriott Hotel,
Zamalek, tel. 3408888 ext. 8266
Ambassador
31 Sharia 26 July, Zamalek, tel. 753342,
743354
Cairo Cellar
22 Sharia Taha Hussein, President Hotel,
Zamalek, tel. 3400652
La Terrace
22 Sharia Taha Hussein, President Hotel,
Zamalek, tel. 3400652
Queen Grill House (Freddy's)
Sharia Midan Segdy, Zamalek,
tel. 3401846

Alexandria, Ismailia, Luxor

Alexander Restaurant
Ramada Renaissance Hotel
544 Sharia el-Geish, Alexandria,
tel. 866111, 868188
Blue Beach Cafeteria
408 Sharia el-Geish, San Stefano,
Alexandria, tel. 5861711
Broost Bamby
7 Midan Saad Zaghloul, el-Ralm Station,
Alexandria, tel. 4827811
Caesar Inn
Corniche Road, Sheraton Montazah
Hotel, Alexandria, tel. 969220, 968550
Cafe Coquillage
Corniche Road, Sheraton Montazah
Hotel, Alexandria, tel. 969220, 968550
el-Bardy
Ramada Renaissance Hotel
544 Sharia el-Geish, Alexandria,
tel. 866111, 868188
Italian Restaurant
544 Sharia el-Geish, Ramada Renaissance
Hotel, Alexandria, tel. 866111, 868188
el-Timsah
Etap Ismailia Hotel, Ismailia, tel. 765322,
768802
Le Coin Du Capitaine
Forsan Island, Etap Ismailia Hotel,
Ismailia, tel. 765322, 768802
La Felouque
Forsan Island, Etap Ismailia Hotel,
Ismailia, tel. 765322, 768802
Le Grill D'Eugenie
Forsan Island, Etap Ismailia Hotel,
Ismailia, tel. 765322, 768802
Palace Coffee Shop
17 Sharia el-Shohada, Winter Palace
Hotel, Luxor, tel. 808700, 808123
Winter Palace Restaurant
17 Sharia el-Shohada, Winter Palace
Hotel, Luxor, tel. 808700, 808123

Travel Agencies

Abydous Tour & Travel
5 Midan Tahrir, tel. 3543559, 3545302
11 Sharia Talaat Harb, tel. 740093
Aerocontact Travel Limited
6A Sharia el-Malek el-Afdal, Zamalek,
tel. 3403908, 3403339
19A Sharia el-Khalifa el-Maamoun,
Heliopolis, tel. 2910380
American Express of Egypt Limited
15 Qasr el-Nil, tel. 750444; tlx. 92715
AMEXT UN
Cairo Airport Terminal 1 & 2, tel. 670895;
tlx. 21388 AMEXT UN
Marriott Hotel, Zamalek, tel. 3408888;
tlx. 92715 AMEXT UN
Meridien Hotel, Garden City, tel. 845444,
844017; tlx. 92715 AMEXT UN
17 Sharia Mahmoud Bassiouni,
tel. 764342, 764353
Telex: 21388 AMEXT UN
Nile Hilton Hotel, Midan el-Tahrir,
tel. 740777, 743383; tlx. 92715 AMEXT
UN
Cairo Sheraton Hotel, Giza, tel. 3488700,
3488937; tlx. 92715 AMEXT UN
Ramses Hilton Hotel, Nile Corniche,
tlx. 92715 AMEXT UN
Residence Hotel, Maadi, tel. 3507817,
3507851; tlx. 92715 AMEXT UN
Amigo Tours
49 Abdel-Aziz el-Seoud el-Roda,
tel. 3625750, 3621321; tlx. 20144 AMIGO
UN
1 Sharia Latin America, tel. 3545292,
3546234
Atoun Travel
Nile Hilton Hotel, tel. 750666, 745520,
740777
Islam Building (opposite Midan el-Ataba),
tel. 906285
Austrian National Tourist Office
13 Sharia Talaat Harb, tel. 742755, 740228
Best Travel
37 Qasr el-Nil, tel. 754654
2 Sherif Basha el-Kebir Abdin, tel. 934547
Cleopatra Tours
4 Sharia Talaat Harb, tel. 747442, 759810
Crystal Travel Centre
9 Midan el-Tahrir, tel. 749707, 775799

Grand Tours (Zamalek)
5 Sharia Barazil, tel. 3404644, 3405333
Marshall International Tours
167 Sharia el-Tahrir, Midan el-Tahrir,
tel. 553213; tlx. 573 HAMBO UN
Misr Travel
1 Sharia Talaat Harb, tel. 750077, 766737,
766984
South Sinai Travel (Garden City)
24 Sharia Hussein Hegazi, tel. 542192;
tlx. 22996
Starco Travel
1 Midan Talaat Harb, 8th Floor,
tel. 741205, 748809
54 Qasr el-Nil, tel. 922701, 937707
3 Midan el-Tahrir, tel. 3548754, 3550831,
3540598
Suez Canal Travel
1 Sharia el-Sherifen, tel. 771595, 751597;
tlx. 93225 SUCT UN
Thomas Cook
4 Sharia Champollion, tel. 743955, 743967
88 Road 9, Maadi, tel. 3511419, 3511438;
tlx. 7147 TCMD UN
Sharia 26 July (next to Zamalek Club),
tel. 802429, 807187
7 Sharia Baghdad, Heliopolis, tel. 696215
Cairo International Airport, tel. 873149

Index of Places